# Data Modeling with Tableau

A practical guide to building data models using Tableau Prep and Tableau Desktop

**Kirk Munroe**

BIRMINGHAM—MUMBAI

# Data Modeling with Tableau

**Publishing Product Manager**: Arindam Majumder
**Senior Editor**: Tazeen Shaikh
**Technical Editor**: Kavyashree K S
**Copy Editor**: Safis Editing
**Project Coordinator**: Farheen Fathima
**Proofreader**: Safis Editing
**Indexer**: Pratik Shirodkar
**Production Designer**: Shankar Kalbhor
**Marketing Coordinators**: Nivedita Singh

First published: November 2022

Production reference: 1301122

Published by Packt Publishing Ltd.
Livery Place
35 Livery Street
Birmingham
B3 2PB, UK.

ISBN 978-1-80324-802-8

www.packt.com

*For my wife and business partner, Candice; thank you for your patience and for keeping things running at Paint with Data while I was working on this book.*

# Contributors

## About the author

**Kirk Munroe** is a Tableau Desktop Certified Professional, Tableau Certified Data Analyst, Tableau Certified Partner Architect, and Tableau Certified Partner Consultant, with over 20 years of work experience in business analytics.

He is the co-founder of Paint with Data, a Tableau partner and visual analytics coaching consulting firm. Kirk works with clients to improve their analytics skills, from data modeling to storytelling and presenting. Kirk has worked at analytics software companies, including Salesforce/Tableau, IBM/Cognos, and Kinaxis, in senior roles in product management, marketing, sales enablement, and customer success.

*I dedicate this book to everyone in the Tableau #DataFam. I've never experienced such support and encouragement from a technical community before. I hope this book adds to the resources and conversations and leads to better dashboards everywhere!*

# About the reviewers

**Michael Warling** is a tenured analytics professional specializing in helping people realize the full value of their analytics investments. With a background in fine arts and statistics, he has been able to develop extensive data visualization skills and has supported a variety of corporate business functions with their analysis needs.

**Dwight Taylor**, with more than 22 years of experience, is the CEO, chief solution architect, and Tableau evangelist of VIZYUL LLC, a certified minority-owned business enterprise and consulting firm that helps clients tell stories with data. Many of VIZYUL LLC's consulting engagements involve building enterprise-scale data sources for use across multiple Tableau dashboards.

*Understanding how to build a professional Tableau data model is critical to the success of enterprise-scale Tableau projects. If you ever wanted to peek behind the curtain to better understand how professional data architects create complex Tableau data models, this book is for you! Thanks for the opportunity to review this book, Packt Publishing!*

**Ethan Lang** is an award-winning data visualization designer and engineer. He is the co-leader of the Veterans Advocacy Tableau User Group, a Tableau User Group ambassador, and a technical reviewer on multiple best-selling Tableau books. His data visualization strategies have been shared in dozens of cities across North America, including Orlando, Portland, Boston, and Kansas City.

# Table of Contents

# Part 2: Tableau Prep Builder for Data Modeling

# Part 3: Tableau Desktop for Data Modeling

## 7

## 8

## 9

## Building Data Models at the Physical Level    191

## 10

## Sharing and Extending Tableau Data Models    209

# Part 4: Data Modeling with Tableau Server and Online

## 11

## Securing Data    239

# 12

## Data Modeling Considerations for Ask Data and Explain Data    269

# 13

## Data Management with Tableau Prep Conductor    285

# 14

## Scheduling Extract Refreshes    305

# 15

## Data Modeling Strategies by Audience and Use Case    317

## Index    327

## Other Books You May Enjoy    334

# Preface

Tableau is powered by a proprietary language, called VizQL. VizQL combines querying, analysis, and visualization into a single framework. Other BI tools offer querying (SQL, MDX), arranging the data through analysis, and then charting the data in three distinct steps. VizQL is what makes Tableau so quick and easy for analysts.

For VizQL to work properly, the underlying data needs to be in a very neat, tabular format with the following characteristics:

- Every column needs to contain values representing a distinct field, ideally free from null values

- The data needs to be at the lowest level of aggregation that the analyst needs to answer questions with no missing rows

From Tableau's release in 2005 to the release of Tableau Prep Builder in 2018, Tableau mostly left the shaping of data to other technologies. In other words, Tableau assumed you, the analyst, would connect to data that was already in the ideal format. Tableau did however let you add rows from more than one table through unions, add additional columns through joins, and adjust the metadata of your data model by renaming fields, changing field types, and creating hierarchies, groups, and folders.

Tableau Prep Builder was released in the first half of 2018. It brought robust data cleaning and shaping to the Tableau platform. Tableau has gained many more data modeling capabilities since that time including relationships, data catalogs and lineage, and virtual connections. Tableau also released artificial intelligence and machine learning features in the form of Ask Data and Explain Data. Each of these has an impact on how we best model our data for Tableau.

This book explores all the data modeling components and considerations of the Tableau platform. It provides step-by-step explanations of essential concepts, practical examples, and hands-on exercises. You will learn the role that Tableau Prep Builder and Tableau Desktop each play in data modeling. The book also explores the components of Tableau Server and Cloud that make data modeling more robust, secure, and performant. Moreover, by extending data models for Ask Data and Explain Data, you will gain the knowledge required to extend analytics to more people in their organizations, leading to better data-driven decisions.

The book wraps up with a final chapter that explains when it is best to use Tableau Desktop and when it is best to use Tableau Prep Builder. To complete your understanding of the topic, the final chapter also goes through four real-world scenarios and the data modeling components needed in each case. This is a practical guide that will help you put your knowledge to the test.

# Who this book is for

This book is equally targeted at data analysts and business analysts looking to expand their data skills. The book offers a broad foundation on which you can build better data models in Tableau to allow for easier analysis and better query performance.

This book is also for those individuals responsible for making trusted and secure data available to their organization through Tableau. These people often carry the title of data steward and work to take enterprise data and make it more accessible to business analysts.

# What this book covers

*Chapter 1*, *Introducing Data Modeling in Tableau*, starts with connecting to data to create our first data model. We will look at the ideal data structure for Tableau and will connect to multiple tables.

*Chapter 2*, *Licensing Considerations and Types of Data Models*, starts with an overview of Tableau product licensing and the impact it has on data modeling. We will then explore the foundational knowledge of how data modeling fits into the overall Tableau platform.

*Chapter 3*, *Data Preparation with Tableau Prep Builder*, focuses on the Prep Builder user interface, the process of connecting to data, and the first step in any data preparation process – the cleaning step. We will also create row-level calculations, including optimizing string fields.

*Chapter 4*, *Data Modeling Functions with Tableau Prep Builder*, explores extending the width of data by adding new columns through joins and extending the length of data by adding rows through unions. We discuss consolidating fields from columns and adding new fields from data in rows. We also cover the strategy and techniques for aggregating data to the proper level for analysis.

*Chapter 5*, *Advanced Modeling Functions in Tableau Prep Builder*, covers two advanced modeling functions, namely, adding new rows and pivoting rows to columns. These are two important data modeling techniques that are unique to Tableau Prep Builder. We also look into extending our flows by integrating data science models.

*Chapter 6*, *Data Output from Tableau Prep Builder*, looks at the four output options available from Tableau Prep Builder. The last step of our flows is always one or more output steps.

*Chapter 7*, *Connecting to Data in Tableau Desktop*, is all about using Tableau Desktop to connect to data, the first step whenever we use Tableau Desktop. This chapter looks at all the different data types that we can connect to in Tableau Desktop.

*Chapter 8*, *Building Data Models Using Relationships*, looks at how to combine multiple data sources into a single data model. The focus in on combining data sources at the **logical layer** through a feature called **relationships**.

*Chapter 9, Building Data Models at the Physical Level*, explores situations where you, the data modeler, need to be one level deeper than the logical layer. For these use cases, we must go to the physical layer of the data source by creating joins.

*Chapter 10, Sharing and Extending Tableau Data Models*, focuses on sharing and extending Tableau data models using published data sources and extending the model using hierarchies, folders, descriptions, grouping, and calculations. We also look at the implications of live versus extracted data models.

*Chapter 11, Securing Data*, covers key concepts and steps for securing data models. We cover adding users and groups and setting up project security, as these are fundamental for understanding access and authorization as they relate to our data models and the data contained in them. We also look at securing the data in our data models through row-level security options.

*Chapter 12, Data Modeling Considerations for Ask Data and Explain Data*, looks at the powerful machine learning features that put analysis in the hands of casual users. For these casual users to get answers to their own questions, the data models and available fields supporting them must be well thought out or users may end up frustrated with answers that don't make sense.

*Chapter 13, Data Management with Tableau Prep Conductor*, explores the additional features of the Data Management that enhance our data models. These features are Tableau Prep Conductor, data catalog, data lineage, and data quality warnings. We will also look at certified data models, which are a standard feature of Tableau Server and Cloud.

*Chapter 14, Scheduling Extract Refreshes*, focuses on keeping data extracts created in both Tableau Desktop and the web client up to date using the scheduling services of Tableau Server and Cloud. We will also look at the role Tableau Bridge plays in making on-premises data available on Tableau Cloud.

*Chapter 15, Data Modeling Strategies by Audience and Use Case*, puts the entire book together by looking first at the general use cases for Tableau Desktop versus Tableau Prep Builder. We will then explore which pieces of the platform we should use based on our audience and use case using four real-world scenarios.

## To get the most out of this book

To get the most of out of this book, you will need to have a basic understanding of querying a database using basic SQL or having used a business intelligence tool in the past. If you have done planning, reporting, or analysis in Excel or another spreadsheet tool before, you will also have a good basis of understanding to get started with this book.

In the book, you will be using Tableau Desktop, Tableau Prep Builder, and the web interface of Tableau Server or Cloud. If you don't already have a license for these products, you can download a free, 14-day trial of Tableau Desktop, Tableau Prep Builder, and Tableau Cloud from https://www.tableau. com/products/cloud-bi. The trial versions of the products are fully featured and can be used in all the exercises in the book. If you need to use the trial version, it is highly recommended that you don't start the trial until you are ready to jump into the book as it only lasts for 14 days.

The files used in the book are found on the GitHub link found below. It is recommended to download all the files as a ZIP file before you start. The easiest way to do this is to click on the green <> **Code** button and select **Download ZIP**.

| Software/hardware covered in the book | Operating system requirements |
| --- | --- |
| Access to Tableau Server or Tableau Cloud | Windows, macOS, or Linux |
| Tableau Desktop version 2022.2 or higher | |
| Tableau Prep Builder version 2022.2 or higher | |

**If you are using the digital version of this book, we advise you to type the code yourself or access the code from the book's GitHub repository (a link is available in the next section). Doing so will help you avoid any potential errors related to the copying and pasting of code.**

## Download the example code files

You can download the example code files for this book from GitHub at `https://github.com/PacktPublishing/Data-Modeling-with-Tableau`. If there's an update to the code, it will be updated in the GitHub repository.

We also have other code bundles from our rich catalog of books and videos available at `https://github.com/PacktPublishing/`. Check them out!

## Conventions used

There are a number of text conventions used throughout this book.

`Code in text`: Indicates code words in text, database table names, folder names, filenames, file extensions, pathnames, dummy URLs, user input, and Twitter handles. Here is an example: "Mount the downloaded `WebStorm-10*.dmg` disk image file as another disk in your system."

**Bold**: Indicates a new term, an important word, or words that you see onscreen. For instance, words in menus or dialog boxes appear in **bold**. Here is an example: "Select **System info** from the **Administration** panel."

> **Tips or important notes**
> Appear like this.

# Get in touch

Feedback from our readers is always welcome.

**General feedback**: If you have questions about any aspect of this book, email us at customercare@ packtpub.com and mention the book title in the subject of your message.

**Errata**: Although we have taken every care to ensure the accuracy of our content, mistakes do happen. If you have found a mistake in this book, we would be grateful if you would report this to us. Please visit www.packtpub.com/support/errata and fill in the form.

**Piracy**: If you come across any illegal copies of our works in any form on the internet, we would be grateful if you would provide us with the location address or website name. Please contact us at copyright@packt.com with a link to the material.

**If you are interested in becoming an author**: If there is a topic that you have expertise in and you are interested in either writing or contributing to a book, please visit authors.packtpub.com.

# Share Your Thoughts

Once you've read , we'd love to hear your thoughts! Scan the QR code below to go straight to the Amazon review page for this book and share your feedback.

https://packt.link/r/1-803-24802-5

Your review is important to us and the tech community and will help us make sure we're delivering excellent quality content.

# Download a free PDF copy of this book

Thanks for purchasing this book!

Do you like to read on the go but are unable to carry your print books everywhere? Is your eBook purchase not compatible with the device of your choice?

Don't worry, now with every Packt book you get a DRM-free PDF version of that book at no cost.

Read anywhere, any place, on any device. Search, copy, and paste code from your favorite technical books directly into your application.

The perks don't stop there, you can get exclusive access to discounts, newsletters, and great free content in your inbox daily

Follow these simple steps to get the benefits:

1.  Scan the QR code or visit the link below

https://packt.link/free-ebook/9781803248028

2.  Submit your proof of purchase

3.  That's it! We'll send your free PDF and other benefits to your email directly

# Part 1: Data Modeling on the Tableau Platform

The Tableau platform has several components that play a role in data modeling. This section covers the way Tableau models and queries data natively. The section sets the stage for all the hands-on learning that continues throughout the book.

This part comprises the following chapters:

- *Chapter 1, Introducing Data Modeling in Tableau*
- *Chapter 2, Licensing Considerations and Types of Data Models*

# 1
# Introducing Data Modeling in Tableau

Welcome to data modeling in Tableau. You might know Tableau as a great self-service analytics tool that provides both powerful analytics and is also easy to use. You might also think that Tableau is light on the key enterprise analytics requirement of data security, data model robustness, and data maintainability. In this book, you will learn that Tableau has all these key data requirements covered. You will learn how data is best structured for Tableau analysis and performance, and understand the functionality of Tableau Prep Builder and Tableau Desktop and the role each plays in building data models. You'll then publish these data models to Tableau Server or Online and optimize them for performance, governance, and security.

By the end of this book, you will have all the strategies and techniques needed to enable individuals in your organization to answer their own questions with data, regardless of their level of expertise. You will also drastically reduce the calls you receive from these same individuals about confusing data and dashboards that are slow to load.

Tableau is very different from most other BI tools in that the model can be either implicit or explicit. For instance, many analysts open Tableau Desktop, connect to data, and immediately begin creating visuals. In this instance, Tableau implicitly created a data model (that is, made a connection, executed a query, and created metadata) without an analyst having to do anything to create the model.

This implicit data modeling works well when your data source has already been prepared for analysis and you are the person creating charts and dashboards. Often, our data is not structured this way. It comes from different sources and needs to be combined and defined in meaningful ways. In these instances, Tableau provides the tools for you to create data models that are scalable, secure, and targeted to the different skills of a broad class of developers and consumers.

Tableau uses a data model as the foundation for the creation of all analyses. A Tableau data model contains the following:

- Connection information to the underlying data source.
- The queries required to retrieve the data.
- Additional metadata, or data about the data, added to the underlying data. Metadata can include more readable field names, field types, the grouping of data into hierarchies, and calculations not in the underlying data.

Tableau works best when your data is in a traditional spreadsheet table format – that is, Tableau assumes that the first row of your data consists of column headers and each column header maps 1:1 to a field name, with additional rows of data each containing one record of data. If the underlying data is not formatted in this way, analysis within Tableau becomes very difficult and performance will suffer. To address this, you can model your data in a format that works best with Tableau. The best practices to model data properly are the primary content of this book.

This chapter demonstrates how Tableau automatically creates a data model when you connect to a data source, how it interprets rows and columns in your data, and how you can shape and combine additional data into your data model.

In this chapter, we're going to cover the following main topics:

- What happens when you connect to data in Tableau Desktop
- The ideal data structure for Tableau
- Shaping data for Tableau
- Connecting multiple tables

# Technical requirements

Tableau Desktop (and Tableau Prep Builder version 2022.2 or higher in future chapters) version 2022.2 or higher is needed to complete the exercises in this chapter.

If you don't have a licensed version of Tableau Desktop, you can obtain a 14-day free trial from `https://www.tableau.com/products/desktop`.

Another alternative is Tableau Public. The free Tableau Public version of Desktop contains almost all the same features as the paid version, with the exception of a small number of data source connection options, and output can only be saved to the Tableau Public site. However, it often has enough features to perform visual analysis as long as the data isn't confidential. The Tableau Public Desktop version can be found at `https://public.tableau.com/s/`.

The files used in the exercises in this chapter can be found at `https://github.com/PacktPublishing/Data-Modeling-with-Tableau/`. We recommend downloading all the files before getting started. The quickest way to do this is to click on the green <>**Code** button and then select **Download ZIP**. Expand the ZIP file and make note of the directory. We will be referencing it throughout the book.

> **Note**
>
> The aforementioned requirements are applicable to all chapters in this book.

## What happens when you connect to data in Tableau Desktop?

When you connect to data in Tableau Desktop, Tableau will begin to interpret your data. First, it will create a field for each column of your data. Second, it will assign a data type to each of the fields. Tableau does this because it is powered by a proprietary query technology, called **VizQL**. VizQL is the technology that underpins Tableau, enabling a visual analytics experience by automatically creating visualizations for a user. This is very different than most business intelligence tools that rely on the user to tell the tool how they would like the data visualized through the picking of a chart type.

For VizQL to work, Tableau needs to know the type of each field. The two main field types in Tableau are discrete and continuous:

- **Discrete fields**: Colored blue in Tableau. By the Oxford Dictionary's definition, discrete means *independent of other things of the same type*. When placed on a Tableau visualization, discrete fields usually create a *header* – similar to a column header in a spreadsheet.

- **Continuous fields**: Colored green in Tableau. Again, using the Oxford Dictionary, continuous is defined as *happening or existing for a period of time without being interrupted*. When placed on a Tableau visualization, continuous fields create an axis – that is, they create a visual display of data.

One way to think about the relationship between discrete and continuous fields is that continuous fields are recording measurements and discrete fields are describing those measurements. In a statement, this can usually be phrased as *continuous by discrete* – for example, sales (continuous) by region (discrete), as shown in *Figure 1.1*.

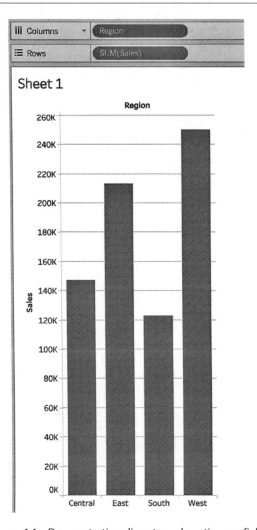

Figure 1.1 – Demonstrating discrete and continuous fields

Within these two main field types, there are additional field types that inform VizQL how to create a visual display when they are brought onto the Tableau canvas. These can be seen in *Figure 1.2* and are as follows:

- **Number (decimal)**: A number that allows fractions. Represented by a # symbol in the Tableau UI.
- **Number (whole)**: An integer or a number with no decimals. Also represented by a # symbol.
- **String**: A field that contains alphanumeric characters. Represented by **abc**.
- **Date**: Tableau accepts several date formatting options. Represented by a calendar icon.

- **Date & Time**: A date field with granularity down to the second of a day. Represented by a calendar icon plus an analog clock.

- **Geographical/Spatial**: A field that can be plotted on a map. There are many subtypes of geographical fields, including country, state/province, city, postal/zip code, airport, congressional district, NUTS (Europe), and a latitude or longitude value. Represented by a globe icon.

- **Binary/Boolean**: A field that takes a true/false or yes/no condition. Represented by a T/F icon.

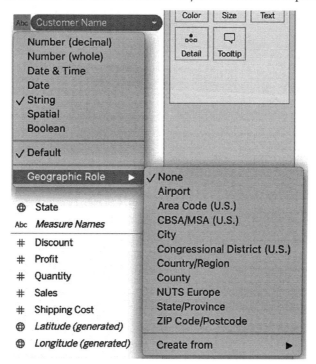

Figure 1.2 – Additional field types

Let's open Tableau Desktop and connect to the `Superstore sales 2022.csv` file. This file contains the sample data that comes along with the Tableau installation. It is a sample (and fictional) retail dataset that is useful for demonstration and learning purposes. We will use this data throughout the book when we can. This will help you as you increase your Tableau learning journey, as most of Tableau's training videos use the same data:

1. Open Tableau Desktop.

2. Click on the **Connect to Data** blue hyperlink near the top-left-hand side of the Tableau Desktop UI:

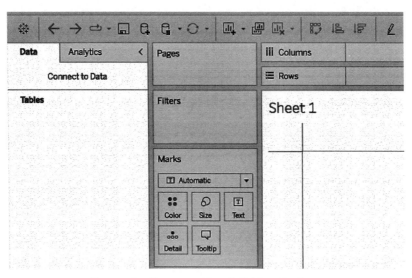

Figure 1.3 – Connect to Data in Tableau Desktop

3.  You are now presented with many different options for data sources. We will discuss some of these in upcoming chapters. For now, find the **To a file** section and click on the **Text file** option. Navigate to the `Superstore sales 2022.csv` file in the location you saved it on your computer. Click **Open**.

4.  Tableau will bring the data in and bring focus to the **Data Source** tab, as follows:

Figure 1.4 – The data pane in Tableau Desktop

The top part of the screen acts as a visual canvas where we can bring in additional data through relationships, joins, and unions. For now, we will look at the bottom part of the screen.

This part of the user interface is broken into two sections. The section on the left displays the metadata for the fields in the data source. The metadata list contains the type, field name, physical table from where the data is being queried, and remote field name.

**Type** is the Tableau field type, which allows VizQL to guide the analyst to the best visual display for the data. **Field Name** is Tableau's attempt to take the remote field name and map it to a business-friendly name. In our dataset, the column names already translate easily to business-friendly names. Imagine if our source file had contained *postal_code* and not *Postal Code* in the first row. Tableau would automatically transform *postal_code* to *Postal Code* in the field name, making our data modeling job easier for us. We can always change the default name Tableau assigns to any field.

The section to the right contains a sample of data that will be queried, called the **Table Details** pane. By default, Tableau returns the first 100 rows as a sample. The sample size can be changed in terms of the number of rows to return.

Next up, we will look at what a table format looks like and why it is so important for Tableau.

## The ideal data format for Tableau – table format

Tableau performs best and is easiest to use when every column in the source data corresponds to a single field and each row represents a record of data at the lowest level required for analysis. As you can see in the following screenshot (*Figure 1.5*), Tableau will put all the field names in columns, including the type of each field. This is the metadata in your data model. Every row below the row of field headers will contain data, with each row representing one record of data:

| Extract Category | Extract City | Extract Country | Extract Customer Name | Extract Discount | Extract Order | r ID | Extract Postal Code | Extract Product Name | Extract Profit | Extract Quantity | Extract Region |
|---|---|---|---|---|---|---|---|---|---|---|---|
| Furniture | Henderson | United States | Claire Gute | 0.00% | 11/8/2016 | CA-2016-152156 | 42420 | Bush Somerset Colle... | $42 | 2 | South |
| Furniture | Henderson | United States | Claire Gute | 0.00% | 11/8/2016 | CA-2016-152156 | 42420 | Hon Deluxe Fabric Up... | $220 | 3 | South |
| Office Supplies | Los Angeles | United States | Darrin Van Huff | 0.00% | 6/12/2016 | CA-2016-138688 | 90036 | Self-Adhesive Addres... | $7 | 2 | West |
| Furniture | Fort Lauderdale | United States | Sean O'Donnell | 45.00% | 10/11/2015 | US-2015-108966 | 33311 | Bretford CR4500 Ser... | ($383) | 5 | South |
| Office Supplies | Fort Lauderdale | United States | Sean O'Donnell | 20.00% | 10/11/2015 | US-2015-108966 | 33311 | Eldon Fold 'N Roll Car... | $3 | 2 | South |
| Furniture | Los Angeles | United States | Brosina Hoffman | 0.00% | 6/9/2 | 014-115812 | 90032 | Eldon Expressions W... | $14 | 7 | West |
| Office Supplies | Los Angeles | United States | Brosina Hoffman | 0.00% | 6/9/ | 014-115812 | 90032 | Newell 322 | $2 | 4 | West |
| Technology | Los Angeles | United States | Brosina Hoffman | 20.00% | 6/9/ | 014-115812 | 90032 | Mitel 5320 IP Phone ... | $91 | 6 | West |
| Office Supplies | Los Angeles | United States | Brosina Hoffman | 20.00% | 6/9/2014 | CA-2014-115812 | 90032 | IXL Anglo-View Bind... | $6 | 3 | West |
| Office Supplies | Los Angeles | United States | Brosina Hoffman | 0.00% | 6/9/2014 | CA-2014-115812 | 90032 | Belkin F5C206VTEL 6... | $34 | 5 | West |
| Furniture | Los Angeles | United States | Brosina Hoffman | 20.00% | 6/9/2014 | CA-2014-115812 | 90032 | Chromcraft Rectang... | $85 | 9 | West |
| Technology | Los Angeles | United States | Brosina Hoffman | 20.00% | 6/9/2014 | CA-2014-115812 | 90032 | Konftel 250 Conferen... | $68 | 4 | West |
| Office Supplies | Concord | United States | Andrew Allen | 20.00% | 4/15/2017 | CA-2017-114412 | 28027 | Xerox 1967 | $5 | 3 | South |
| Office Supplies | Seattle | United States | Irene Maddox | 20.00% | 12/5/2016 | CA-2016-161389 | 98103 | Fellowes PB200 Plas... | $133 | 3 | West |
| Office Supplies | Fort Worth | United States | Harold Pawlan | 80.00% | 11/22/2015 | US-2015-118983 | 76106 | Holmes Replacement... | ($124) | 5 | Central |

Figure 1.5 – The Tableau data format

When data is structured in this manner, it allows Tableau to perform optimally based on query performance, the ease of building analyses, and combining data from different sources.

Tableau will automatically *assume* your data is stored this way when you connect to a new data source. We saw this in the previous exercise. Tableau took the first row from the comma-separated values file and used it to create field names, restarting after the comma separator. Next, Tableau assumed after the first carriage return that the second row would be a row of values, neatly falling into the columns above it. For each additional carriage return, Tableau assumed another data record.

It turned out that Tableau was right in the assumptions it made. Data prepared for analysis is often already stored in this format, with each row being a unique record of data, separated into individual fields based on fields in database tables or headings in flat files and Excel.

What happens when it isn't? This puts an analyst in the position of creating more complicated analyses (calculations, sheets, dashboards, and stories) and query performance almost always suffers.

In the next section, we will look at one of the most common ways where we see data structured in a manner that is not Tableau-friendly.

## Shaping data for Tableau

In the previous section, we looked at the data format that works best in Tableau. We will now look at one of the two main examples where data is shaped ineffectively for Tableau and how we can easily change it to the correct format before beginning our data analysis.

Time-based data, especially financial data, is often stored in Excel with the dates in the column headers, the fields spread across columns in the first row, and values falling in the cells in the intersection. We can see this in *Figure 1.6*. This is a planning sheet for sales targets for the year 2022 for category sales of our SuperStore data:

| | A | B | C | D | E | F | G | H | I | J | K | L | M |
|---|---|---|---|---|---|---|---|---|---|---|---|---|---|
| 1 | | Jan-22 | Feb-22 | Mar-22 | Apr-22 | May-22 | Jun-22 | Jul-22 | Aug-22 | Sep-22 | Oct-22 | Nov-22 | Dec-22 |
| 2 | Furniture | 8,000 | 10,000 | 12,000 | 14,000 | 16,000 | 18,000 | 20,000 | 22,000 | 24,000 | 26,000 | 28,000 | 30,000 |
| 3 | Office Supplies | 15,000 | 15,000 | 15,000 | 15,000 | 15,000 | 15,000 | 20,000 | 20,000 | 20,000 | 20,000 | 20,000 | 20,000 |
| 4 | Technology | 12,000 | 14000 | 16,000 | 18000 | 20,000 | 22000 | 24,000 | 26000 | 28,000 | 30000 | 32,000 | 34000 |
| 5 | | | | | | | | | | | | | |

Figure 1.6 – SuperStore sales targets format

If we connect this data to Tableau, it gives us the following metadata:

〈

**Name**

Sheet1

**Fields**

| Type | Field Name | Physical Table | Remote Field Name |
|------|-----------|----------------|-------------------|
| Abc | F1 | Sheet1 | F1 |
| # | Jan-22 | Sheet1 | Jan-22 |
| # | Feb-22 | Sheet1 | Feb-22 |
| # | Mar-22 | Sheet1 | Mar-22 |
| # | Apr-22 | Sheet1 | Apr-22 |
| # | May-22 | Sheet1 | May-22 |
| # | Jun-22 | Sheet1 | Jun-22 |
| # | Jul-22 | Sheet1 | Jul-22 |
| # | Aug-22 | Sheet1 | Aug-22 |
| # | Sep-22 | Sheet1 | Sep-22 |
| # | Oct-22 | Sheet1 | Oct-22 |
| # | Nov-22 | Sheet1 | Nov-22 |
| # | Dec-22 | Sheet1 | Dec-22 |

Figure 1.7 – SuperStore target default metadata

Thinking back to having fields in columns, a field type, and values in rows, we can see that this interpretation of the data is not helpful at all. What we want are three fields of the following types:

- `Date`: Type – date. There are 12 values, one for each month in 2022.
- `Category`: Type – string. There are three values: Furniture, Office Supplies, and Technology.
- `Revenue target`: Type – whole number

In order to get these fields into the right format, we need to *pivot* those date columns into rows and then rename two fields. Tableau makes this easy for us. Here are the steps:

1. Open Tableau Desktop.
2. Click on the **Connect to Data** blue hyperlink near the top left-hand side of the Tableau Desktop UI.

3.  Choose **Microsoft Excel**. Navigate to the `SuperStore 2022 Budget.xlsx` file in the location you saved it on your computer. Click **Open**.

4.  You will be presented with a screen similar to *Figure 1.6*.

5.  In the **Table Details** pane, click on the header of **Jan-22**, hold down the *Shift* key, and click on the **Dec-22** header to select all the date columns. You might find this easier if you first collapse the metadata pane:

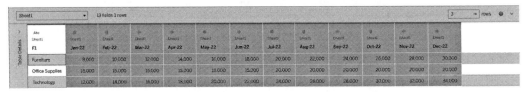

Figure 1.8 – Multiselecting columns in the Table Details pane

6.  Hold your cursor over the top-right-hand corner of the **Dec-22** header to bring up the down arrow.

7.  Click on the down arrow to bring up the menu of options. Choose **Pivot**.

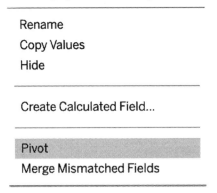

Figure 1.9 – Menu options from the Table Details pane

8.  You will now be presented with three fields. We are almost there!

| Abc Sheet1 **F1** | Abc Pivot **Pivot Field Names** | # Pivot **Pivot Field Values** |
|---|---|---|
| Furniture | Apr-22 | 14,000 |
| Furniture | Aug-22 | 22,000 |
| Furniture | Dec-22 | 30,000 |
| Furniture | Feb-22 | 10,000 |
| Furniture | Jan-22 | 8,000 |
| Furniture | Jul-22 | 20,000 |
| Furniture | Jun-22 | 18,000 |
| Furniture | Mar-22 | 12,000 |
| Furniture | May-22 | 16,000 |
| Furniture | Nov-22 | 28,000 |

Figure 1.10 – Table Details after the pivot

9. Our last step is to rename our three fields. We can do this by clicking on the field name and typing over the ones that are there, or by clicking on the same down arrow that we used in *step 8* and using the **Rename** option.

10. Let's rename our fields as follows: **F1** to Category, **Pivot Field Names** to Date, and **Pivot Field Values** to Sales Target:

| Abc Sheet1 **Category** | Abc Pivot **Date** | # Pivot **Sales Target** |
|---|---|---|
| Furniture | Apr-22 | 14,000 |
| Furniture | Aug-22 | 22,000 |
| Furniture | Dec-22 | 30,000 |
| Furniture | Feb-22 | 10,000 |
| Furniture | Jan-22 | 8,000 |
| Furniture | Jul-22 | 20,000 |
| Furniture | Jun-22 | 18,000 |
| Furniture | Mar-22 | 12,000 |
| Furniture | May-22 | 16,000 |
| Furniture | Nov-22 | 28,000 |

Figure 1.11 – Table details after renaming

11. Our last step is making sure our field types are correct. **Category** is a string field (alphanumeric) so it should show **Abc**, which it does. Similarly, **Sales Target** is a number and Tableau has it correct. **Date** is showing as a string. We would really like this as a date field because Tableau has special date-handling capabilities to make analysis much easier for us. To change the **Date** field to a type of date, click on **Abc** over **Date** and change the field type to **Date**:

| Abc | Abc | Number (decimal) | |
| Sheet1 | Pivot | Number (whole) | |
| **Category** | **Date** | Date & Time | |
| | | Date | |
| Furniture | Apr- | ✓ String | 14,000 |
| Furniture | Aug- | Spatial | 22,000 |
| Furniture | Dec- | Boolean | 30,000 |
| Furniture | Feb- | | 10,000 |
| Furniture | Jan- | ✓ Default | 8,000 |
| Furniture | Jul-2 | | 20,000 |
| | | Geographic Role ▶ | |
| Furniture | Jun-22 | | 18,000 |
| Furniture | Mar-22 | | 12,000 |
| Furniture | May-22 | | 16,000 |
| Furniture | Nov-22 | | 28,000 |

Figure 1.12 – Table details – changing the data type

Don't close this workbook; we will pick up from this point in the exercise in the next section, where we will combine data to our data model from other tables.

In this section, we looked at how we may need to reshape our data to make better data models in Tableau. In the next section, we will look at a use case where we need to add additional columns (fields) of data from other data sources to our model.

## Connecting multiple tables to add new columns

Now that we understand the ideal format of data for Tableau, we can look at ways to expand the size of our data model by connecting to multiple tables. We have connected independently to two different tables in this chapter. We will now combine those tables, along with a third table.

There are two ways in which we can add multiple tables to a single data model. The first is by joining data. We join data when we want to add additional columns to our model for additional context. Think of our sales target data. We want to join that data to our SuperStore sales data to add the additional context of sales targets. That will allow analysts to create views to see how the different categories are performing against their targets.

The second way to add additional data to our model is by adding additional rows (with the same columns). The SuperStore data we used earlier in this chapter was for 2022. What if we wanted to add in sales from 2021? That is where a union would be the answer.

For our next exercise, it should be noted that we are creating a relationship to add the new column and not a join. Using a relationship allows Tableau to create the proper join at runtime based on the data being analyzed. You can think of a relationship as a dynamic, smarter join. We will explore the details and differences between relationships and joins in *Chapter 7*, *Chapter 8*, and *Chapter 9*.

To add the additional column of sales target, we will pick up from the end of the previous exercise:

1.  Click on the blue **Add** hyperlink to the right of **Connections**:

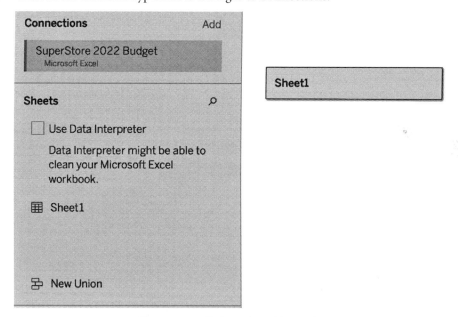

Figure 1.13 – Clicking the Add hyperlink

2.  Select **To a file** | **Text file** | Superstore Sales 2022.csv | **Open**.

3.  Under **Files**, drag Superstore Sales 2022.csv onto the canvas until the orange *noodle* shows, and then let go.

4.  At this point, Tableau tries to create a relationship between these tables. Sometimes, Tableau can figure out how to create this relationship. In this case, we can see Tableau was unable to do this from the exclamation mark in a red triangle:

Figure 1.14 – Creating a relationship between two tables

5.  We need to tell Tableau that the two relationships it should create are **Date** with **Order Date** and **Category** with **Category**. Let's relate the two category fields first. We do this by selecting **Category** and **Category1** and making sure the operator is set to equals (=):

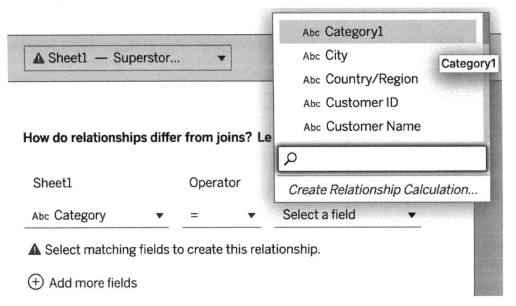

Figure 1.15 – Creating a relationship by linking fields

6.  To complete the relationship, we will also need to link **Date** fields to ensure that the sales targets are aligned with the proper dates for analysis. In this specific case, the dates are not at the same grain (one is at the month level and one is at the day level). This will require us to create a relationship calculation, which we will explore in future chapters.

7.  Now that we have joined additional data sources (tables) to add additional columns for analysis, we will explore adding new rows of data through a union.

8.  Hover your cursor on the right side of the `Superstore Sales 2022.csv` file rectangle on the canvas, and click on the down arrow when it appears. Select **Convert to Union…**:

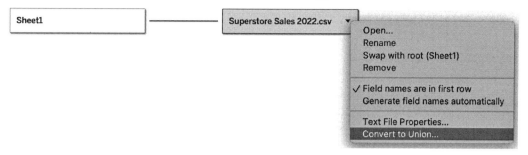

Figure 1.16 – Convert to Union…

9.  Drag the `Superstore Sales 2021.csv` file from the files section on the canvas into the union dialog box. After clicking **OK**, all the rows from both 2021 and 2022 will be available for analysis:

Figure 1.17 – Dragging files to the union dialog box

We have now covered the two core methods of expanding our data model through relationships and unions.

## Summary

Congratulations! We are only one chapter in and you have already created a data model in Tableau. We now know how to structure the ideal data model for Tableau. We looked at connecting to data, exploring how Tableau interprets that data, reshaping data for analysis, and adding additional data. With this learning foundation, we are well-positioned for more advanced topics in the following chapters, where we will build security, maintainability, and robustness into our data models.

In the next chapter, we will look at Tableau licensing models and how licensing impacts data modeling. We will also explore the difference between embedded and published data models and the difference between data models that connect live to data and those that extract data for analysis.

# 2
# Licensing Considerations and Types of Data Models

Tableau licensing has an impact on how a person can create and maintain data models. First, Tableau has role-based pricing for individual users of the platform. Second, Tableau has different tiers for how organizations license Tableau, which impacts data modeling capabilities.

Tableau data models are used by analysts and developers to create Tableau **workbooks**. Workbooks are a series of **sheets**, **dashboards**, and **stories**. Every workbook must be connected to a minimum of one data model. These data models can be embedded in the workbook, meaning they are only available in the workbook. Alternatively, they can be published separately and made available in many workbooks; these are called **published data sources**. We will create both types in this chapter.

Data models can also connect live to data sources. This means the queries from the model are serviced by the underlying data server. Data can also be extracted into the Tableau data engine, called **Hyper**. We will learn about both types of connections in this chapter.

Tableau also provides the capability to put a layer between the data model and the underlying data server through a **virtual connection**. We will also explore virtual connections in this chapter.

This chapter will give you the foundational knowledge of how data modeling fits into the Tableau platform. This knowledge is a crucial foundation for the exercises we will be doing in future chapters. The main topics we will be discussing are how Tableau connects to and publishes data and the licensing considerations for which users can perform these tasks.

In this chapter, we're going to cover the following main topics:

- Tableau roles – Viewer, Explorer, and Creator

- Tableau Data Management

- Tableau virtual connections

- Tableau published data sources

- Tableau embedded data sources

- Live versus extracted data

- The Tableau Hyper engine

For the complete list of requirements to run the practical examples in this chapter, please see the *Technical requirements* section in *Chapter 1*. The files used in the exercises in this chapter can be found at https://github.com/PacktPublishing/Data-Modeling-with-Tableau/.

## Tableau roles – Viewer, Explorer, and Creator

The method Tableau uses for product licensing is important to understand as it has ramifications on the data modeling capabilities available to the user of the Tableau platform.

For Tableau Cloud and most Tableau Server deployments, Tableau's first and primary licensing method is by user role. The three Tableau roles are:

- **Viewer** – This role is aimed at executives and other information consumers. A person who is assigned a Viewer role has a robust set of capabilities available to them for exploring and sharing data. As the Viewer role is aimed at the information consumer, it does not allow for the creation and maintenance of the data modeling capabilities we will learn in this chapter and throughout this book.

- **Explorer** – This role is aimed at business users. A person who is assigned an Explorer role can create data visualizations for themselves and others and do everything someone with a Viewer license can do. A person with an Explorer role has very limited access to data modeling features. They do not have access to Tableau Desktop and Tableau Prep Builder, two of the main components we cover in this book. They can connect to published data sources and create their own embedded data sources from flat files.

- **Creator** – This role is aimed at analysts. A person who is assigned a Creator role has the full capabilities of the Tableau platform. One of the primary jobs of Creators is to create and manage the data models for Explorers (and other Creators), assuming the role of Data Management and governance for the organization. The audience for this book is Creators.

Before leaving this section, we should acknowledge that two other roles exist and can determine some of the capabilities available to Viewers, Explorers, and Creators. These two roles are **Server**

**Administrator** and **Site Administrator**. Neither of these roles is a licensed role, rather they are additional roles that are layered on top of the licensed roles. The Server Administrator role is a specific role to administer a Tableau Server on-premises deployment. The Site Administrator is a role intended for the management of content and users within a Tableau site. Tableau Server has both roles and Tableau Cloud only has the Site Administrator role, as the Server Administrator roles of installation, upgrade, and management are included in the Tableau Cloud service.

To have the role of Site Administrator, you must first be licensed either at the Explorer or Creator level.

Although we do not cover server and site administration functions in this chapter, it is important to know of the existence of these roles because both Site and Server Administrators have access to settings that could affect your ability to perform some of the tasks we do in this book. If you are working on these exercises and find you don't have access, reach out to a Site Administrator for help.

## Tableau Data Management

Starting with the 2019.3 release, Tableau enhanced Data Management capabilities with the introduction of Tableau Prep Conductor and Tableau Catalog. Since the initial release of Data Management, Tableau has continued to add and enhance capabilities. The virtual connections functions we mentioned in the first part of this chapter are an example. These Data Management features require additional licensing costs.

It is important to understand this product add-on as it enables some of the Data Management functions that layer onto the modeling capabilities we will learn about in this book. As it is a set of bundled features that are licensed *on top* of user roles, you might not have these capabilities available to you if your organization has not purchased Data Management licenses. To get access to these features, you can download a 14-day free trial of Tableau Cloud with Data Management enabled, as described in the *Technical requirements* section in *Chapter 1*.

*Table 1.1* outlines which capabilities are available with and without Data Management licensing. For all capabilities listed, the user role is Creator:

| Base Tableau Creator license | Capabilities requiring Data Management |
| --- | --- |
| <ul><li>Creating and publishing data models in Tableau Desktop and from the web client</li><li>Scheduling extract refreshes on Tableau Server and Tableau Cloud</li><li>Creating and publishing Tableau Prep flows from both Tableau Prep Builder and from the web client</li></ul> | <ul><li>Virtual connections</li><li>Tableau Catalog</li><li>Tableau Prep Conductor (scheduling Tableau Prep flows)</li></ul> |

Table 1.1 – Additional capabilities with Data Management

In addition to the data modeling capabilities that are only available with this add-on, there are also some key data governance capabilities that are included. Data lineage, data catalog, and data warnings are all included with Data Management. We will look at these features in *Chapter 13*.

# Tableau virtual connections

Prior to the Tableau 2021.4 release, data model creation started with a direct connection to the underlying data source. This meant that data modelers would most often connect directly to enterprise database tables in their organization. This approach works well when the data modeler understands databases, but it falls short in several important ways, especially when the organization wants to delegate the role of data modeling to less technical users in the business.

If the organization is going to delegate data model creation to business users, the information technology, data engineering, and security teams will often want to ensure that the data modeler:

- Cannot have access to all the data in the database for confidentiality reasons
- Limits access to the number of tables in the database
- Ensures that analytics are not run against live tables, that is, ensures that data is extracted to an analytics store so impacting performance of the database is minimized to a scheduled window

**Tableau virtual connections** can only be created in the web client of either Tableau Server or Tableau Cloud. Virtual connections are intended for large organizations. For this reason, they are only available with Data Management and are only available for data servers and cloud data drives.

We will now go through the starting process for creating a virtual connection:

1. Start by signing into your organization's Tableau Server or to Tableau Cloud from your browser. If you are using your organization's Tableau Cloud or signed up for a trial as described in the *Technical requirements* section in *Chapter 1*, the URL to enter in your browser is `https://online.tableau.com`.

2. After entering your sign-in credentials, navigate to the home page of the Tableau interface. Once there, you will find a button labeled **New**. Click on this button to bring up the menu seen in *Figure 2.1*. From this menu, choose **Virtual Connection.** ( In this case, if you want to follow along in this section, taking the trial option described in the *Technical Requirements* section in *Chapter 1* will allow you to.):

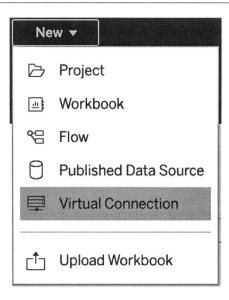

Figure 2.1 – New options on Tableau Server and Tableau Cloud

3.  Tableau will take you to a screen to create a connection. Unlike Tableau Desktop and Tableau Prep Builder, virtual connections are designed to work exclusively with data stored in database server technology. This means that the options for flat files, Tableau published data sources, web data connectors, and others aren't available.

We will stop at this point, for now, and look at virtual connections in more detail in subsequent chapters. The most important takeaway from virtual connections is that they are not data models per se but a layer that sits between underlying databases and Tableau data models. Virtual connections are also not always needed in the data modeling pipeline, meaning you can create Tableau models directly on top of data sources without first creating a virtual connection.

## Tableau published data sources

**Published data sources** are the primary method of sharing data models between analytics users. A published data source contains all the information a person will need to start creating visualizations, namely, a published data source can have the following:

- The connection string to the underlying database or the reference to a Tableau virtual connection
- Metadata changes relating to the renaming and casting of fields into new data types
- Descriptions of fields
- Embedded flat files

- Organization of fields into hierarchies and folders for easier navigation
- Reusable calculations

Published data sources can be created in three different places in Tableau: Tableau Desktop, Tableau Prep Builder, and from the home page in the web client. In this chapter, we will look at the creation of published data sources from Tableau Desktop and the home page in the web client. We will create a published data source from Tableau Prep Builder in *Chapter 6, Data Output*.

Let's open Tableau Desktop and connect to the same `Superstore sales 2022.csv` file we used in the previous chapter:

1.  Open Tableau Desktop.

2.  Click on the **Connect to Data** blue hyperlink near the top left-hand side of the Tableau Desktop user interface.

3.  Find the **To a File** section and click on the **Text file** option. Navigate to the `Superstore sales 2022.csv` file at the location you saved it at on your computer. Click **Open**.

4.  Follow the prompt in the bottom left-hand corner of the application to go to **Sheet 1**, as seen in *Figure 2.2*:

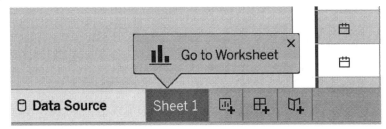

Figure 2.2 – Go to Worksheet prompt upon connecting to data

5.  When we go to **Sheet 1**, we will be presented with our data model in the data pane on the left-hand side of the user interface:

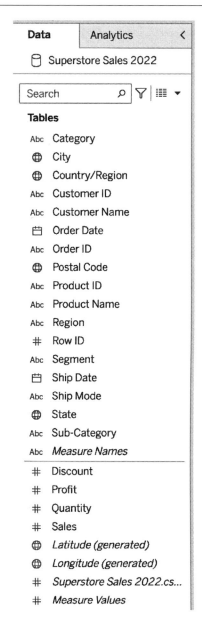

Figure 2.3 – The Tableau Desktop data pane

6.  In *Chapter 7, Connecting to Data in Tableau Desktop*, we will explore the ways in which we can enhance metadata using the data pane. For now, we want to introduce the concept of a Tableau published data source and demonstrate how to create one. From the menu bar in Tableau Desktop, select **Server** and then the **Publish Data Source** selection. Select **Superstore Sales 2022**, as seen in *Figure 2.4*. If you aren't signed into Tableau Server or Tableau Cloud, you will be first prompted to sign in. Enter your credentials to continue:

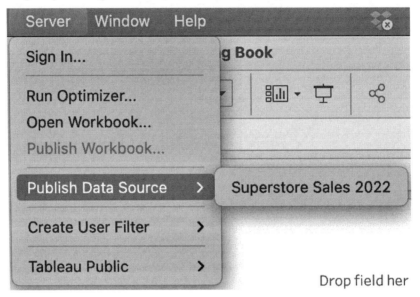

Figure 2.4 – Publish Data Source

7.  We are now presented with a dialog box for settings of our published data source, as seen in *Figure 2.5*. The first part of the dialog box asks for a **Project** location. Projects are the method that Tableau uses to organize and secure content on Tableau Server and Tableau Cloud. Choose the project where you want to save the published data source:

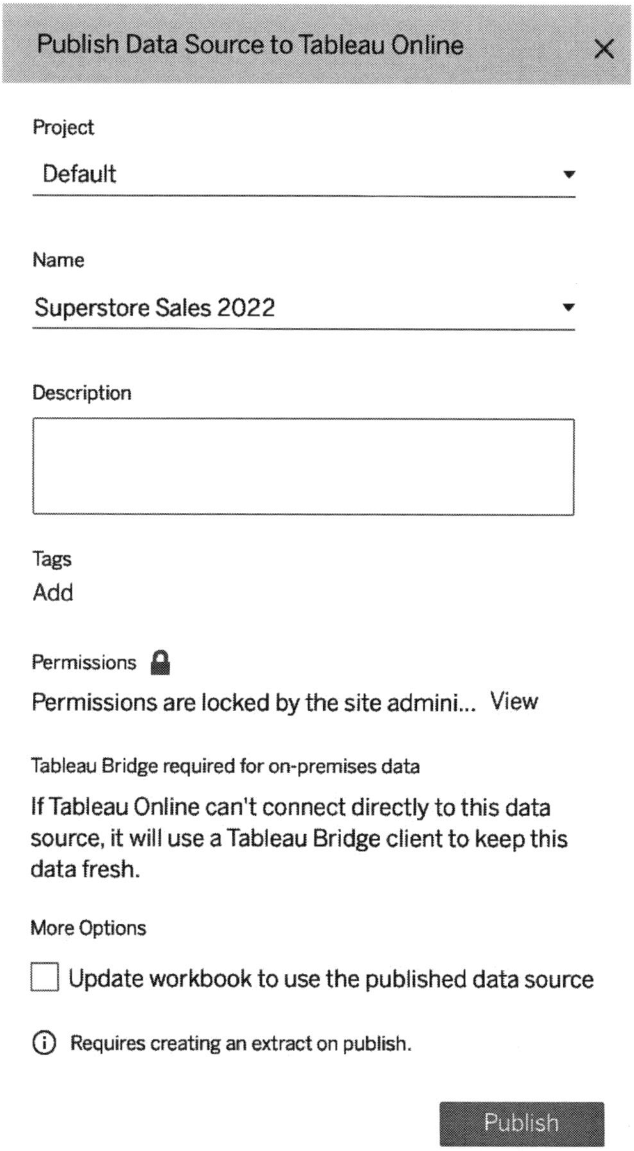

Figure 2.5 – Publish Data Source dialog box

8.  The next three selections are name, description, and the ability to add tags. **Tags** are keywords used to add in searching for content on Tableau Server and Tableau Cloud. Take the default name and leave the description and tags blank for now.

9.  **Permissions** give the ability to determine which users can access the published data source on Tableau Server or Tableau Cloud. In *Figure 2.5*, you will see that permissions are locked by the Site Administrator. One way to manage Tableau Server and Tableau Cloud content, including published data sources, is to lock permissions to projects. The reason for this is to separate the roles of content creators from security administrators. If the project you are publishing is not locked by a Site Administrator, you will have access to a dialogue box, as seen in *Figure 2.6*. You can use this to add security to your data model:

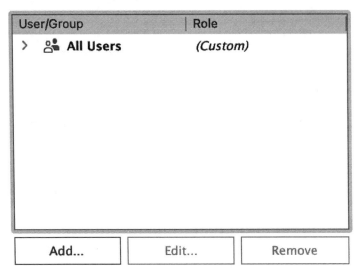

Figure 2.6 – Adding security to a data model

The last option is a checkbox that says **Update workbook to use published data source?** If you plan to create visual analyses in this workbook, you should check the box. This ensures that the analysis will be kept up to date when the published data source is updated. In this case, we are only using the workbook to create a published data source so leave the box unchecked.

Before we hit the **Publish** button, you might notice two warnings. The first is specific to Tableau Cloud. If you use Tableau Cloud with data sources that are housed within your organization's network or on your individual computer, you will need **Tableau Bridge** to create a connection between the data source and Tableau Cloud. We will explore Tableau Bridge in detail in *Chapter 14, Scheduling Extract Refreshes*. The other message might be **Requires creating an extract on publish**. We will discuss extracts later in this chapter.

10. Click the **Publish** button to publish your data source.

Tableau will now open the page to your published data source in a browser. Please keep Tableau Desktop open in the background as we will begin the next section where we left off here.

In your browser, you might see the dialogue box in *Figure 2.7*. For now, please disregard this dialogue box by clicking on the cross in the top-right corner.

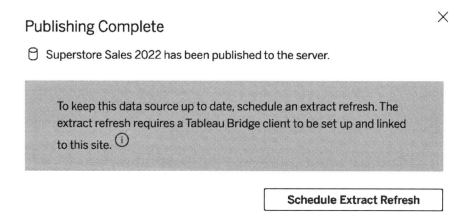

Figure 2.7 – Publishing Complete dialogue

Now that we have seen how to create and publish a Tableau published data source from Tableau Desktop, let's look at published data sources on Tableau Server and Tableau Cloud.

## Working with published data sources on Tableau Server and Tableau Cloud

We will now look at working with published data sources from the Tableau web user interface, that is, working with published data sources without needing to use Tableau Desktop:

1.  Click on the dropdown next to the **New** box. You should see the options that are available in *Figure 2.8*. This screenshot is from Tableau Cloud version 2022.1. One of the options is to create a new published data source and another is to upload a workbook. The other three are important to this published data source. You can create a new workbook starting with all the data modeling work you put into the data source. You can also leverage the data source as a starting point for creating a **flow**, which we will be discussing in the next chapter, and a **lens**, which we will be exploring in *Chapter 12, Data Modeling Considerations for Ask and Explain Data*, with **Ask Data**:

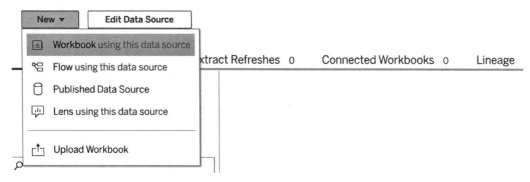

Figure 2.8 – The New button from the published data source in the browser

2.    Click away from the new dropdown options. You will see a button that enables you to edit this published data source in the browser without having to download it to Tableau Desktop first. Only the owner of the data source can edit it.

3.    Click on the **Connections** tab. This tab will show you all the information about the underlying data connections within your published data source. In our example, it is a simple connection to a CSV file. In your organization, these data connections can get more complex.

4.    Click on the **Extract Refreshes** tab and then on the **New Extract Refresh** button. This will bring up a dialogue box, as seen in *Figure 2.9*:

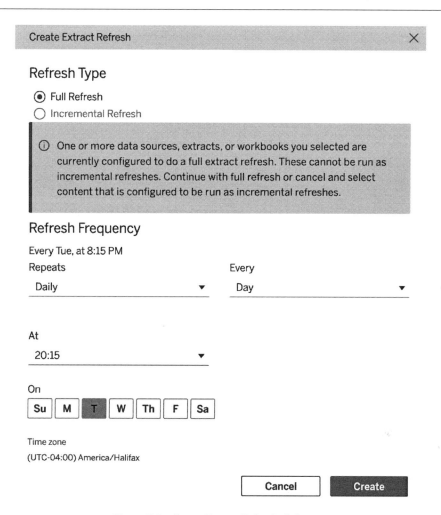

Figure 2.9 – Create Extract Refresh dialogue

5.  This dialogue allows you to schedule a regular refresh of your data source if you are extracting data into Tableau's high-performance **Hyper** engine. You set whether you want to extract your data when you create it. You also set whether you want the refresh to be full (replace existing data) or incremental (only add new rows since the last refresh). You can schedule your refresh to run on a finely tuned schedule through this dialogue and you can always come back and change it. We discuss extracts in more detail later in this chapter.

6.    For now, click **Cancel** on the **Create Extract Refresh** dialogue box. The next tab we see is **Connected Workbooks**. We do not yet have any connected workbooks at this point. As people create workbooks from our published data source, we will be able to see them on this tab in the web user interface.

7.    The last tab where we see whether our Tableau Server or Tableau Cloud has Data Management enabled is **Lineage**. The **Lineage** tab shows the descriptions of all the fields in our data model as well as all the upstream and downstream connections of our model. As we see in *Figure 2.10*, we have not yet added descriptions to our data model, nor have we connected workbooks. We will look at these features in *Chapter 13*.

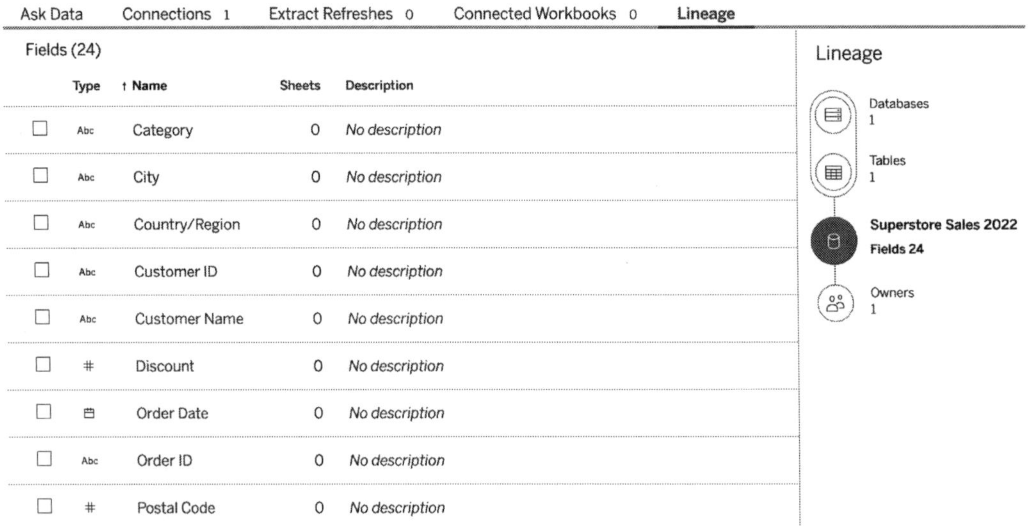

| | Type | ↑ Name | Sheets | Description |
|---|---|---|---|---|
| ☐ | Abc | Category | 0 | *No description* |
| ☐ | Abc | City | 0 | *No description* |
| ☐ | Abc | Country/Region | 0 | *No description* |
| ☐ | Abc | Customer ID | 0 | *No description* |
| ☐ | Abc | Customer Name | 0 | *No description* |
| ☐ | # | Discount | 0 | *No description* |
| ☐ | ▤ | Order Date | 0 | *No description* |
| ☐ | Abc | Order ID | 0 | *No description* |
| ☐ | # | Postal Code | 0 | *No description* |

Ask Data    Connections 1    Extract Refreshes 0    Connected Workbooks 0    **Lineage**

Fields (24)

Lineage

Databases 1

Tables 1

**Superstore Sales 2022**
**Fields 24**

Owners 1

Figure 2.10 – Data Lineage

8.    Let's look at the process of creating a published data source in the web user interface versus Tableau Desktop. Click on the **New** button.

9.    This time, we will select the option for **Published Data Source**. We will be asked to connect to the data source, as seen in *Figure 2.11*. Click on the **Files** tab and then upload from computer. Then find the `Superstore Sales 2022.csv` file that we used earlier in this chapter and click **Open**:

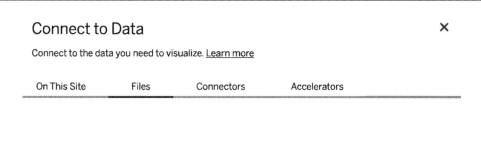

## Connect to Data                                                    ✕

Connect to the data you need to visualize. <u>Learn more</u>

On This Site          Files          Connectors          Accelerators

Drag and drop a file

or

**Upload from computer**

Figure 2.11 – Connecting to a data source in the browser

10. Once you have connected to the file, you will see the user interface, as shown in *Figure 2.12*. This user interface works almost the same as the Tableau Desktop experience with a slight change in the way you publish and manage user access. To publish, click on the **Publish As** button and select the name of the project where you wish to publish the data source:

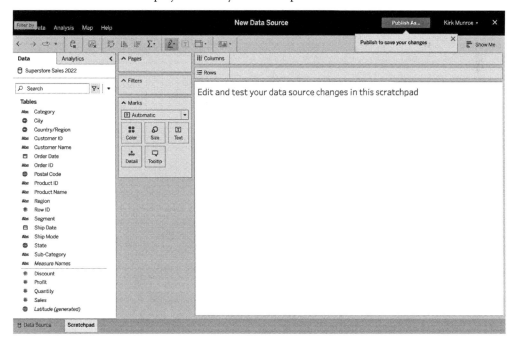

Figure 2.12 – Web client version UI to create a published data source

That covers the basics of understanding and creating published data sources, the primary method of creating shareable data models. In future chapters, we will look at creating more complex data models and publishing and maintaining them. Next, we will look at **embedded data sources**.

## Tableau embedded data sources

The other main data source type in Tableau is an embedded data source. An embedded data source has the data model embedded within the Tableau workbook. What does this mean?

When we publish an embedded data source, we don't publish the data source, but rather we publish a workbook that is not connected to a previously published data source. This is what makes the data source embedded. It is embedded in the workbook that has been published.

To see how this works, let's go back to where we left off in Tableau Desktop in the previous section, namely, *step 10*:

1. Before we publish a workbook, we need to create a chart on at least one sheet. From **Sheet 1**, double-click on **Sales** in the data pane. This will create a single bar representing all sales. Next, double-click on **Region** in the data pane. This will break sales up into four bars, one representing each region, as seen in *Figure 2.13*:

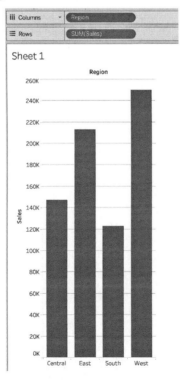

Figure 2.13 – Sales by region

2.  Now we have a very basic workbook that we can publish. We should rename our sheet before we publish it. On the **Sheet 1** tab on the bottom right of the screen, right-click, choose **Rename**, and then type Sales by Region over **Sheet 1** (*Figure 2.14*):

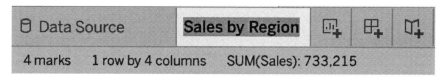

Figure 2.14 – Renaming a sheet

3.  We are now ready to publish. Go back to the **Server** option in the menu bar. This time, we will pick the option **Publish Workbook…** instead of **Publish Data Source**, as seen in *Figure 2.15*. At this point, you might be presented with a dialog recommending to create a data extract. If you are, please click on **Publish Without Extract** before continuing:

Figure 2.15 – Publish Workbook… menu item

4.  You will be presented with the dialogue box seen in *Figure 2.16*. Choose a project that you want to publish and change the name of the workbook to Sales by Region. Ensure that the **Data Sources** option says **1 embedded in workbook** and click **Publish**:

Figure 2.16 – Publish Workbook to Tableau Online dialog box

If the **Data Sources** option says **1 published separately**, first **edit** this option to **Embedded in workbook** as per *Figure 2.17*:

Manage Data Sources

| Data Source | Publish Type ⓘ | Authentication |
| --- | --- | --- |
| 🗄 Superstore Sales 2022<br>Requires creating an extract on publish. | Published separately ▾<br>Embedded in workbook<br>Published separately | |

Figure 2.17 – Changing the data source type

5.  This action publishes your workbook to Tableau Server or Tableau Cloud with your data source embedded. This means that other people, with the right permissions, can download or edit a version of our workbook but they cannot connect directly to our data source. This means that if they want to leverage the data modeling work we may have done in the workbook, they have to take the entire workbook to do so.

Embedded data sources have their place in the Tableau infrastructure. For individual analysts creating workbooks where the data model is not likely to be used by others, embedded data sources make sense to avoid the overhead of managing the workbook and its data source separately.

As the main goal of this chapter is Tableau data modeling, we will spend the rest of our time focusing on creating data models that will be available for your entire organization and perhaps beyond your organization. For this reason, we are going to focus exclusively on published data sources, but it is important for you to understand embedded data sources and when they make logical sense.

## Live versus extracted data

Tableau broadly gives two options for connection types for the data behind your data models. These are **Live** and **Extract**.

If you choose a live connection, Tableau will query your data source every time a user interacts with a visualization when it needs to get additional data that isn't in the view. If you choose to extract the data, Tableau will move the data from where the data is sourced to a high-performance analytical store.

The most basic use case for live connections is when the analysis being performed needs to occur on up-to-the-minute data. When the analysis is slightly delayed, as of the end of the close of business of the previous day, for example, an extract will often make the most sense as it allows for faster query time and less impact on operational databases. These use cases often simplify the many nuisances that determine the best option between live connections and extracts. We will explore each of these considerations as they come up in the use cases we cover throughout the rest of this book.

Another use case for live connections is when your data is stored in a highly performant database that is already optimized for analytic analysis. Traditionally, this included cube technologies and in-memory database appliances. More recently, all the major cloud vendors, as well as companies such as Snowflake and Databricks, offer analytical databases as a service.

To create an extract in Tableau Desktop, navigate to the **Data Source** tab in the bottom left-hand corner of the screen. Near the top right-hand corner of the data source screen, you should see the option for a **Live** or **Extract** connection as per *Figure 2.18*:

Figure 2.18 – Changing the connection type

It is as simple as clicking the appropriate radio button and Tableau will handle the rest for you. Next up, we will discuss Tableau Hyper, the database engine that powers Tableau extracts.

## The Tableau Hyper engine

Tableau extracts are stored in a proprietary database engine called **Hyper**. The Hyper engine is included with Tableau Desktop, Tableau Prep Builder, Tableau Server, and Tableau Cloud and therefore does not have any additional licensing requirements. In a technical sense, the term **extract** refers to data that is moved from its original source for the purposes of analysis. The term **Hyper** refers to the Tableau technology that houses and manages the extracted data. However, the terms are often used interchangeably or even together as **Hyper extract**. In fact, the extracted data will sit on a disk with a .hyper extension.

It is important to mention Hyper in this chapter as it is an important piece of the data modeling stack in Tableau. For the purposes of this book, we never interact with Hyper directly, but it is often at work behind the scenes when our data models are from extracted data. We have now explored published and embedded data sources and live and extract connections. We are now ready to tackle Tableau Prep Builder in *Chapter 3*.

## Summary

In this chapter, we explored the different Tableau licensing options and how they impact us as data modelers.

We then looked at how Tableau uses data models in workbooks. We looked at embedded data sources, which are data models that are linked to one workbook and cannot be used in others. We explored published data sources as a way to share our data models to be used by many analysts and developers in the creation of their workbooks. We also looked at live and extract connections and when to use each of them.

In the next chapter, we will build on what we learned by working with Tableau Prep Builder and understanding the role it plays in creating data models.

# Part 2: Tableau Prep Builder for Data Modeling

This part of the book focuses on the Tableau data preparation client, Tableau Prep Builder. In this part of the book, you will get an in-depth understanding of the tool and its ideal use cases.

This part comprises the following chapters:

- *Chapter 3, Data Preparation with Tableau Prep Builder*
- *Chapter 4, Data Modeling Functions with Tableau Prep Builder*
- *Chapter 5, Advanced Modeling Functions in Tableau Prep Builder*
- *Chapter 6, Data Output from Tableau Prep Builder*

# 3

# Data Preparation with Tableau Prep Builder

**Tableau Prep Builder** is Tableau's product for preparing data and creating simple to complicated data models. Tableau Prep Builder extracts data via data connectors and allows the user to transform the data through several different functions and load the data on Tableau Server, Tableau Online, and other destinations. Tableau Prep Builder, first released in 2018, is different than Tableau Desktop in that it is solely focused on preparing data for analysis.

Tableau Prep Builder can be used via a downloadable software client that you install on your local computer. It is available for both Windows and Mac. Tableau Prep Builder is also available as a web client on Tableau Server and Tableau Cloud for individuals with a Creator license. Tableau Prep Builder will create an object called a **flow**. The term flow is used because it describes how data flows from originating data sources through a data transformation process, ending with the transformed data being stored via an output step.

This chapter is focused on the Tableau Prep Builder user interface, the process of connecting to data, and the first step in any data preparation process – the clean step. The chapter will also focus on row-level calculations, including optimizing string fields. The functions in this chapter are the most foundational data preparation functions to master. With the foundation you build in this chapter, you will be able to create your first data models in Tableau Prep Builder and gain the knowledge required to master the more complex modeling functions that we explore in *Chapter 4* and *Chapter 5*.

In this chapter, we're going to cover the following main topics:

- Using Tableau Prep Builder to connect to data
- Profiling, cleaning, and grouping data
- Row-level calculations and hiding and removing fields
- Recommendations and changes

To view the software requirements for this chapter, please see the *Technical requirements* section in *Chapter 1*.

All the exercises and images in this chapter will be described using the Tableau Prep Builder client software, except where noted. You can also recreate all the exercises in this chapter using the Tableau Prep Builder web client, which has a near-identical experience to the installed client. There are also very minor differences in the look and feel of the user interface between macOS and Microsoft Windows. The images in this and future chapters that come from the client software are created on macOS. The images from the web client are generated from Chrome on macOS.

## Using Tableau Prep Builder to connect to data

To run the exercises in this chapter, we will need the following downloaded files:

- `Bad Measures.xlsx`
- `Mobile Phone Plans.xlsx`
- `Product Database.xlsx`
- `Sales Argentina.csv`
- `Sales Chile.csv`
- `Sales Colombia.csv`
- `Sales Targets.xlsx`
- `Superstore Sales Orders - Canada.xlsx`
- `Superstore Sales Orders - US.xlsx`

We are using these files as they give us a good representation of the types of data cleaning that we typically run into in our daily jobs and they align well with Tableau Prep Builder features. When possible, they also include data related to Tableau's sample data, `Superstore`.

Let's open Tableau Prep Builder and explore the user interface. If you are using the installed client, please open the program. If you are using the web client, you can launch it by creating a new flow. You can create a new flow from the home page on Tableau Server or Tableau Cloud, as shown in *Figure 3.1*:

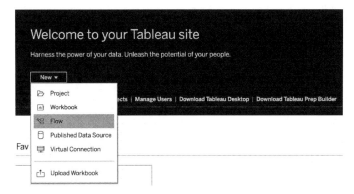

Figure 3.1 – Create a new flow

We will now start the process of creating our first Tableau flow:

1.  Open the Tableau Prep Builder client or begin a new flow from your browser, as shown in *Figure 3.1*. You will be presented with the screen shown in *Figure 3.2* from the client, or *Figure 3.3* if you're using your browser:

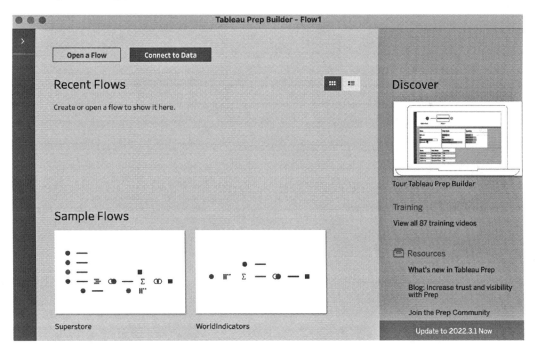

Figure 3.2 – Initial screen in Prep Builder client

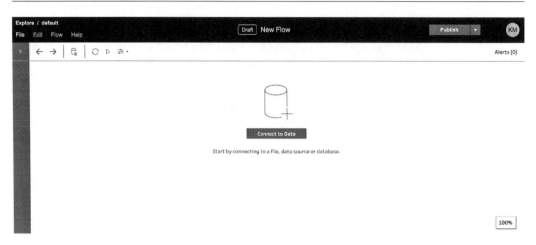

Figure 3.3 – Initial screen from web client

2.  The first step in any Tableau Prep Builder flow is connecting to data. Press the **Connect to Data** button to get started.

3.  Select **Microsoft Excel**, locate the Superstore Sales Orders - US.xlsx file where you copied it from the GitHub repository to your local computer, and click **Open**. Tableau will now open the file and create the first step in a flow, as shown in *Figure 3.4*:

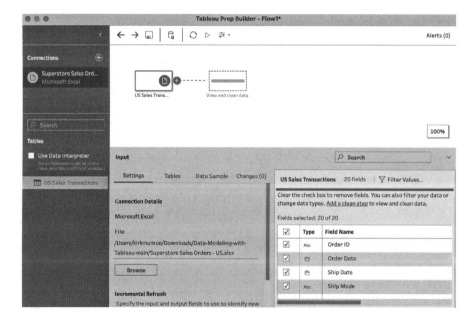

Figure 3.4 – Tableau Prep Builder UI after connecting to data

4.  In the left-hand pane (shaded in blue), Tableau presents all the data **connections** in the flow first. This area is called the **Connections** pane. At this point, we have the single data source that we just connected to. We will connect to additional data sources as we continue through this and the next few chapters. Below the connections, Tableau lists all the tables in the selected connections. In this case, our Excel workbook contains a single sheet, so we only see a single table, **US Sales Transactions**. If we had multiple sheets in our Excel workbook, each sheet would show up as an individual table. We can also see the **Use Data Interpreter** option. This option is designed to clean up formatting in Excel and text files. Our Excel file is already well formatted, so we don't need this option. If our file had additional formatting, such as information above the rows containing file headers, we could select the data interpreter and Tableau would clean up the file for us when it could interpret it correctly.

5.  The pane on the top of the screen is the flow pane. This is where we will visually build out our data preparation flow.

6.  Most of the screen is taken up with the input pane. On the **Settings** tab, we can see the details of our connection. Since we used Excel, our connection is to a file. If we had connected to a database, the connection information would be shown here. This is where we also have the option to set the data source to **Enable incremental refresh**. Incremental refreshes allow us to add to our output without needing to reload historical data each time. We will discuss this option in more detail in *Chapter 6* when we explore the output action.

7.  The input pane is also where we can **filter** our data. Filtering data is key for data storage and performance and is often overlooked when building data models. We do not want to load data that will never be used for analysis. This clutters the user experience for analysts and consumers, leads to slower loading times, and can take a lot of unnecessary space on disk.

8.  Thinking back to our exploration of the way Tableau likes data in *Chapter 1*, there are two methods for filtering down our data. The first is to filter the width of the data model. The width is determined by the number of columns in the data model. The quickest way to eliminate columns from our data source is to deselect them from the **Settings** tab in the **Input** step of the flow creation. A way of filtering out the Segment and Ship Mode columns is shown in *Figure 3.5*. The Tableau Prep Builder user interface makes it clear that 18 of the 20 fields will be brought into the data model.

---

**Note**

We will be using all 20 fields in the rest of this exercise, so please make sure all 20 fields are checked. We will eliminate fields from our model later in this chapter.

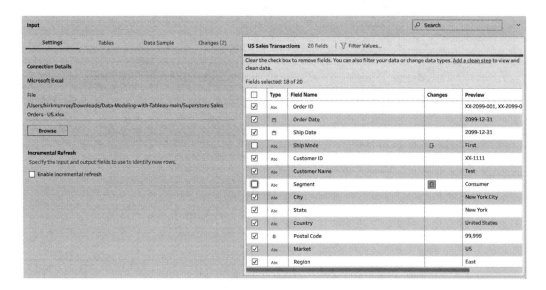

Figure 3.5 – Filtering columns

9.    The other way we can filter the amount of data in our model is by filtering values. This will constrain the length of the data. Filtering values decreases the number of rows in the model. Filtering out data the analysts don't need can significantly increase query performance. To filter rows, click on the **Filter Values** button. A dialog box will appear, letting you input a **Boolean** calculation, that is, a value that returns either true or false. As an example, if we were creating a data model for a team that was only looking at data for the state of New York, we could enter the calculation shown in *Figure 3.6*. This is telling Tableau to filter data to the condition where the State field only contains the value New York. In other words, this is instructing Tableau to eliminate all rows that contain all other US states. As in the previous step, we do not want to apply this filter right now. Please click on the **x** in the top right-hand corner of the dialog box to dismiss our changes:

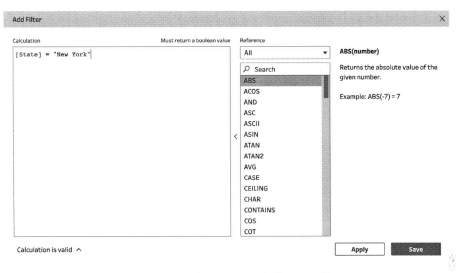

Figure 3.6 – Creation of a Boolean calculation to filter rows

10. The next tab in the input pane is the **Tables** tab. This is where we can tell Tableau Prep Builder to automatically add data from other files and tables through a **union**. We will be looking at unions in *Chapter 4*. For this exercise, leave the default option of **Single table**, as shown in *Figure 3.7*:

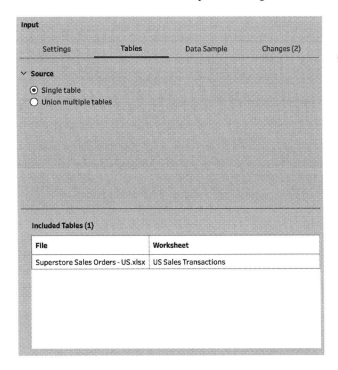

Figure 3.7 – The Tables tab of the input pane

11.  Moving from left to right, the next tab we see is **Data Sample**, as shown in *Figure 3.8*:

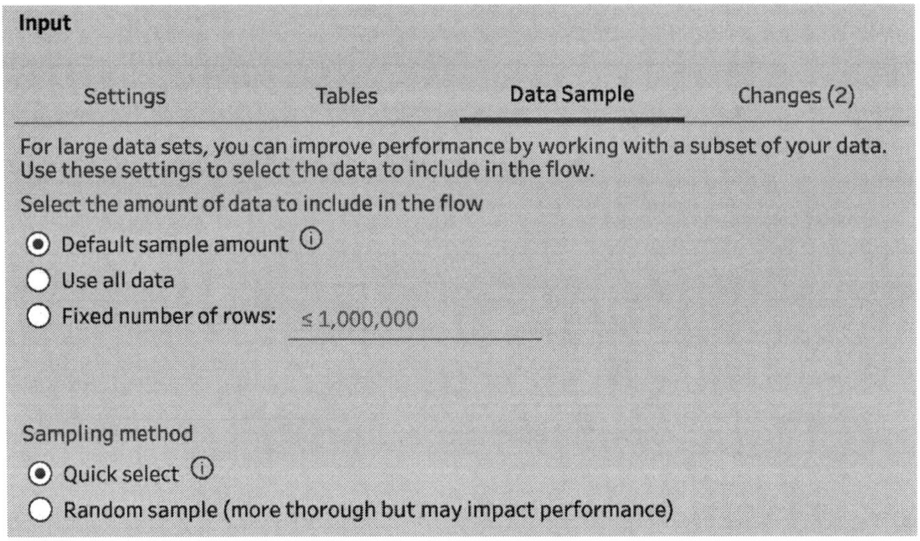

**Input**

| Settings | Tables | **Data Sample** | Changes (2) |
|---|---|---|---|

For large data sets, you can improve performance by working with a subset of your data. Use these settings to select the data to include in the flow.

Select the amount of data to include in the flow

⦿ Default sample amount ⓘ

◯ Use all data

◯ Fixed number of rows:    ≤ 1,000,000

Sampling method

⦿ Quick select ⓘ

◯ Random sample (more thorough but may impact performance)

Figure 3.8 – Data Sample tab of the input pane

When we have very large datasets, we might want or need to set up **data sampling**. If the memory on our computer is less than that which would hold the entire dataset, Tableau Prep Builder will run very slowly as it will have to swap data from memory to disk. This can render the data modeling experience very slow and difficult, or even impossible. The amount of data you should sample varies depending on the speed and memory of your computer and the structure of the data you are bringing in.

In large datasets, it can be a bit of a trial and error to get the sample size correct. Using the defaults of **Default sample amount** and **Quick select** sampling methods is usually the best choice. The challenge of sampling data is that the sample data might not be representative of all the data that you work to clean in your flow. We will look at some examples when we look at grouping data later in this chapter.

For this reason, Tableau Prep Builder allows you to control how sampling works through the **Fixed number of rows** and **Random sample (more thorough but may impact performance)** options. If you know that your data is well represented in, say, the first 2 million rows, you can select that option. If your data is very heterogeneous, you can select the random sample option.

As shown in the user interface, this option will be slower to retrieve data than just fetching rows via the **Quick select** method. For our exercise, you can leave the default checks or select **Use all data** as our dataset is very small and this sample will be equal to using all data.

12. The last tab in the input pane is **Changes**. As we build out our flows, Tableau keeps track of all changes we make. This is a great feature as it allows us to change or delete previous steps in our flow. If you think about the Windows clipboard features of undo and redo or the back and forward buttons in Tableau Desktop, the changes feature of Tableau Prep Builder is even more powerful. It allows you to go back and undo changes you made in the past without having to undo all the changes you made after it, provided the changes after the one you are deleting aren't impacted by that change. At this point, we have not made any changes, which is why there is a **0** in parentheses after **Changes** in the user interface. We will look at how changes work later in the chapter.

In the next section, we are going to be looking at the most important and most common step in a Tableau Prep Builder flow, the clean step. Please leave Tableau Prep Builder open as it is right now. We will be picking up from this point.

## Profiling, cleaning, and grouping data

In this section, we are going to begin the process of profiling, cleaning, and grouping data in Tableau Prep Builder. Of all the functions in Prep Builder, the clean step is the one we will use most often. In fact, it is recommended to add a clean step after any other type of step to see if the previous step transformed the data in the manner we were expecting.

Let's pick up where we left off in the previous section:

1. The top right-hand section of the Tableau Prep Builder user interface is the flow pane. It gets this name because it is the area where we get a graphical representation of how our data flows through the preparation process. Continuing from the previous section, your flow pane should look like *Figure 3.9*:

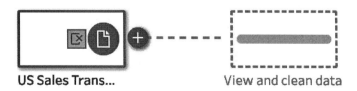

US Sales Trans...                 View and clean data

Figure 3.9 – The flow pane

2.  To create a clean step, click on the + symbol to the right of the box. When the drop-down menu appears, select **Clean Step**, as shown in *Figure 3.10*:

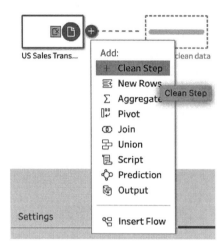

Figure 3.10 – Starting a clean step

3.  Once **Clean Step** is selected, the user interface changes into four distinct sections:

    A.  To the left, stretching down the entire user interface, we see the **Connections** pane that we explored in the previous section.

    B.  On the top right, we have the flow pane that we discussed in the first step of this exercise.

    C.  On the middle right, we have the profile pane. This is where we get a profile of our data before and after any changes we make.

    D.  On the bottom right, we have data details. This is a sample of the rows of data that will change as we make changes in the profile pane.

4.  To see how we use the profile pane to clean and transform our data, find the **Order Date** field, which is the second field from the left, right after **Order ID**. The **card** for the Order Date field, shown in *Figure 3.11*, immediately profiles a lot of information about this field in our dataset:

Figure 3.11 – The Order Date card

First, above the field name, there is a little calendar icon that tells us that Tableau is treating this as a date field. Click on the calendar icon to see the other field type options, as shown in *Figure 3.12*. Selecting the proper field type is important as it tells Tableau how to treat the data when creating a visualization in Tableau Desktop. In this case, Tableau correctly interpreted the field to be a date field so we will not change anything:

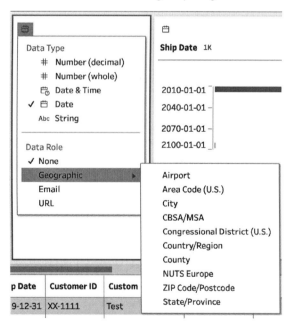

Figure 3.12 – Data types

The next two things you will notice are the **1K** to the right of **Ship Date** and the distribution of values shown in a histogram below the line under the field name. The **1K**, representing approximately one thousand values, is helpful for understanding our data. For instance, if we find the Order ID field, we will see **5K** representing the number of records in the data. This means that there were approximately 5 order IDs generated per day. (Remember this is only sample data; it's not representative of a successful business!)

5. Looking at the histogram of date distributions, we can see there is clearly something not right with our data. It looks like most of our data is in the decade 2010-2020, but we have some data in the decade 2090-2100. This is clearly not possible as those dates haven't happened yet. To address this, let's click on the small bar that shows to the right of **2100-01-01**, as shown in *Figure 3.13*, and then watch what happens in data details, as shown in *Figure 3.14*:

Figure 3.13 – Select the bottom bar in the histogram

| Order ID | Order Date | Ship Date | Customer ID | Customer Name | City | State | Country | Postal Code | Market | Region | Product ID | Sales |
|---|---|---|---|---|---|---|---|---|---|---|---|---|
| XX-2099-001 | 2099-12-31 | 2099-12-31 | XX-1111 | Test | New York City | New York | United States | 99,999 | US | East | XX-XX-0001 | 99,999 |
| XX-2099-002 | 2099-12-31 | 2099-12-31 | XX-1111 | Test | New York City | New York | United States | 99,999 | US | East | XX-XX-0002 | 99,999 |
| XX-2099-003 | 2099-12-31 | 2099-12-31 | XX-1111 | Test | New York City | New York | United States | 99,999 | US | East | XX-XX-0003 | 99,999 |

Figure 3.14 – Data details for Order Date selection

6. Looking at this data, we can see that test data was mixed in with our production data and should not be there. We don't want this data in our data model or it could cause confusion for analysts. Tableau Prep Builder makes it easy to filter this data out of our model. Going back to the histogram bar from the previous step, right-click and choose **Exclude**, as shown in *Figure 3.15*:

Figure 3.15 – Excluding test data

7.  Once we exclude the data, the **Order Date** card has a distribution that shows data across four years, as shown in *Figure 3.16*. It is important to note that Tableau does not write back to your database. As we create our flow, we are giving Tableau instructions on what data to bring into our data model and how to transform that data. In this case, it means that the three records we just excluded are not deleted from the database (in this case, our database is Excel). It is important to remember that nothing we do in Tableau Prep Builder or Tableau Desktop can change the underlying data source.

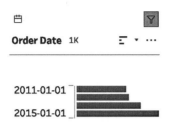

Figure 3.16 – Date distribution after excluding 2099

8.  Moving along the fields in our model, we can see that things also don't look right in the **Ship Mode** field. In this field, we can see that **First** and **First Class**, **Second** and **Second Class**, and **Standard** and **Standard Class** are probably meant to represent the same ship mode. This can be seen in *Figure 3.17*:

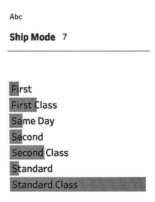

Figure 3.17 – Ship Mode distribution

9.  One of the most important and common functions of Tableau Prep Builder is to group values in fields exactly like this one. To begin cleaning this field, we will look at the manual method. Click on **First** in the **Ship Mode** card, right-click, and choose **Edit Value**. This is shown in *Figure 3.18*:

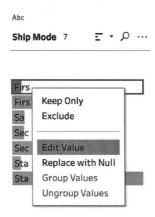

Figure 3.18 – Manually editing a value

10. Type First Class over the **First** value and press *Enter/Return*. You will see that Tableau groups all the values that were previously **First** into **First Class**, as shown in *Figure 3.19*. This will make our analysis in Tableau Desktop much easier. The other two things to notice are the value after **Ship Mode** is now **6** (it was 7 before), and there is a little paper clip icon in the top right-hand corner of the card letting us know that values are grouped:

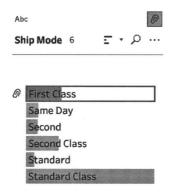

Figure 3.19 – Ship Mode after manual grouping

11. The manual method of editing and grouping values is very direct and powerful but not always practical. In this case, we only have 7 values, which we want to put in 4 groups. If we had hundreds or thousands of values, this method would not be practical and would often be error prone. To help solve this issue, Tableau Prep Builder has machine learning algorithms embedded to make this task run automatically. Going back to the **Ship Mode** card, hover your mouse just below the paper clip icon until the more options dialog appears. Click on **More options | Group Values** and let's look at our options for grouping. The result of these steps can be seen in *Figure 3.20*:

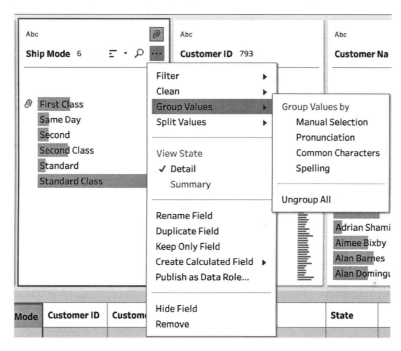

Figure 3.20 – Grouping options

We looked at the manual selection in *step 12* of this process. The three machine learning options are as follows:

A. **Pronunciation** – useful for fixing data errors where words sound similar. The dataset we are providing is a good example.

B. **Common Characters** – useful for fixing capitalization or formatting issues. An example would be a field where the data input was done by different people who weren't consistent with capitalizing proper nouns or leaving spaces between words.

C. **Spelling** – useful for values that are entered manually as spelling mistakes inevitably happen, or when people are using American and UK English, for example, *favour* and *favor*.

12. To see this in action, click on **Pronunciation** and watch the remaining fields group automatically. The result can be seen in *Figure 3.21*:

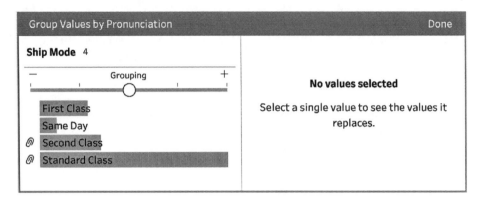

Figure 3.21 – Resulting grouping after the Pronunciation method

13. After running the grouping function, Tableau allows you to tweak the specificity of the machine learning results when Tableau doesn't do a perfect job. If we click on **Second Class**, we see how Tableau came up with the grouping as seen in *Figure 3.22*. In our example, Tableau did the job perfectly. If it hadn't, you could slide the circle on the bar below **Grouping** in this card to refine the results. Since Tableau got it right in our case, click on **Done** in the top right-hand corner to dismiss the grouping card:

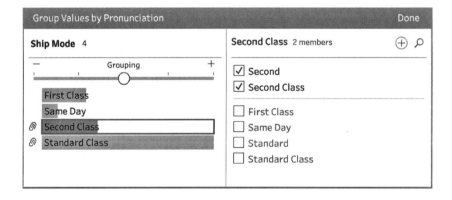

Figure 3.22 – Refining the Grouping algorithm

14. Before moving on from grouping, let's look at the **Clean** function of Tableau Prep Builder by again clicking on more options on the **Ship Mode** card. As you can see in *Figure 3.23*, Tableau gives you a number of options to clean your data:

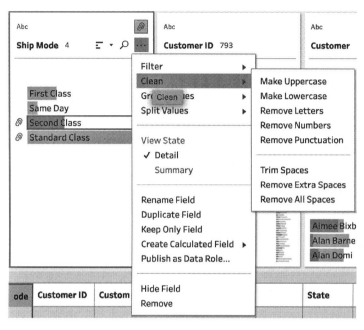

Figure 3.23 – Clean options

Let's see one of these options in action by clicking on **Make Uppercase**. The result is shown in *Figure 3.24*. The options to **Remove Extra Spaces** (that is, spaces between words) and **Trim Spaces** (that is, spaces before and after words) are particularly useful as spaces are characters to a computer. In other words, values with extra spaces can be very difficult to debug. Please leave Tableau Prep Builder in this state or save your flow so we can pick up from this point in the next section of this chapter:

Figure 3.24 – Results of Make Uppercase

In this section, we learned how to profile, group, and clean data. In many cases, these will be the most common functions used in data preparation for building data models in Tableau. If our data is not cleaned and grouped properly, we can end up with misleading results in the analysis we do on that data.

We will now move to the next section, where we focus on row-level calculations.

## Row-level calculations and hiding and removing fields

Creating calculations in our data model can be of great benefit to analysts, who will use it to get answers to questions they have about the data. It makes more sense for some calculations to happen during analysis. These types of calculations relate to use cases where the data modeler can't predict the questions the analysts will have. Typical examples are running totals, differences between values, period-to-date, and percentage of totals. These calculations are hard to perform ahead of the analysis phase because we don't know the filters and the level of aggregation the analyst will be using ahead of time. These aggregate calculations are usually best left to the analyst and not put in the data model. However, there are some exceptions to this rule, so we will be looking at aggregate calculations in Tableau Prep Builder in *Chapter 4*.

Many other calculations only need to be performed once. These calculations tend to occur on the row level, that is, these calculations happen before any aggregation of the data occurs. Almost all calculations on string fields occur at this level. An example would be combining a field containing the first (given) name with a field containing the last name (surname) to create a full name field. It is much better to perform these calculations in our data model because they will slow down analysis if left for that phase. It takes a lot of computing power to deal with string fields and they must be performed on every row which could easily be in the millions. We are going to look at some row-level calculations in this section.

Another useful feature of Tableau Prep Builder is the ability to *hide* and *remove* fields. Hiding a field will result in it not being visible in your Tableau Prep Builder flow, but it will still be in the data model and available to analysts. You may want to hide fields if you have a lot of fields and know you no longer need to perform any functions on those fields. Much like excluding values, removing fields does not impact your underlying data source but it does remove the field from your data model. This is a very useful function to eliminate unnecessary columns from our data model. Extra fields make our data model wider. If they aren't needed, leaving them in can often impact query performance and make analysis harder as the analyst will have to look through a list of fields that they will never use. For this reason, removing fields is key to filtering data.

Let's pick up from where we left off in our flow from the previous section:

1.  Find the **Customer Name** field in the profile pane. It should be the sixth field from the left. Highlight the card for the field and notice that the ribbon bar between the flow and profile pane changes dynamically based on the field type we select, in this case, a string field. Click on the ellipses on this pane to see additional options, as shown in *Figure 3.25*:

Figure 3.25 – Options for string fields

In addition to **Filter Values**, let's look at the rest of the options:

A.  **Automatic Split** – using this function tells Tableau Prep Builder to split out our field using embedded logic in the product.

B.  **Custom Split** – this also splits a field but we get to decide the condition to split on. We will do this in the next step.

C.  **Rename Field** – as it sounds this allows us to rename the field. Imagine this field was called **CUS_NAME** in our data source. We could change it to **Customer Name** with this function.

D.  **Create Calculated Field** – this allows us to use Tableau's extensive calculation language to manually write a calculation.

E.  **Duplicate Field** – this function gives us another copy of the same field.

F.  **Keep Only Field** – this function removes all other fields. It's not commonly used.

G.  **Hide Field** – as mentioned in the introduction to this section, this function hides the field in our flow but does not remove it from the data model.

H.  **Remove Field** – as mentioned in the introduction to this section, this function removes the field from our data model.

2.    To split our **Customer Name** field into first and last name, select **Automatic Split**. The result is shown in *Figure 3.26*. You will find any new calculated fields in the leftmost position on the profile pane. You can reorder fields in the profile pane by clicking on its card and dragging it to the position where you wish it to be. In this case, we will leave the two new fields, **Customer Name – Split 1** and **Customer Name – Split 2**, where Tableau Prep Builder puts them:

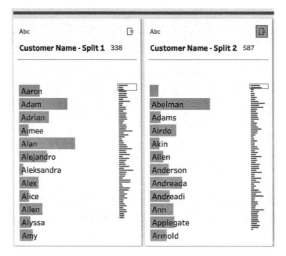

Figure 3.26 – Two new fields from the split function

3.    Now we get to use the **Rename Field** function. Highlight the **Customer Name – Split 1** field and click on the **Rename Field** function. You will then be able to type over the existing field name to add the new name you want. Alternatively, if you double-click on the field name in the card, you will also be given the same ability, saving the step of clicking on **Rename Field** in the user interface. You can see this in *Figure 3.27*:

Figure 3.27 – Rename Field

Please rename the field `First Name` and repeat the process with **Customer Name – Split 2**, renaming it `Last Name`, as shown in *Figure 3.28*:

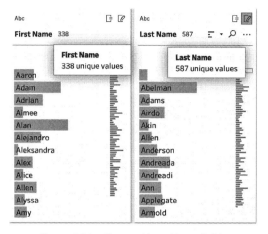

Figure 3.28 – First and Last Name fields

4.  In addition to string calculations, we can perform other calculations in Tableau Prep Builder using the same calculation language and engine available in Tableau Desktop. One example is date calculations. Let's add a date calculation by finding the **Create Calculated Field** function on the same ribbon between the flow and profile panes. This will bring up a calculation dialog box. When the box comes up, scroll down until you find the **DATEDIFF** function. Tableau provides this useful reference for the calculation language without needing to go to an external reference guide. Your screen should now look *Figure 3.29*:

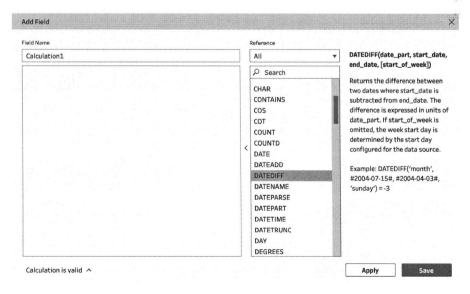

Figure 3.29 – Tableau calculation dialog box

We will now create a calculation for the number of days each row took to ship. In the field name, type `Days to Ship` and, in the calculation window, type `DATEDIFF('day', [Order Date], [Ship Date])`, as shown in *Figure 3.30*. Tableau will help us here. For example, when you start typing `Ship Date`, Tableau will find the field for you, and you can hit the *Enter/Return* key to autocomplete. Tableau will also let you know if there is a problem with your syntax and how to fix it. Click on **Save** and we have a new calculated field:

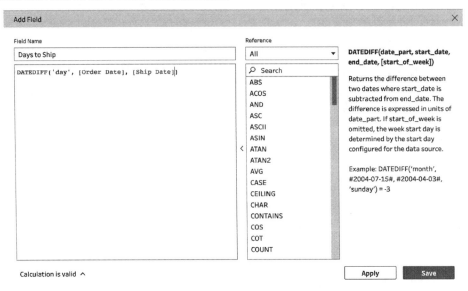

Figure 3.30 – Days to Ship calculation

5.    After clicking on **Save**, you should notice a new card for the `Days to Ship` field, as shown in *Figure 3.31*:

Figure 3.31 – Days to Ship field

We have just learned the importance of creating row-level calculations in our data model and have created our first two calculations, one each of a string and date calculation. In the next and final section of this chapter, we are going to look at Tableau Prep Builder **changes** and **recommendations**.

## Recommendations and changes

Tableau Prep Builder has two powerful features that help direct us to items to put in our flow and give us an audit trail of our flow. They give us the ability to go back and delete or change anything in our flow without having to undo all the changes we have made since that action. The changes also automatically create documentation for the development work done in Prep Builder. If anyone else needs to work with our flow, they can use the changes pane to see everything we have done in the flow.

Let's first look at **Recommendations**, picking up from where we left off in the previous section:

1. Looking at the ribbon between the flow and prep panes, you will see a **Recommendations** button. Clicking on this button will bring up a list of recommendations, as shown in *Figure 3.32*:

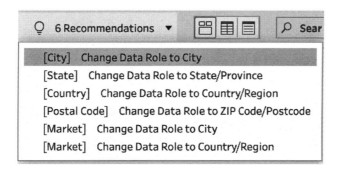

Figure 3.32 – Recommendations

2. As we can see in this example, sometimes these recommendations are useful and point out things we might have missed. Specifically, changing the **data role** of City to City, State to State, and Postal Code to ZIP Code/Postcode all make a lot of sense. For now, we are going to ignore these recommendations, but we would implement them if we were going to publish this flow in our organization.

3. Next, we will look at the changes pane. If the data pane is not already open, find the **Changes (8)** option to the left of the leftmost field to open it. You will then see all the changes you have made in your flow, as shown in *Figure 3.33*. Note that the changes pane might be collapsed. In this case, click on the > that is to the left of the profile pane and above the **Changes** text to expand the changes pane.

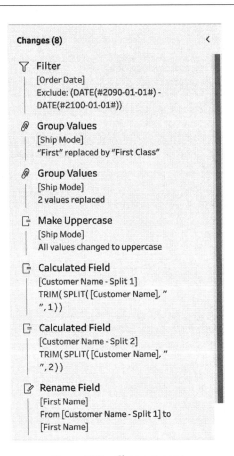

Figure 3.33 – Changes pane

4.  Tableau Prep Builder and Tableau Desktop have back and forward buttons that work very similarly to undo and redo in the Microsoft Windows and macOS operating systems. Changes is a much more powerful version of this. Back and forward (undo and redo) require you to undo/redo every step to get back or forward to the one you wish to change. With changes, you can go back in time and make a change without having to undo all the great work you've done since, as long as subsequent changes aren't dependent on that step. By clicking on any step, you will be able to see what Tableau Prep Builder did at that stage. Let's click on **Make Uppercase** and see what Tableau did at that point. First, click on **Make Uppercase** and then click on the pencil icon in the top-right corner of the card. You will see the **Edit Field** pane open, as shown in *Figure 3.34*:

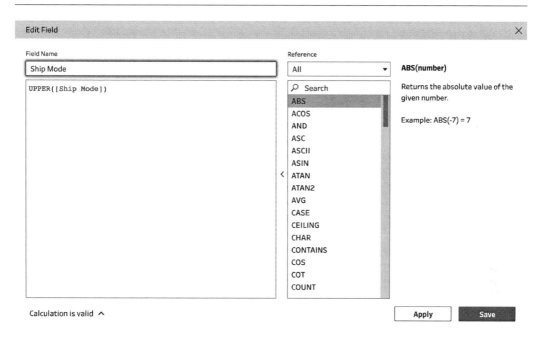

Figure 3.34 – Step to make Ship Mode uppercase

5.  When we made the change to make this field uppercase, we used the Tableau clean function to do it in *step 15* of the *Profiling, cleaning, and grouping data* section of this chapter. The changes pane is also great for understanding the Tableau calculation language generated by automated functions. We don't want to make a change to this, so press the **x** in the upper right-hand corner to dismiss the dialog box.

6.  Let's delete the last five steps we made in our flow. To do this, go to each of these steps and click the **x**, as shown in *Figure 3.35*:

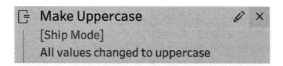

Figure 3.35 – Delete a step

After deleting the last five steps, you should be left with the changes shown in *Figure 3.36*. Remember, if you make a mistake, you can use the back button too:

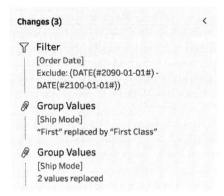

Figure 3.36 – Final state of changes

7.  Our final step is to save our flow. We will pick up from this point in the next chapter. Remember the name you give the flow in case you close Tableau Prep Builder between now and starting the next chapter. Tableau makes this easy by providing a **Recent Flows** option when you open Tableau Prep Builder.

In this section, we looked at recommendations and changes. These two features act as a *safety net* to make sure we don't miss a step and to provide the ability to easily fix a step that we made earlier in our flow.

## Summary

In this chapter, we learned about the foundational capabilities of Tableau Prep Builder. The main function is to create flows, which refer to the way data moves through a data preparation process. Every flow begins with connecting to data. In addition to the connection pane, flows have three key panes to help us with data preparation: the flow pane, which gives us a visual representation of the stages of our flow; the profile pane to profile the shape and contents of our data; and data details to get samples of what is in our data sources and the impact of our changes.

We also learned how to group, filter, and clean data. We learned about the impact of creating row-level calculations in our model and created string and date calculations. In the final section of the chapter, we learned how the recommendations and the changes pane can drive our efficiency, ensuring we don't miss steps and giving us an easy way to modify or delete steps that we later realize weren't right.

In the next chapter, we will build off this foundation knowledge and begin the more advanced data preparation functions of joins and unions, pivots, aggregate calculations, and creating new rows in our data.

# 4

# Data Modeling Functions with Tableau Prep Builder

In the previous chapter, we were introduced to Tableau Prep Builder, Tableau's product for preparing data and creating data models. We explored connections, filtering, cleaning, grouping, and several functions Tableau Prep Builder uses to make our modeling jobs easier.

Beyond extracting, filtering, and cleaning data, Prep Builder has functions for combining different data sources and reshaping data to optimize in the table format preferred by Tableau. This chapter focuses on extending the width of data by adding new columns through joins and extending the length of data by adding rows through unions. The chapter also covers consolidating fields from columns and adding new fields from data in rows. Additionally, we cover the strategy and technique for aggregating data to the proper level for analysis.

In this chapter, we're going to cover the following main topics:

- Adding additional data through unions – including wildcard unions

- Joining new data

- Consolidating fields from columns – pivoting columns to rows

- Understanding the level of detail and aggregating data

---

**Note**

To view the complete list of requirements to run the practical examples in this chapter, please see the *Technical requirements* section of *Chapter 1*.

---

All the exercises and images in this chapter are described using the Tableau Prep Builder client software except where noted. You can also recreate all the exercises in this chapter using the Tableau Prep Builder web client, which has a near identical experience to the installed client.

> **Note**
>
> The colors that you see in the screenshots in the chapters might not match the colors you see on your UI when you run the flow.

# Adding rows to our data model with unions and wildcard unions

Before beginning our exercises in Tableau Prep Builder, as mentioned in *Chapter 3*, in the *Using Tableau Prep Builder to connect to data* section, please make a note of the directory name where you have stored these files from GitHub:

- `Sales Argentina.csv`
- `Sales Chile.csv`
- `Sales Colombia.csv`
- `Superstore Sales Orders - Canada.xlsx`
- `Superstore Sales Orders - US.xlsx`

Create a sub-directory in the directory where you downloaded the files from Github. Call the sub-directory `South America Sales` and move the `Sales Argentina.csv`, `Sales Chile.csv`, and `Sales Colombia.csv` files into this new sub-directory. In this section, we will explore **unions**. Thinking back to our exploration of how Tableau likes data in *Chapter 2*, unions are a method of adding additional rows of data. This makes our data model longer. In the next section of this chapter, we will look at **joins**. Joins are a way to add new columns. Joins make our data wider.

We are using the previously mentioned files to demonstrate unions because they represent the Tableau sample data, Superstore. The main characteristic of tables (or files) that are good candidates for unions are tables that have the same columns. The columns do not always need to have the same names. We will look at resolving the cases where the field names (column names) don't match exactly but contain the same type of data in this section.

To begin, open the flow we created in the previous chapter. If you haven't closed Tableau Prep Builder since the exercise in the previous chapter, you are good to pick up where you left off. If you have closed Tableau Prep Builder, when you launch the application, you should see your saved flow on the home screen in the upper-left corner, as shown in *Figure 4.1*. In this case, the flow is called **Book Chapter 3**. Double-click on the flow to open it. If the flow doesn't show in **Recent Flows**, click on the **Open a Flow** button to locate the flow on your computer, then click on the **Open** button after highlighting the file:

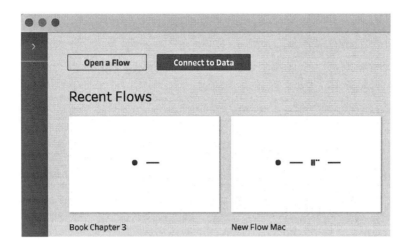

Figure 4.1 – Recent Flows in Tableau Prep Builder

We will now start the process of creating our first union in Tableau:

1.  To begin, we need to add a new connection to the data source we will union the `Superstore Sales Transactions - US.xlsx` data source, which is in our flow. To add a new connection, click on the + symbol in the connections pane, as shown in *Figure 4.2*.

> **Note**
>
> The colors might not match those seen in the screenshots in this chapter.

Figure 4.2 – Adding a new connection

Now select **Microsoft Excel** from the **To a File** section and, from the location where you saved the files from GitHub, find and select the file called `Superstore Sales Orders - Canada.xls`. Click on the **OK** button. Your screen should now look like the one shown in *Figure 4.3*:

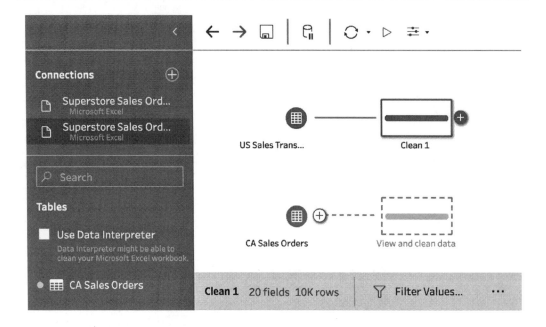

Figure 4.3 – Superstores Sales Orders Canada addition

Before going further, we will rename the **Clean 1** step as a good name practice. To do this, double-click on the **Clean 1** text in the flow and then enter Clean US Sales over **Clean 1**. Press *Enter* as shown in *Figure 4.4*:

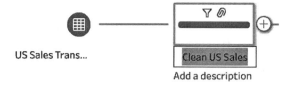

Figure 4.4 – Rename clean step

2.  Now we will create our first union. Hold down the left mouse key while clicking on the + symbol to the right of **CA Sales Orders**. Then, drag it just below the **Clean US Sales** box until the **Union** text appears in the user interface. Release the left mouse key to drop the CA Sales Orders table on **Union**, as shown in *Figure 4.5*.

> **Note**
>
> To the right of the **Clean US Sales** box, you should also see **Join**. Make sure you do not release the left mouse button when hovering over the join option. We will be exploring joins in the next section of this chapter.

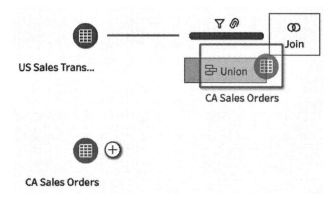

Figure 4.5 – Dragging to Union

3.  After releasing your left mouse button, your flow pane and profile pane should look like *Figure 4.6*. Remember that a union means adding new rows, which means that all field (column) names must match for Tableau to add the new rows in the right place:

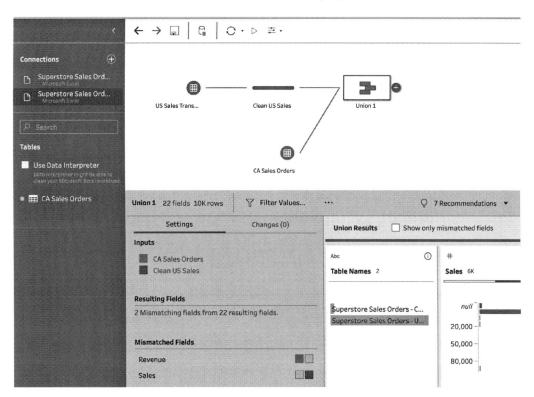

Figure 4.6 – Creating a union

To help with this, the profile pane shows us that we have two mismatched fields, `Sales` and `Revenue`. To make this easier to see, click on the **Show only mismatched fields** checkbox, which sits over the field cards in the profile pane, as shown in *Figure 4.7*:

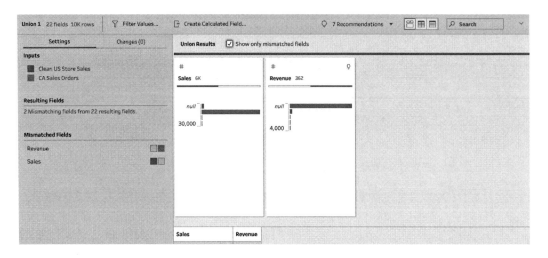

Figure 4.7 – Showing only mismatched fields

4.    These two mismatched fields clearly represent the same values. In Canada, company sales are captured in a field called `Revenue`. To be consistent with the US field, we want the values to fall under the field, `Sales`. This process is called **merging** fields. Tableau Prep Builder makes it easy to merge. Left-click and hold on to the `Revenue` field and drag and drop it on the `Sales` field, and Tableau will make the change for you! You can see the result in *Figure 4.8*. We now have a complete union of the US and Canada sales tables:

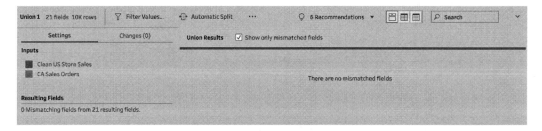

Figure 4.8 – No mismatched fields

Now that we have the sales of our two North American tables unions, we will next bring in the sales tables for our three South American divisions. Each of these tables is represented in a **comma-separated file (CSV)**, and they already have field names matching the US table. Since all the files are already in the correct format, we can bring them all in at once using a **wildcard union**. To ensure the wildcard union works as expected, we need to make sure the three South America sales files are in a directory with no other files.

5.  Click on the + symbol in the connections pane, then click on the **Text file** option under the **To a File** heading. Locate and highlight the `Sales Chile.csv` file and click on the **OK** button.

6.  Tableau Prep Builder should now focus on `Sales Chile` in the flow pane. In the input pane, click on the **Tables** tab and then select **Union multiple tables**. This will bring up a few options, as shown in *Figure 4.9*:

    A.  **Search in**: In the case of using files, this will let you pick wherever your files are saved. In *Figure 4.9*, they are in a file folder called `South America Sales`. It doesn't matter which folder the files are in but it is much easier if they are all in the same folder.

    B.  **Include subfolders**: Tick this box if you want all the files in this folder and every subfolder below it on the filesystem. In our case, all the files are already in the same folder, so this can be left unchecked.

    C.  **File Filters**: This allows you to filter files by filename, file size, date created, and date modified. In our example, we don't need to set file filters.

7.  Tableau Prep Builder gives a visual indication of which files will be included. After any changes, when the files look as expected, click on the **Apply** button. Click on the **Apply** button now and our wildcard union is complete. Now the icon for this step in the flow should change to include a + symbol to indicate that there are multiple files in the step:

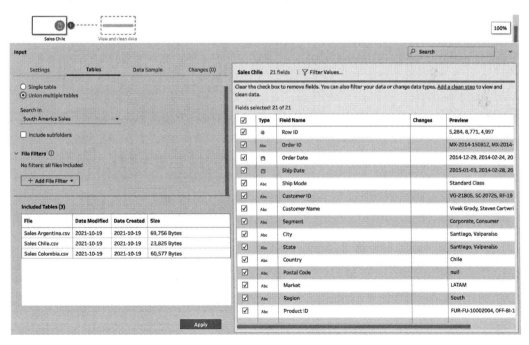

Figure 4.9 – Wildcard union

8.  Now we have two union steps in our flow, one for the North American files and the other for South American files. We will create a third union that will create a union of all five country files. Before taking that step, it is always a good practice to add a clean step after any other type of step because the data is easier to profile from a clean step. Click on + after the `Sales Chile` step and add a clean step. Rename the clean step, `SA Sales`. Then, click on + after the **Union** step and add a clean step. Rename this clean step, `NA Sales`. The results should look like those in *Figure 4.10*:

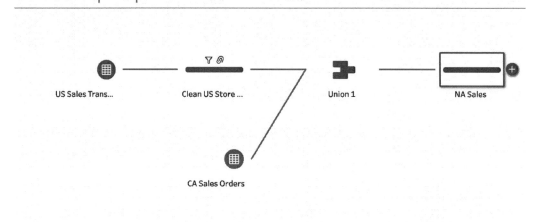

Figure 4.10 – Clean steps after unions

9.  To complete the third union to bring all five files together, left-click and hold on to the + symbol to the right of the `SA Sales` step and drag it below the `NA Sales` step to create a union in the same manner we used in *step 3* of this exercise. Release the mouse button to create our union. At this point, you might notice that there are three mismatched fields, namely, `Table Names`, `Row ID`, and `File Paths`. We would want to clean up these files if we were creating a model to be used in our organization. We will leave them here for now. Finally, add a clean step to the end of this new union step and rename it `All Sales`. The results should look like that in *Figure 4.11*. We now have all our five files in a single step:

Figure 4.11 – All files in a single step

10. Another great way to check our progress is to open the flow in Tableau Desktop to see whether the data model is what we expect at any point along our flow. Tableau makes this easy for us. Right-click on the All Sales step. In the drop-down menu, select **Preview in Tableau Desktop** as shown in *Figure 4.12*.

> **Note**
>
> This feature is not available when creating flows in the web client.

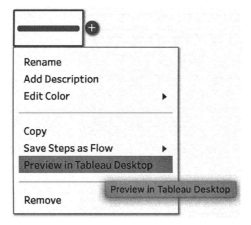

Figure 4.12 – Preview in Tableau Desktop

11. Tableau Desktop will now open with the data model we have created. To get a look at how the model will look to analysts, double-click on **Country** in the data pane. You should now see a dot on the map for each of the five countries we have added, as shown in *Figure 4.13*. Close the Tableau Desktop application without saving the workbook. Save the flow in Tableau Prep Builder and we will pick it up at this point in the next section:

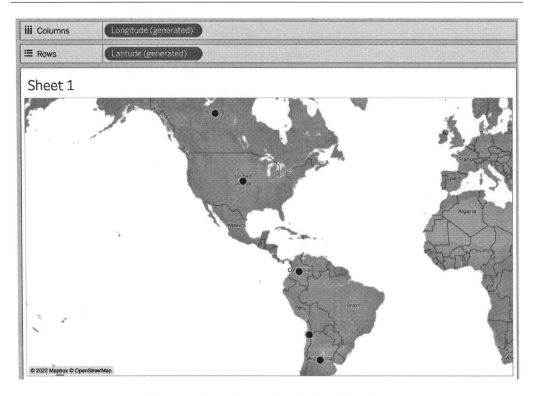

Figure 4.13 – The data model in Tableau Desktop

In this section, we have explored how to add additional rows to our data model using unions. We saw how Tableau makes unions easy by merging fields when the field names don't match. Additionally, we created wildcard unions, a method of easily adding multiple tables to our data model. Where the purpose of unions is to lengthen our data model by adding new rows, we can also add to the width of our data model by adding additional columns. We do this through joins. We will look at joins in the next section.

## Adding new columns by joining data

In this section, we are going to create a join to add additional fields (or columns) of data to add the width of the data model. Adding new columns opens the opportunity for richer analysis. In our case, from the previous section, we only have *Product ID* in our data. If we want to analyze our sales by product category, product sub-category, and even product name, we need to join those fields to our data model.

We will be using the following file in this section:

- `Product Database.xlsx`

We will now start the process of creating our first union in Tableau:

1.  Picking up from where we left off in our flow, click on the + symbol in the connection pane, select **Microsoft Excel** from the **To a File** section and, from the location where you saved the files from GitHub, find and select the file called `Product Database.xlsx` and click on **OK**.

2.  Hold down the left mouse key on the + symbol to the right of the **Product DB** box in the flow. Then, drag it and release it on the right-hand side of the `All Sales` step when the **Join** option appears, as shown in *Figure 4.14*. Release the mouse button to complete the first step of the join:

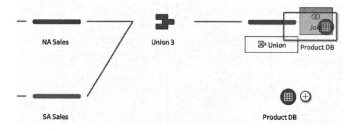

Figure 4.14 – Creating a join

3.  After releasing the mouse button, you will see a join pane like the one shown in *Figure 4.15*:

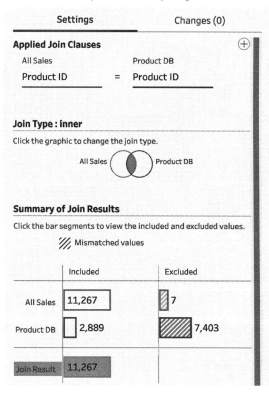

Figure 4.15 – The Join pane

In the **Join** pane, you will see a few options to optimize your join as follows:

A.   **Applied Join Clauses** – To create a join, you need at least one field that is the same between the tables you are joining. Tableau Prep Builder will find fields for us to join when possible. In our case, since **Product ID** is in both tables, Tableau automatically made the join clause for us. To override this join, or if Tableau did not determine the proper join, you can click on the + symbol to the right of the applied join clauses text and bring up the fields you want to join on, as shown in *Figure 4.16*. Again, in our case, we can accept the recommendation:

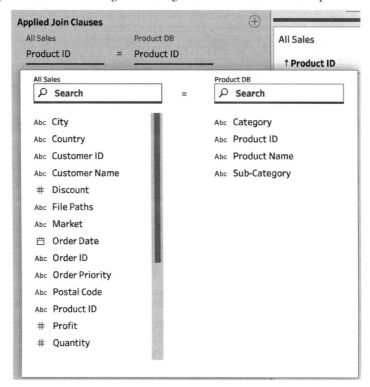

Figure 4.16 – Applied join clauses

B.   **Join Type** – You can set up the join type you want here. The most common are **left join** and **inner join**. A left join tells Tableau to include all the rows from the left table, even if the values don't match in the right table. An inner join returns the rows only when there is a match in both tables. A **right join** is like a left join except that it includes all the rows of the table to the right of the join. The other four possible join types are **right only**, **left only**, **not inner**, and **outer join**. An outer join returns all the rows from both tables. The right-only and left-only joins don't really serve a purpose as they don't result in the joining of new fields (columns). A not-inner join returns the values from both tables when they don't match the join field.

C. **Summary of Join Results** – When deciding on a join type, it can be difficult to know which rows will be added and which will be excluded. Tableau Prep Builder makes this easier with the visual summary of join results. As you click on the different circles in the join type, you will see the resulting join results here. Let's try it out by clicking on the circle on the left-hand side (**All Sales**). This shows how we will get all the rows from the sales database even though some of them have **Product IDs** that are not in the product database.

D. **Join Clause Recommendations** – Tableau gives recommendations on which fields to join. It doesn't always get them right, like in our example. However, sometimes, they can be helpful, so they are always worth exploring. For now, we will ignore them.

4.  Let's look at the different join types available to see which fits best:

A. Click on the left circle (**All Sales**) under the join type, ensuring the overlap of the circle is also selected, as shown in *Figure 4.17*. To select and deselect any of the two circles and the overlap in the circle, click on it in the image. The user experience works as a toggle where each click will highlight or unhighlight. This join is a left join. By looking at the join results, we see that a small number of records from the All Sales table will be unmatched with any records of the Product DB table. Thinking about the questions we want business analysts to be able to answer with our data model, choosing a left join will let them answer questions about products that have sold but not about products that haven't sold. The reason is that we are excluding all products (right table) that have not been sold (left table):

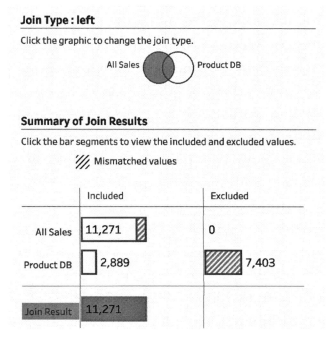

Figure 4.17 – Result of the left join

B.  Click on the right circle while also ensuring the left circle is unselected and the overlap is still selected, as shown in *Figure 4.18*. This is a right join. Thinking about the questions we want business analysts to be able to answer with our data model, choosing a right join will let them answer questions about all products, including those that haven't sold, except for any sales records that don't have `Product ID` in `Product DB`. The reason is that we are including all products (the right table) whether they have sold or not (the left table):

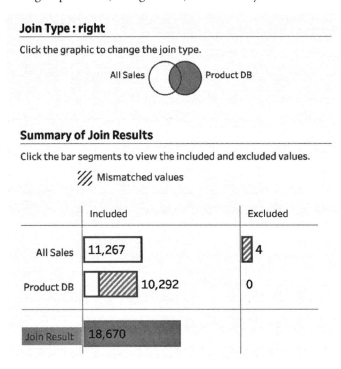

Figure 4.18 – The results of a right join

C.  Click on the left-hand (`All Sales`) table and make sure both circles and the overlap are selected, as shown in *Figure 4.19*. In Tableau Prep Builder, this is referred to as a full join. Sometimes, it is also referred to as an outer join or a full outer join. Thinking about the questions we want business analysts to be able to answer with our data model, choosing a full join will let them answer questions about sales without linked products and products that haven't sold. It might seem like a full join is always the best option since it does not eliminate any answers. However, full joins are rarely the best option because they result in large data models that will have a negative impact on query performance and generate a lot of NULL values, which makes analysis difficult. For instance, in our case, if we published this data model, analysts might become confused as to why some products don't have sales. They might think there is a problem with the data model, which could erode their trust in it. Often, it would make sense to publish two distinct models for each business case, that is, one for sales by product and the second for product sales, including those that haven't sold. That is not to say that full joins do not have a purpose. It's just that how to use them should just be very well documented:

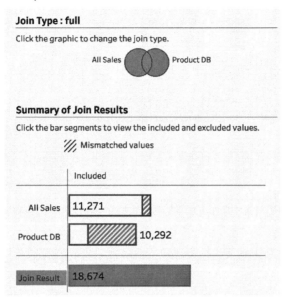

Figure 4.19 – Results of an outer (full) join

5.  For the purpose of our exercise, we are going to take the left join, knowing that it will not let us answer questions about products that have not sold. Before we continue, note that there is a shaded area next to the bar by `All Sales`. Hover your mouse over the shaded area, as shown in *Figure 4.20*. This is telling us that there will be four (4) rows added that do not have a match in the `Product DB` table. This is not ideal as it means we have four (4) sales transactions with a bad `Product ID` value:

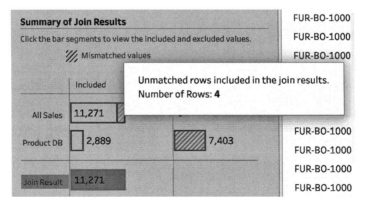

Figure 4.20 – Clicking on the shaded areas to filter

6.  Click on the shaded bar from the last step and ensure that **Show profile pane** is selected from the icons to the immediate left of the search bar. You will then see the four (4) records that do not have a match in the products database. This makes it easy for you to explore why the records are incorrect in the underlying sales database. You also have the option to go back to a previous clean step and update (clean) the *Product ID* for these four (4) records:

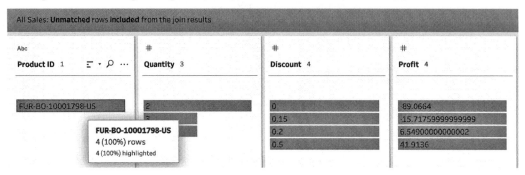

Figure 4.21 – Bad Product ID

7.  As the final step of our join, click on + on the right-hand side of the join result box and add a clean step. It is always a good idea to add a clean step after any other type of step to make profiling the results easy. Rename the join step `Join Sales and Product` and the new clean step as `Sales & Product` to make the flow easier to follow:

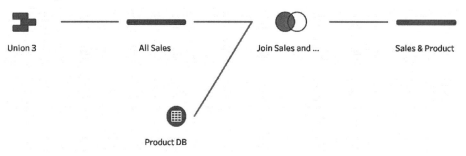

Figure 4.22 – The results of our join

8.  Add an output step to the right of the `Sales & Product` clean step we just created. Do this by clicking on the + and selecting the **Output** option. We will go into the output step in greater detail in *Chapter 6*. We are adding the output step as a placeholder for now because this point marks the end of our first data model, that is, the sales for five (5) countries combined with a product database:

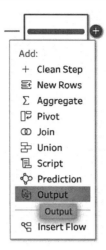

Figure 4.23 – Adding an output step

Now that we know how to add additional columns to our existing data model with joins, next, we will look at what we need to do when our source data does not have distinct fields represented in each column. The next section looks at the specific use case of columns containing values that need to be pivoted into rows to make the data model work properly in Tableau.

# Dealing with data when columns contain values and not distinct fields

In this section, we are going to create a **columns-to-rows pivot**. Thinking back to the columnar data source, Tableau performs best when every column is a field and each row is a record. Sometimes, we are presented with input data sources that are not structured that way. Financial information, often in spreadsheets, is organized in a format like that shown in *Figure 4.24*. This data contains monthly sales targets for each country. This is the data that can be found in the Sales Targets.xlsx file:

| | A | B | C | D | E | F | G | H | I | J | K | L | M |
|---|---|---|---|---|---|---|---|---|---|---|---|---|---|
| 1 | Country | 2014-01-01 | 2014-02-01 | 2014-03-01 | 2014-04-01 | 2014-05-01 | 2014-06-01 | 2014-07-01 | 2014-08-01 | 2014-09-01 | 2014-10-01 | 2014-11-01 | 2014-12-01 |
| 2 | United State | $50,000.00 | $52,500.00 | $55,125.00 | $57,881.25 | $60,775.31 | $63,814.08 | $67,004.78 | $70,355.02 | $73,872.77 | $77,566.41 | $81,444.73 | $85,516.97 |
| 3 | Canada | $ 1,000.00 | $ 1,050.00 | $ 1,102.50 | $ 1,157.63 | $ 1,215.51 | $ 1,276.28 | $ 1,340.10 | $ 1,407.10 | $ 1,477.46 | $ 1,551.33 | $ 1,628.89 | $ 1,710.34 |
| 4 | Argentina | $ 1,000.00 | $ 1,050.00 | $ 1,102.50 | $ 1,157.63 | $ 1,215.51 | $ 1,276.28 | $ 1,340.10 | $ 1,407.10 | $ 1,477.46 | $ 1,551.33 | $ 1,628.89 | $ 1,710.34 |
| 5 | Chile | $ 500.00 | $ 525.00 | $ 551.25 | $ 578.81 | $ 607.75 | $ 638.14 | $ 670.05 | $ 703.55 | $ 738.73 | $ 775.66 | $ 814.45 | $ 855.17 |
| 6 | Columbia | $ 1,000.00 | $ 1,050.00 | $ 1,102.50 | $ 1,157.63 | $ 1,215.51 | $ 1,276.28 | $ 1,340.10 | $ 1,407.10 | $ 1,477.46 | $ 1,551.33 | $ 1,628.89 | $ 1,710.34 |

Figure 4.24 – Sales targets in Excel

Looking at the data in this file, we see the Country field in column A. The range of row 1, B1:M1, represents a Date field. The range from B2:M6 represents the Sales targets field. As you can see, this is not the columnar format that Tableau likes.

Now, we will begin the exercise of pivoting this data into a columnar format:

1. From the connections pane, click on the + in the connection pane, select **Microsoft Excel** from the **To a File** section, and from the location where you saved the files from GitHub, find and select the `Sales Targets.xlsx` file and click on **Open**.

2. You should now see a **Sheet1** data source in the flow pane. Click on the + symbol on the right-hand side of the **Sheet1** data source and add a clean step. Rename the clean step as `Sales Targets`. Again, it is always a good idea to add clean steps between other steps to better profile our data throughout the flow.

3. Let's create our pivot to create the three (3) fields we need from the data source, namely, `Country`, `Date`, and `Sales Target`. To begin, click on the + symbol on the right-hand side of the newly created `Sales Targets` clean step. From the drop-down menu, choose **Pivot** as shown in *Figure 4.25*:

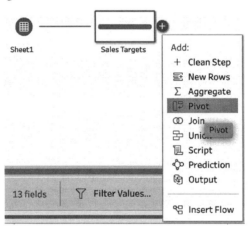

Figure 4.25 – Adding a pivot step

Now, we must tell Tableau which fields to pivot. Ensure the drop-down box to the left of **Pivoted Fields** is set to **Columns to Rows**. We will look at pivoting **Rows to Columns** in *Chapter 5*. We can drag the fields over one-by-one or we can use the **Search** feature. Since all of the fields have **14** in them, we can type **14** in the search box, as shown in *Figure 4.26*, and press *Enter*. Unselect the checkbox in front of **Automatically rename pivoted fields and values**. Click on the top field in the list (2014-01-01), hold down the Shift key, and select the bottom field (2014-12-01) in the list to select all 12 fields:

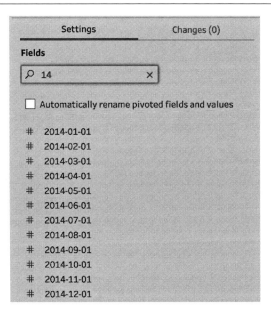

Figure 4.26 – The list of fields to pivot

4. Drag the fields to the **Pivoted Fields** area where the text shows **Drop fields here to pivot them**. The result should look like the screenshot in *Figure 4.27*:

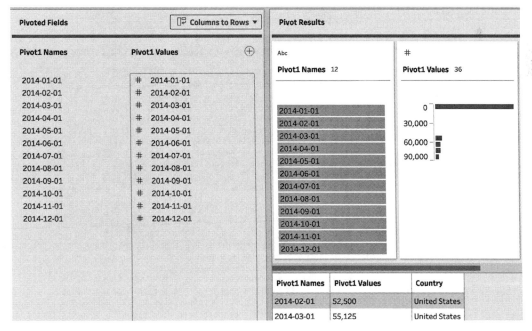

Figure 4.27 – Pivot date columns

5.  Again, let's add a clean step by clicking on the + symbol to the right of the **Pivot 1** step. Change the view to **Show list view** by clicking on the icon to the rightmost side of **1 Recommendation**, as shown in *Figure 4.28*:

Figure 4.28 – Show list view

Let's change the field name for **Pivot1 Names** to Date and **Pivot1 Values** to Sales Target by clicking on the field name to get them to highlight. Then, type over the original name and enter the new names:

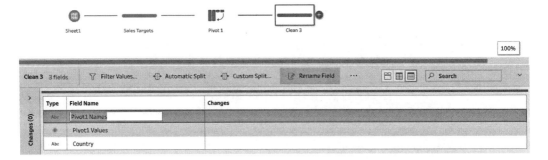

Figure 4.29 – Renaming the pivot fields

After renaming the fields, change the type of the Date field to Date by clicking on **Abc** in front of the field named Date and selecting **Date** from the drop-down menu. Rename the clean step to Pivoted Sales Targets:

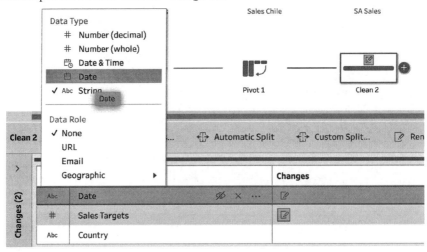

Figure 4.30 – The result of renaming and changing a string to date

We now have our fields pivoted into the columnar format that works with Tableau. We started with an Excel spreadsheet with 13 columns and 6 rows as our input data source. After our pivot, we have 3 columns (fields) and 60 rows of data. Each row contains a sales target for each month and country. With our data in this format, we will have a much easier time creating a data model, which we will see in the next section of this chapter.

## Aggregating data

To create impactful data models in Tableau, it is important to understand the level of detail in your data sources. In the previous sections of this chapter, we looked at sales data. This sales data had a row for every product sold in each sales transaction. That is, if a customer had an order that had 11 products in it, that would generate 11 rows of data. That creates the level of detail of the data source.

In the previous section of this chapter, we pivoted data to create a row of sales targets for each country for each month. This defines the level of detail of the data.

For an analyst, understanding the level of detail is essential to know what answers you can get from your data model. As someone creating data models, you need to understand the level of detail when combining data sources into a single data model. To join two or more data sources into a single data model, they typically need to be at the same level of detail.

Let's imagine that we want to give financial analysts and sales managers the ability to see how each country is performing against its sales targets. To do this, we need to **aggregate** the sales data to the level of country and month so that we can join it with the sales target.

Why not disaggregate the sales targets down to the transaction level to make the join at that level of detail? In most cases, it isn't possible to disaggregate data because we don't typically have a formula to use. In our case, finance set targets at the monthly level. It would not make a lot of sense to set targets at the product and transactional levels. Often, targets only make sense at a higher level of detail than the transactional level.

So, what about sales and marketing analysts who want to analyze sales trends? The easier way to accomplish these two use cases is to use two (2) distinct data sources. Looking back at *step 9* in the joins section of this chapter, we can say that this is why we added an output step. As promised, we will revisit this output in *Chapter 6* making it a data model for analyzing sales transactions.

Let's aggregate our sales data as our first step in joining our sales targets:

1. Click on the + symbol to the immediate right of the `Sales & Product` step in our flow and add an **Aggregate** step, as shown in *Figure 4.31*. Make sure you click on the + to the immediate right side of the step and not the + symbol on the line connecting the `Sales & Product` step to the **Output** step:

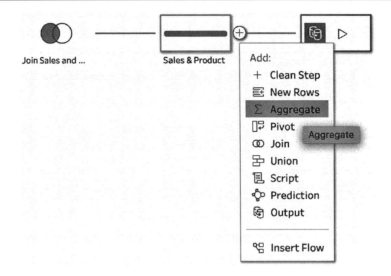

Figure 4.31 – Inserting an aggregate step

Clicking on the + symbol attached to the Sales & Product step will branch out our flow (*Figure 4.32*), which is what we intend here. We are branching to create a new, aggregated data model:

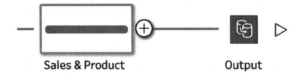

Figure 4.32 – Click here to branch a flow

If we click on the + symbol on the line (*Figure 4.33*), we will insert a new step between the two steps:

Figure 4.33 – Click here to insert in the middle of the steps

2.  In the aggregate step, we will be directed to drag and drop fields into **Grouped Fields** and **Aggregated Fields**. The aggregated fields are the measure(s) that we want to aggregate. In our case, we want to aggregate Sales with SUM. That is, we want to add up our sales. Drag and drop Sales into the **Aggregated Fields** area. The default aggregation should be SUM. The grouped fields are the ones that define our level of detail. In our case, we want to group by both Order Date at the month level and Country. These define the level of detail in our Sales Targets data source that we want to join. Find Country and Order Date and drag and drop them into the **Grouped Fields** area. The results should match the screenshot in *Figure 4.34*:

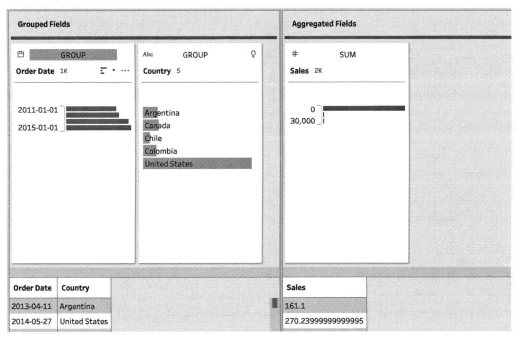

Figure 4.34 – Grouped and aggregated fields

3.  We have one more step in our aggregation before we can join. By default, Tableau will group date fields to the day level. We want the aggregation to occur at the month level. If you look back at our pivot of sales targets from the previous section of this chapter, you will notice that Tableau put the monthly numbers on the first day of each month. To group all Sales at the same level in our aggregation step, click on **GROUP** above Order Date, select **Group by level**, and then pick **Month Start**, as shown in *Figure 4.35*:

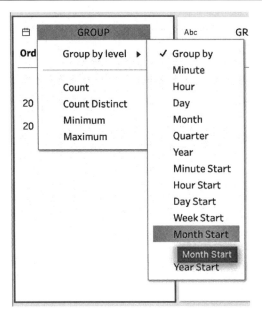

Figure 4.35 – Date group by the Month Start level

Tableau might also convert the field into *Date & Time* type. To make sure the type is set properly to **Date**, click on the calendar icon above **Order Date** and select **Date**, as shown in *Figure 4.36*:

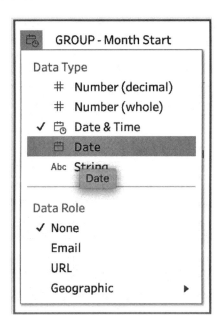

Figure 4.36 – Set the type to Date

4. Click on the + to the right of the aggregate step and add a clean step. Rename the clean step to `Monthly Sales`, as per the diagram in *Figure 4.37*:

Aggregate 1                    Monthly Sales

Figure 4.37 – Add a clean step and rename it "Monthly Sales"

5. Now that we have our sales aggregated to the month level, we can join it with our pivoted sales targets. Going back to our `Pivoted Sales Targets` step, left-click and hold on to the + symbol to the right of `Pivoted Sales Targets` and drag and drop it to the right of the `Monthly Sales` step where the **Join** drop area appears. The result should look like *Figure 4.38*.

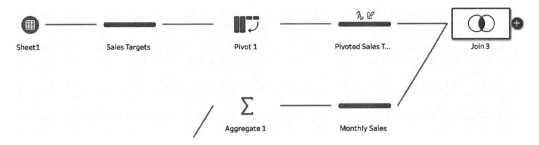

Figure 4.38 – Monthly Sales and Sales Targets Join

6. Click on the new join step to see what Tableau is suggesting. Tableau should be looking to join with `Country`. When you look at the profile pane of the join, you should see that there is a problem with `Colombia` and `Columbia` as shown in *Figure 4.39*. The spelling of `Columbia` in `Pivoted Sales Targets` is incorrect. We need to fix it to the proper spelling of `Colombia` before we can join:

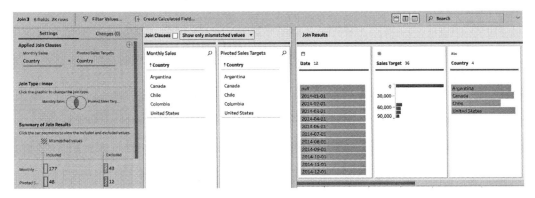

Figure 4.39 – Columbia and Colombia

7.  To address this issue, click on the `Pivoted Sales Targets` step, right-click on `Columbia` in the `Country` field, and click on **Edit Value** to correct the spelling of `Columbia` to `Colombia`, as shown in *Figure 4.40*. After correcting the spelling, click on the **Join** step again. All five (5) countries should now match with no red text:

Figure 4.40 – Editing Columbia to fix spelling to Colombia

8.  To make our join work, we need to add a second join clause because we want to join on both the country and date levels. In other words, we want to ensure the sales targets match each country by the proper month. Click on the + symbol to the right of **Applied Join Clauses** and match **Order Date** to **Date**, as seen in *Figure 4.41*:

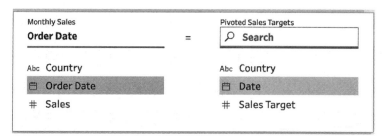

Figure 4.41 – Creating a join clause for dates

9.  Leave the join as an inner join. The left-hand side of the profile pane should now look like *Figure 4.42*. This is telling us that we are getting all 60 records of our `Pivoted Sales Targets` (5 countries by 12 months) along with 60 records from `Monthly Sales` leaving out 160 rows. These 160 rows represent the 32 months of sales data outside the year 2014. That is, the months of sales for which we don't have sales targets:

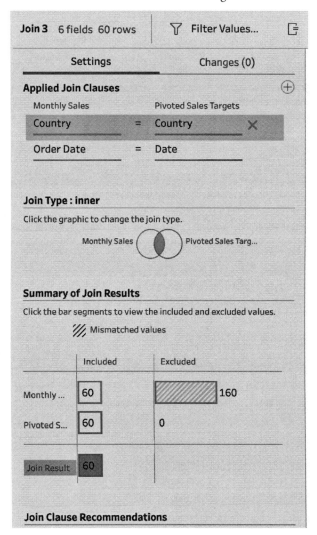

Figure 4.42 – Join results

10. To finalize this new data model, add a clean step at the end of our new join step by clicking on the + symbol and renaming it to `Sales & Targets`. From the + symbol to the right of `Sales & Targets`, add an output step, as shown in *Figure 4.43*. We are going to leave our flow here and pick up the output steps in *Chapter 6*. Make sure you save your flow at this point, calling the file `Chapter 4.tfl`:

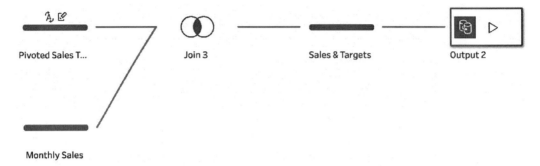

Figure 4.43 – Adding a clean and output step

In this section, we learned about the level of detail of data sources and how to aggregate a data source if we need to join it to another data source that is at a higher level of detail. We used the aggregate step in Tableau Prep Builder and explored how to use group and aggregated fields in the aggregate step. Understanding how to resolve different levels of details is a key skill for building effective data models in Tableau.

## Summary

In this chapter, we learned about extending the data in the data model through unions and joins. Unions are a method of adding additional rows to our data model when two or more data sources have the same fields. Joins are a method of adding additional fields to our data model by linking one or more fields between data sources.

Additionally, we learned about pivoting columns to rows. Data sources are often in the format of crosstabs, which don't work well with Tableau data models. Tableau likes the data to be in a table format. Pivoting the rows of a crosstab format neatly into columns allows Tableau to map the columns into fields for data model creation for easy analysis.

In the final section of the chapter, we learned about the level of detail of data sources and how we can aggregate the data source to join with other data sources at the same level of detail.

In the next chapter, we will add to the foundational knowledge we learned in this chapter by exploring additional data modeling capabilities. The methods we will explore are pivoting columns to rows, adding additional rows to our data model, and integrating data science models and technologies into our data preparation flows.

# 5
# Advanced Modeling Functions in Tableau Prep Builder

In the previous chapter, we learned about extending our data model by adding rows via unions and adding columns via joins. We also learned about pivoting columns to rows to transform our data into the format that works best with Tableau, and about the level of detail in data sources and how we can aggregate a data source to join with other data sources with the same level of detail.

In this chapter, we will cover two advanced modeling functions, namely, *adding new rows* and *pivoting rows to columns*. Sometimes, our data will be too sparse to enable a smooth analysis experience. In this case, we will want to add rows to our data model to make it much easier for analysts and dashboard developers when they use our model in Tableau Desktop. Our source data might also have multiple measures in the same column, making the measures conditional.

Dealing with conditional measures in Tableau Desktop requires calculations that both slow down and limit analysis options. The best way to deal with this type of data is to pivot the rows to columns first, making each column represent a single field. This results in a data format that is optimal for Tableau. These features are unique to Tableau Prep Builder on the Tableau platform – that is, neither of these functions can be done in Tableau Desktop.

Beyond these functions, Tableau Prep Builder has functions for more advanced data modeling, including using **artificial intelligence** (**AI**) and **machine learning** (**ML**) in our flows. Tableau Prep Builder has some built-in ML models, but the cases for ML are endless. This chapter explores how Prep Builder models can be extended by embedding scripts created in R or Python and the predictive models of Salesforce Einstein Predictions.

In this chapter, we're going to cover the following main topics:

- Adding new rows
- Pivoting rows to columns
- Inserting data science models

To view the software requirements for this chapter, please see the *Technical requirements* section in *Chapter 1*.

All the exercises and images in this chapter will be described using the Tableau Prep Builder client software except where noted. You can also recreate all the exercises in this chapter using the Tableau Prep Builder web client, which has a near-identical experience to the installed client.

## Adding new rows

As mentioned in *Chapter 3*, in the *Using Tableau Prep Builder to connect to data* section, please make a note of the directory name where you have stored these files: `Mobile Phone Plans.xlsx` and `Bad Measures.xlsx`.

In this section, we will explore **adding new rows** when the **level of detail** (**LOD**) of the source data is higher than the level we need to analyze. Looking at the data in the `Mobile Phone Plans.xlsx` file, as shown in *Figure 5.1*, we can see data that is easy to understand. We have the customer's name, the plan they have enrolled in, their monthly plan charge, the number of years of their contract, and the start date of their contract. However, while the data is easy to understand by viewing it, it is not easily consumable for analytical purposes. Imagine the difficulty of answering questions such as, *"How many of these customers are still active on January 1, 2023?"* or *"How much money will we be collecting in the third quarter of 2023?"* This is where the adding new rows feature of Tableau Prep Builder can help. Let's jump in and see for ourselves:

| | A | B | C | D | E |
|---|---|---|---|---|---|
| 1 | Name | Plans | Rate | Years | Start Date |
| 2 | Kirk | Unlimited 20 | 80 | 2 | 01-Jul-21 |
| 3 | Candice | Unlimited 40 | 85 | 1 | 02-Jun-21 |
| 4 | John | Unlimited 60 | 95 | 2 | 03-Aug-21 |
| 5 | Susan | Unlimited 40 | 85 | 3 | 04-Sep-21 |

Figure 5.1 – Mobile phone plan data

To begin, we are going to create a new flow in Tableau Prep Builder:

1.  Open the Tableau Prep Builder client software or select **New** and then **Flow** from the web client, and click the **Connect to Data** option to add a new connection. In the client software, under the **To a File** section, click on **Microsoft Excel**, locate the `Mobile Phone Plans.xlsx` file, and click on **Open**.

2.  Tableau Prep Builder will automatically add **Sheet1** to our profile pane. Let's begin by adding a clean step, by clicking on + to the right of the **Sheet1** step and selecting **Clean**. Rename the new clean step `Phone Plans Input`, as shown in *Figure 5.2*:

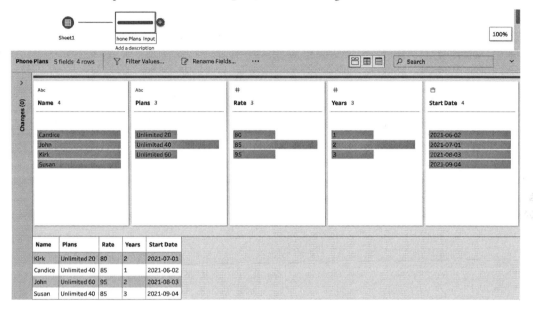

Figure 5.2 – Renaming the clean step

3.  Before adding new rows, we will need to give Tableau the logic to create the new rows. To do this, we will put an end date in our data through a row-level calculation. Click on **Create Calculated Field** from the ribbon between the flow and profile panes. Create a calculated field called `End Date` with the `DATEADD('month', ([Years]*12)-1, [Start Date])` logic, as shown in *Figure 5.3*. The reason we use this calculation is that we want data at the month level. Since we don't have months in our data, we can make them by multiplying the `Years` field by `12`. We then need to take one month away from this number to account for the fact that we already have the first month in our data. Now that we have an end date, we can move to the next step to add rows between our first and final month:

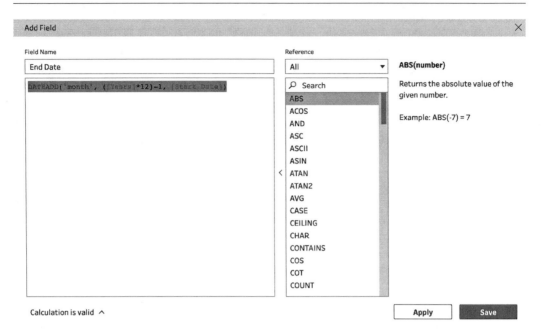

Figure 5.3 – Creating an end date

Note that your **End Date** field might be of **Date & Time** type and not **Date**. If so, click on the calendar icon on the **End Date** card and change the type to **Date**.

4.   Now, we will add new rows to fill in the gaps in the data to make analysis easier. Click on the + symbol to the right of the **Phone Plans Input** step and select **New Rows**, as shown in *Figure 5.4*:

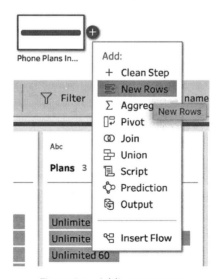

Figure 5.4 – Adding new rows

5. You should now see an alert. We can ignore the alert for now because it is telling us we have *no fields selected to generate new rows*, which we are about to address. You should see a radio-button dialog asking you **How do you want to add new rows?** Select the **Value ranges from two fields** option and choose **Start Date** as the start field and **End Date** as the end field, as shown in *Figure 5.5*. Leave the operator as <=:

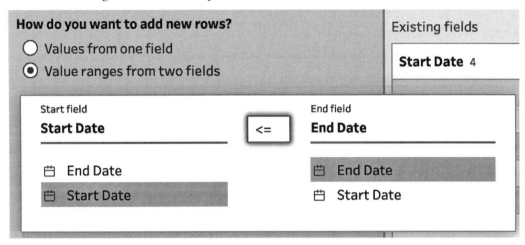

Figure 5.5 – Start and end dates to generate rows

6. Now that we have the start and end dates for our range, we need to tell Tableau what we want to happen between the ranges. Click away from the dialog box with the dates. You will see we have three more options:

   A. **Field name**: Change the field name to `Month of Contract`.

   B. **Specify your value increment**: This is the increment of the rows. Leave the number at one and change the date increment to **Month** – this is the level of granularity of the mobile plan billing.

   C. **What values should your new rows have?**: Set this to **Copy from previous row**, as the amount of the monthly billing is the same for each month for the duration of the contract.

   Your settings for adding new rows should match the screenshot in *Figure 5.6*:

Figure 5.6 – Settings for adding new rows

7.  Finally, click on the + symbol to the right of the **New Rows 1** step in the flow plan and add a clean step. Our data is now ready to be output to a data model that can be used to analyze the state of our mobile plans in the past, present, and future with ease. No complex calculations are needed. You can now close this flow without saving, as we will not be building additional steps with it.

In this section, we learned how to add new rows to our data models to make it easier for analysts to ask and answer questions about their data, when the granularity of their source data is higher than that needed for practical analysis.

In the next section, we will look at a case where we need to pivot values from rows to columns. This is the opposite of the more common use case of pivoting columns to rows, which we explored in *Chapter 4*.

## Pivoting rows to columns

In this section, we will explore **pivoting rows to columns**. There are instances when our data sources have multiple, conditional fields contained in the same column. This structure of data will cause problems because Tableau likes every column to be a unique field. If we look at the structure of our `Bad Measures.xlsx` file, as shown in *Figure 5.7*, you can see that there is a column called **Measure** and another column called **Value**. The ideal data structure would have four columns, one for the date and one each for sales, profit, and volume:

| | A | B | C |
|---|---|---|---|
| 1 | Date | Measure | Value |
| 2 | 01-Jan-21 | Sales | 543019 |
| 3 | 01-Jan-21 | Profit | 119765 |
| 4 | 01-Jan-21 | Volume | 4100 |
| 5 | 01-Feb-21 | Sales | 645225 |
| 6 | 01-Feb-21 | Profit | 131221 |
| 7 | 01-Feb-21 | Volume | 4765 |
| 8 | 01-Mar-21 | Sales | 775945 |
| 9 | 01-Mar-21 | Profit | 143444 |
| 10 | 01-Mar-21 | Volume | 5321 |

Figure 5.7 – The Bad Measures file

If we don't pivot these rows to columns, analysts using Tableau Desktop don't have an easy way to create views and dashboards in Tableau. The best they could hope for is to create three calculated fields, one for each of the measures, as shown in *Figure 5.8*:

| Sheet1 Date | Sheet1 Measure | Sheet1 Value | Calculation Volume | Calculation Sales | Calculation Profit |
|---|---|---|---|---|---|
| 2021-01-01 | Sales | 543,019 | null | 543,019 | null |
| 2021-01-01 | Profit | 119,765 | null | null | 119,765 |
| 2021-01-01 | Volume | 4,100 | 4,100 | null | null |
| 2021-02-01 | Sales | 645,225 | null | 645,225 | null |
| 2021-02-01 | Profit | 131,221 | null | null | 131,221 |
| 2021-02-01 | Volume | 4,765 | 4,765 | null | null |
| 2021-03-01 | Sales | 775,945 | null | 775,945 | null |
| 2021-03-01 | Profit | 143,444 | null | null | 143,444 |
| 2021-03-01 | Volume | 5,321 | 5,321 | null | null |

Figure 5.8 – Result of calculated fields

This approach is not ideal because it creates a lot of null values, which take up room in our data model and make analysis very difficult. For example, we cannot do a row-level calculation such as Profit Margin because Sales and Profit are not on the same row.

The good news is that this problem is easily solved in Tableau Prep Builder:

1.  Open the Tableau Prep Builder client software or select **New** and then **Flow** from the web client, and click on the **Connect to Data** option to add a new connection. In the client software, under the **To a File** section, click on **Microsoft Excel**, locate the Bad Measures.xlsx file, and click **Open**.

2.  Tableau Prep Builder will automatically add **Sheet1** to our profile pane. Let's begin by adding a clean step by clicking on the + symbol to the right of the **Sheet1** step and selecting **Clean**. Rename the new clean step Pre-Measures, as shown in *Figure 5.9*:

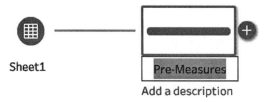

Figure 5.9 – Adding and renaming a clean step

3.  Now, we will add our pivot to transform the data to make analysis easier. Click on the + symbol to the right of the **Pre-Measures** step and select **Pivot**, as shown in *Figure 5.10*:

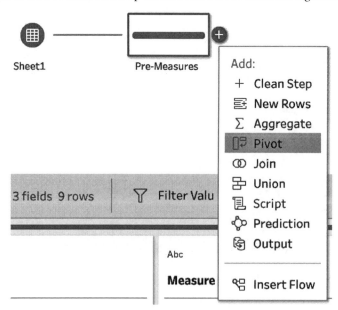

Figure 5.10 – Adding a pivot step

4.  After selecting *Pivot*, note in the **Pivoted Fields** card that the default pivot type is **Columns to Rows**. Click on the dropdown to the right of the **Pivoted Fields** text and select **Rows to Columns**, as shown in *Figure 5.11*:

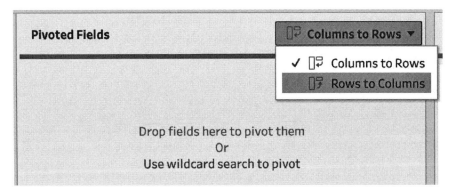

Figure 5.11 – Pivoting rows to columns

5.  The user interface will now change to two sections, **Field that will pivot rows to columns** and **Field to aggregate for new columns**, as shown in *Figure 5.12*:

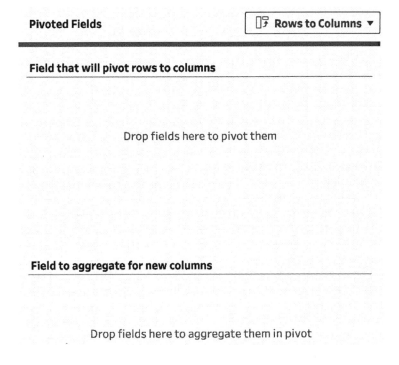

Figure 5.12 – Areas to drop fields for the Rows to Columns pivot

Drag and drop the **Measures** field to the area that says **Drop fields here to pivot them**, and drag and drop the **Values** field to the area that says **Drop fields here to aggregate them in pivot**. The result should look like the screenshot in *Figure 5.13*:

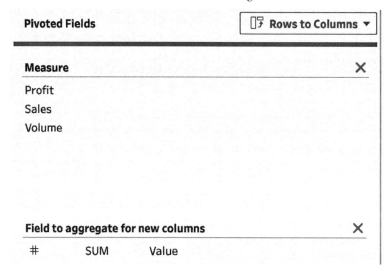

Figure 5.13 – Fields to pivot

6.  Our pivot is now complete. To see the transformed data, click on the + symbol after the **Pivot 1** step and add a clean step. You should now see the data transformed, as shown in *Figure 5.14*:

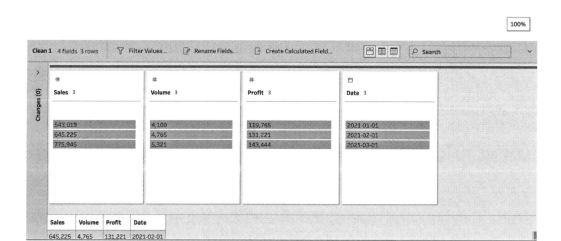

Figure 5.14 – Data transformed after the Rows to Columns pivot

In this section, we learned how to pivot rows to columns when we need to get conditional measures out of a single column into a column of their own. Each field being contained exclusively within its own column is essential for great Tableau data models.

In the next and final section of this chapter, we will look at integrating AI and ML into our flows.

## Inserting data science models

In this section, we will explore how we can incorporate data science models into our flows. Your organization might already have data-cleaning code written in R or Python. Your organization might also be using R, Python, or Einstein Discovery and Prediction Builder to score data. For example, you might have a model that looks at customer data and, using an ML algorithm, scores a customer's propensity to churn. Within a Tableau Prep flow, you can pass your data to any of these technologies to get back new or transformed data and then continue with your flow in Tableau Prep Builder.

It is beyond the scope of this textbook to create and integrate with R, Python, or Einstein models, as each of these technologies requires an extensive combination of installation and/or configuration. For this reason, we will look at the steps to add the models into a flow in the user interface without creating a connection. This will enable you to understand the process and options when integrating Tableau Prep Builder flows with ML models in the future:

1.  Continuing from the flow in the previous section, click on the + symbol to the right of the last clean step and choose **Script**, as shown in *Figure 5.15*:

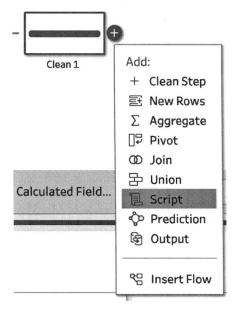

Figure 5.15 – The script step to integrate with R or Python

2.  The user interface will now look like the screenshot in *Figure 5.16*. From here, you can choose your connection type as either **Rserve** or **Tableau Python (TabPy) Server**:

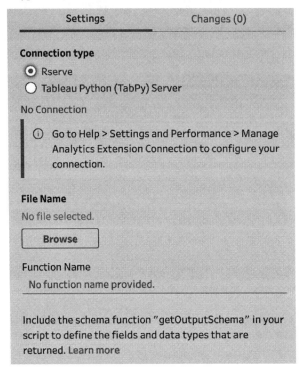

Figure 5.16 – The script interface in Tableau Prep Builder

**Rserve** is an open source server that runs code written in the programming language R. **TabPy** is a program available from Tableau, at no cost, that runs Python code. Both require a level of configuration. If you are interested in the steps to configure these, Tableau Prep Builder always includes links to the most current documentation available. After selecting either of these options, the next step would be to browse for the file containing the R or Python code. After completing these steps, Tableau Prep Builder will take the output, and you can continue building your data model with the results.

Using Einstein Predictions serves a similar purpose to R or Python with two main differences. First, Predictions does not require additional installation or configuration of any services because Einstein runs in the Salesforce cloud. Second, Predictions is a commercial product that has a cost associated with it. Again, it is beyond the scope of this textbook to configure a model in Einstein Prediction Builder, but you can sign up for a trial version if you want to see it in action. For now, we will look at how to integrate Predictions into a Tableau Prep Builder flow:

3.   Continuing from our previous step, click on the + symbol to the right of the **Script 1** step and select **Prediction** from the dropdown, as shown in *Figure 5.17*:

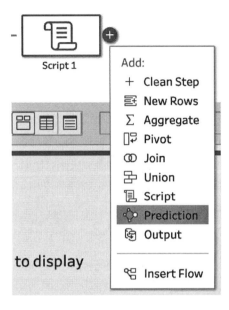

Figure 5.17 – Adding a prediction to a flow

4.   The user interface will now present you with a **Connection** option, where you can select a server where the prediction is housed in the cloud. At the time of this writing, the only server type is **Salesforce**, as shown in *Figure 5.18*. For now, we will stop at this point. If you had a predictive model that you could receive data from, the user interface would guide you through the necessary steps after authenticating with your Salesforce organization:

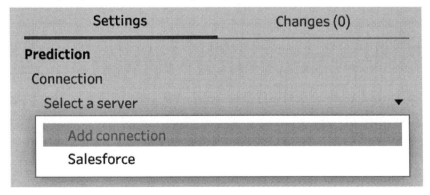

Figure 5.18 – Connecting to Salesforce

In this section, we learned how Tableau can incorporate ML algorithms created in R, Python, and Einstein Predictions to add additional features to our data preparation flows. This allows Tableau Prep Builder to be extended beyond the features it has natively, expanding the usefulness of the data flows it can create.

## Summary

In this chapter, we learned about the more advanced capabilities of Tableau Prep Builder, including adding new rows, pivoting rows to columns, and integrating with data science models.

Sometimes, the level of detail of the source data is higher than the level we need to analyze. Specifically, there are cases where the data has a range of values that are contained in the same row, based on the value of one of the fields. In these cases, to make analysis easier in Tableau, we can add new rows to expand the data to a lower level of detail.

We also learned about pivoting rows to columns. Data sources sometimes have multiple conditional measures contained in a single column. Pivoting the rows within these fields into their own columns, each representing a unique field, allows for much easier analysis in Tableau.

In the final section of the chapter, we learned that Tableau Prep Builder can extend its capabilities to include data science models created in R, Python, or Salesforce Einstein predictive models.

In the next chapter, we will wrap up the features of Tableau Prep Builder by exploring the **Output** option. This is how we output our data models so they can be consumed by analysts and dashboard developers.

# 6

# Data Output from Tableau Prep Builder

In the previous three chapters, we learned about preparing, cleaning, and transforming data using Tableau Prep Builder. In this chapter, we will look at the final step of creating a data model in Tableau Prep Builder, *the output step*.

When using Tableau Prep Builder to create our data models, the transformed data always needs to have a destination location. This means that when using Tableau Prep Builder, after preparing our data for analysis, it needs to be loaded to a new location before it can be consumed. This is different than Tableau Desktop and Tableau web editing, which also allow the option of creating a data model on a live connection.

Tableau Prep Builder gives four choices for where we can load our data through the **output step**. These are flat files, Tableau published data sources, database tables, and CRM analytics.

> **Note**
>
> The option to output to CRM analytics was added in the 2022.3 release of Tableau Prep Builder. To use this output option, we need a Salesforce organization for our output. As the requirement for a Salesforce organization is beyond the scope of this book, we do not have an exercise with this output option.

This chapter will explore each of the other three output options and when to use them.

In this chapter, we're going to cover the following main topics:

- Outputting our data models to files
- Outputting our data models to published data sources
- Outputting our data models to database tables

To view the software requirements for this chapter, please see the *Technical requirements* section in *Chapter 1*.

## Outputting our data models to files

The first option we will look at is data output to a flat file. This is a great option when prototyping and when we are still in development and want to check our progress. The other use case for the file output type is when we are creating a data model for our own analysis and do not have a plan to share the data model more broadly.

The **comma-separated values (CSV)** and **Microsoft Excel (.xlsx)** file outputs serve very similar purposes. The CSV values option is the more lightweight option, meaning you can use it if you don't use Microsoft Excel.

The **Tableau Data Extract (.hyper)** option will load your data into Tableau's high-performance analytical data store, **Hyper**. This is the best option when we are creating a data model for personal analysis. The Hyper file gives us the balance of low maintenance with the fastest query performance.

Before beginning the exercise in this section, please open the Tableau Prep Builder client and open the Chapter 4.tfl file we created in *Chapter 4*:

1. We can open our saved flow by clicking on the **Open a Flow** button, finding the file, and pressing **OK**. Alternatively, if the **Chapter 4** card is shown under **Recent Flows**, we can double-click on the image associated with the **Chapter 4** card, as seen in *Figure 6.1*:

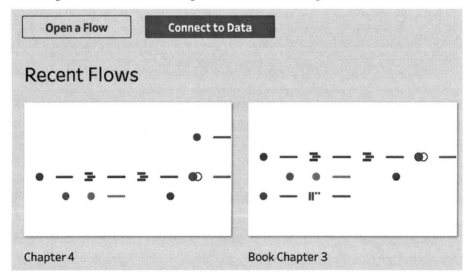

Figure 6.1 – Selecting from recent flows

2. In this flow, we have two output steps that we created in the exercises in *Chapter 4*. Find the step labeled **Output**. This step should be to the right of the **Sales & Product** step, as seen in *Figure 6.2*. Click on the **Output** step with the left mouse button:

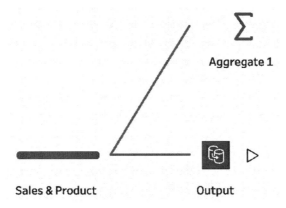

Figure 6.2 – Find the Output step

3.   The bottom of your screen should now show the output pane, as seen in *Figure 6.3*. Let's look at each of the options available in the **Output** step when you choose **Save output to** with the **File** option:

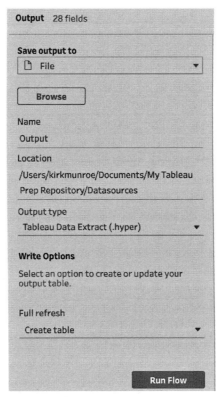

Figure 6.3 – Output pane options

Once you select **File**, the following options are available to you:

- **Browse** – the **Browse** button will open a dialog box, allowing you to name your file and save it to a file system location of your choice.

- **Name** – the name of the file. This will change after you select a file name in the **Browse** section.

- **Location** - the location of the file on your file system.

- **Output type** – we have three options for file output types:

  - **Comma Separated Values (CSV)**

  - **Microsoft Excel (XLSX)**

  - **Tableau Data Extract - the Tableau proprietary database engine, Hyper (.hyper).**

- **Write Options** – the two options are **Create Table** and **Append Table**. The **Create** option will load all data into the file, overwriting the file if a file with the same name in the same location exists. The **Append** option will add new rows to the file if it already exists, otherwise, it will create the file.

4. After selecting the file name and type that you would like, click the **Run Flow** button at the bottom of the output pane and Tableau Prep Builder will create the file for you. Leave your Tableau Prep Builder client in this state. In the next section, we will pick up from this point.

In this section, we discussed the file output options from Tableau Prep Builder. Tableau Prep Builder allows for three different file types: CSV, Microsoft Excel, and Tableau Hyper files. These flat file options are used for prototyping and analysis in Tableau when the data model does not need to be shared with others.

In the next section, we are going to explore Tableau published data sources, the best practices method of sharing our data model with a broader data analyst community.

## Outputting our data models to published data sources

The second output option is a Tableau published data source. This is the best option when we are sharing our data model more broadly. When we output to a published data source, other analysts can connect to our data model without needing to recreate all the data modeling work we have done every time they create a new workbook. It also allows us to have organizational definitions for data and standardized calculations, and allows us to decide which fields from the underlying data source we will make broadly available. We will now create a published data source by connecting to Tableau Server or Tableau Cloud:

1. To begin the process of a published data source output, we are going back to our last step from the previous section, but we will change our **Save output to** option to **Published data source**, as seen in *Figure 6.4*:

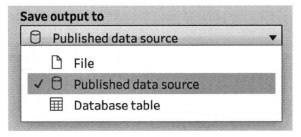

Figure 6.4 – Changing output to a published data source

2.  We should now see our output pane change to ask for different options, namely to connect to a Tableau Server (or Cloud), as seen in *Figure 6.5*:

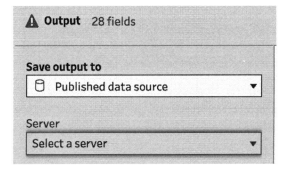

Figure 6.5 – Output pane with the Published data source option

3.  The first thing we need to do is to sign into our Tableau Server or Tableau Cloud. Click on the dropdown next to **Server** and click on **Sign in…**, as seen in *Figure 6.6*. When prompted for a username and password combination, please enter your credentials. If you are using Tableau Cloud, you may get prompted with a multi-factor authentication as well:

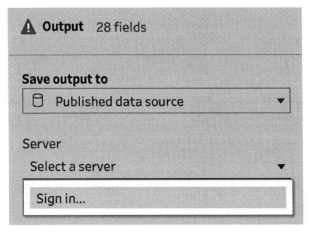

Figure 6.6 – Sign in dialog for the published data source

4.  After connecting to your Tableau Server or Tableau Cloud, your input pane should change to match the image in *Figure 6.7*:

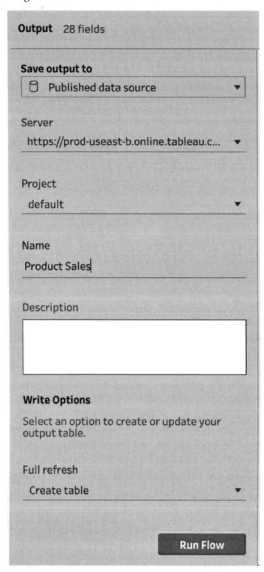

Figure 6.7 – Output to the published data source after connection

The options are as follows:

*   **Project** – a project on Tableau Server and Tableau Cloud is analogous to a file folder in most file systems. It is a place to put content and can be secured to users and groups of users. Select a folder to publish your data source.

- **Name** – the name of your data source. In this case, type in `Product Sales`.

- **Description** – this is an optional field that you can use to describe your published data source. The text will appear next to the published data source in the web user interface of Tableau Server and Tableau Cloud.

- **Write Options** – the two options are **Create Table** and **Append Table**. The **Create** option will load all data into the published data source, overwriting the published data source of the same name and location, if it exists.. The **Append** option will add new rows to the published data source if it already exists, otherwise, it will create a new published data source.

5.  After selecting the project and typing in the published data source name, click the **Run Flow** button at the bottom of the output pane and Tableau Prep Builder will create the published data source for you. Make note of the project where you published the data source as we will connect to it from Tableau Desktop in the next chapter. Leave your Tableau Prep Builder client in this state. In the next section, we will pick up from this point when we look at outputting to database tables.

In this section, we discussed the published data source option. This is the best option when you want to share your data model with others in your organization, leading to the best scale and data governance. We will talk more about extending Tableau published data sources in the next chapter.

## Outputting our data models to database tables

The third and final output option is the option to output to a database table. If you want to leverage the enterprise security and scalability of a database server, this option provides you the ability to output your data to a single database table. This option may also make sense if you are consuming your data model in other analytics tools in addition to Tableau:

1.  To begin the process of a database table output, we are going back to our last step from the previous section, but we will change our **Save output to** option to **Database table**, as seen in *Figure 6.8*:

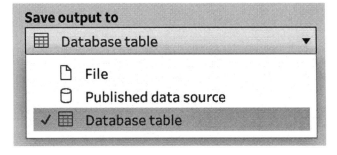

Figure 6.8 – Publishing to a database table

2. We should now see our output pane change to **Add a connection** to a database server, as seen in *Figure 6.9*. The list of available database servers is always being updated. At the time of writing, the list of supported databases matches the list in *Figure 6.9*:

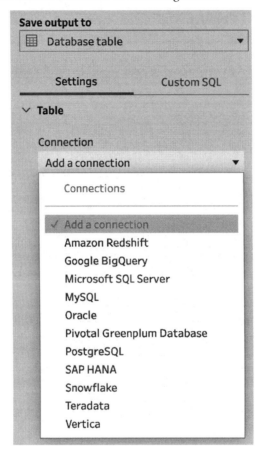

Figure 6.9 – Database server options

3. It is beyond the scope of this book to install and/or configure a database server. If we were to connect to a database server, we would be asked for similar information to the published data source from the last section, namely, the database to publish to, the name of the table, and whether to create a new table or append an existing table. Running the flow to generate the output matches the process for both file and published data source outputs.

In this section, we learned about the third and final output option for Tableau Prep Builder: output to database tables. This option allows us to leverage the enterprise security and scalability features of enterprise database servers and makes our model available for applications in addition to Tableau.

# Summary

In this chapter, we learned about the output options for Tableau Prep Builder.

The output to a flat file option works well when prototyping and when we are still in development and want to check our progress. It also meets the use case of creating a data model for our own analysis.

The Tableau published data source output is the best option when we are sharing our data model more broadly. It allows other analysts to connect to our data model without needing to recreate the work that went into the data modeling. It also allows us to have organizational definitions for data and standardized calculations, and allows us to decide which fields to make available for analysis.

The output to database table option allows us to leverage the enterprise security and scalability features of enterprise database servers. It also allows access to our model from tools and applications in addition to Tableau.

This was the final step of our Tableau Prep Builder learning, which started in *Chapter 3* and continued through *Chapters 4* and *5*. While the output step is the final step in the Tableau Prep Builder journey, it is not the final step for creating data models in Tableau. The next chapter is the first of four chapters that explore the role of Tableau Desktop in creating and extending data models.

In the next chapter, we will explore basic data modeling in Tableau Desktop, including connecting to the published data source that we created in this chapter.

# Part 3: Tableau Desktop for Data Modeling

This part of the book focuses on creating data models in Tableau Desktop. You will get an in-depth understanding of the tool and its ideal use cases.

This part comprises the following chapters:

# 7

# Connecting to Data in Tableau Desktop

The two primary tools for connecting to data in Tableau are Tableau Prep Builder and Tableau Desktop. Building off the previous four chapters, which covered Tableau Prep Builder, this chapter focuses on connecting to data in Tableau Desktop.

Tableau Desktop has connectors to many different data sources. These broadly fall into the categories of flat files, database servers, data from the web, and Tableau data servers, called **published data sources**.

In this chapter, we're going to check out how to connect to each of these data sources through the following main topics:

- Connecting to files in Tableau Desktop
- The data interpreter feature and pivoting columns to rows
- Connecting to data servers – on-premises, cloud, applications, and file shares
- Web data connectors and additional connectors
- Connecting to data sources that aren't listed
- Connecting to Tableau published data sources

> **Note**
> All the exercises and images in this chapter will be described using the Tableau Desktop client software except where noted. Additionally, you can recreate all the exercises in this chapter using the Tableau web client, which has a very similar experience to the Desktop client.

# Technical requirements

To view the complete list of requirements needed to run the practical examples in this chapter, please view the *Technical requirements* section of *Chapter 1*.

To run the exercises in this chapter, we will need the following downloaded files:

- `GrainDemandProduction.xlsx`
- `Contribution_Amounts_for_Fiscal_Years_2002-03_to_2015-16.csv`
- `DETROIT_BIKE_LANES.geojson`
- `unece.json`
- `hcilicensed-daycare-center760narrative11-13-15.pdf`
- `SIPRI-Milex-data-1949-2021.xlsx`

Most of the files we are using in this chapter come from `data.gov`, which has over 300,000 data files that are free to use and offer a wide range of file types and examples.

The `SIPRI-Milex-data-1949-2021.xlsx` file is associated with a Tableau community project, Makeover Monday, from week 35 of 2022. The file was generated SIPRI Military Expenditure Database. Makeover Monday, found at `https://www.makeovermonday.co.uk`, is also a great source of data to practice your Tableau skills.

The `unece.json` file comes from the **United Nations Economic Commission for Europe** (UNECE).

The files used in the exercises in this chapter can be found at `https://github.com/PacktPublishing/Data-Modeling-with-Tableau/`.

# Connecting to files in Tableau Desktop

Tableau Desktop has the flexibility to connect to many different types of data sources. First, we are going to look at flat files. **Flat files** have a lot of use cases from the personal analysis of downloaded files to prototyping development before connecting to enterprise databases.

The different types of flat files that Tableau can connect to include the following:

- Microsoft Excel
- Text files (including delimited and character-separated files)

- Spatial files (including Esri, GeoJSON, KML, KMZ, MapInfo, and TopoJSON files)

- Statistical files (including SAS, SPSS, and R output)

- JSON files (JavaScript Object Notation files)

- PDF files (tables from Adobe's Portable Document Format files)

We will begin by connecting to a Microsoft Excel file.

## Getting data from Microsoft Excel files

Microsoft Excel has become an almost ubiquitous method of collecting and analyzing data. Compared with Tableau, Microsoft Excel has very limited visual analytics capabilities and limits on the amount of data that can be analyzed. In cases where the data might only exist in Microsoft Excel, it often makes sense to take that data and extend it with other data in a Tableau data model to provide a rich analysis experience. We will be looking at combining Excel data with other data sources in *Chapter 8* and *Chapter 9*. For now, we will look at bringing Excel files into Tableau.

Before we begin this exercise, locate the `GrainDemandProduction.xlsx` file from the location you saved it in on your computer. Open the file in Microsoft Excel (or another program of choice that will open an `xlsx` file) and notice the spreadsheet table format, as shown in *Figure 7.1*:

| | A | B | C | D | E | F |
|---|---|---|---|---|---|---|
| 1 | Dataset | Element | Region | Sub-region | Year | Millions of metric tons |
| 2 | Grain food demand, other demand, total demand, prodi | Food grain demand | IFSA Countries | IFSA Countries, Total | 2021 | 694.5 |
| 3 | Grain food demand, other demand, total demand, prodi | Food grain demand | IFSA Countries | IFSA Countries, Total | 2031 | 911.3 |
| 4 | Grain food demand, other demand, total demand, prodi | Other grain demand | IFSA Countries | IFSA Countries, Total | 2021 | 349.0 |
| 5 | Grain food demand, other demand, total demand, prodi | Other grain demand | IFSA Countries | IFSA Countries, Total | 2031 | 465.3 |
| 6 | Grain food demand, other demand, total demand, prodi | Total grain demand | IFSA Countries | IFSA Countries, Total | 2021 | 1,043.5 |
| 7 | Grain food demand, other demand, total demand, prodi | Total grain demand | IFSA Countries | IFSA Countries, Total | 2031 | 1,376.5 |
| 8 | Grain food demand, other demand, total demand, prodi | Grain production | IFSA Countries | IFSA Countries, Total | 2021 | 770.0 |
| 9 | Grain food demand, other demand, total demand, prodi | Grain production | IFSA Countries | IFSA Countries, Total | 2031 | 982.0 |
| 10 | Grain food demand, other demand, total demand, prodi | Implied additional supply required | IFSA Countries | IFSA Countries, Total | 2021 | 273.5 |
| 11 | Grain food demand, other demand, total demand, prodi | Implied additional supply required | IFSA Countries | IFSA Countries, Total | 2031 | 394.5 |
| 12 | Grain food demand, other demand, total demand, prodi | Food grain demand | Asia | Asia, Total | 2021 | 481.0 |
| 13 | Grain food demand, other demand, total demand, prodi | Food grain demand | Asia | Asia, Total | 2031 | 618.2 |
| 14 | Grain food demand, other demand, total demand, prodi | Other grain demand | Asia | Asia, Total | 2021 | 171.2 |
| 15 | Grain food demand, other demand, total demand, prodi | Other grain demand | Asia | Asia, Total | 2031 | 227.2 |
| 16 | Grain food demand, other demand, total demand, prodi | Total grain demand | Asia | Asia, Total | 2021 | 652.2 |
| 17 | Grain food demand, other demand, total demand, prodi | Total grain demand | Asia | Asia, Total | 2031 | 845.4 |
| 18 | Grain food demand, other demand, total demand, prodi | Grain production | Asia | Asia, Total | 2021 | 546.5 |
| 19 | Grain food demand, other demand, total demand, prodi | Grain production | Asia | Asia, Total | 2031 | 668.6 |
| 20 | Grain food demand, other demand, total demand, prodi | Implied additional supply required | Asia | Asia, Total | 2021 | 105.6 |
| 21 | Grain food demand, other demand, total demand, prodi | Implied additional supply required | Asia | Asia, Total | 2031 | 176.8 |
| 22 | Grain food demand, other demand, total demand, prodi | Food grain demand | Asia | Commonwealth of Independent States | 2021 | 13.5 |
| 23 | Grain food demand, other demand, total demand, prodi | Food grain demand | Asia | Commonwealth of Independent States | 2031 | 16.2 |
| 24 | Grain food demand, other demand, total demand, prodi | Other grain demand | Asia | Commonwealth of Independent States | 2021 | 23.8 |
| 25 | Grain food demand, other demand, total demand, prodi | Other grain demand | Asia | Commonwealth of Independent States | 2031 | 31.8 |
| 26 | Grain food demand, other demand, total demand, prodi | Total grain demand | Asia | Commonwealth of Independent States | 2021 | 37.3 |

Figure 7.1 – Grain Demand Production table

Let's bring the Excel file into Tableau:

1.  Open Tableau Desktop. When you open Tableau Desktop, you will see the **Connect** pane on the left-hand side of the user interface, as shown in *Figure 7.2*:

Figure 7.2 – The Connect pane in Tableau Desktop

2.  From the **Connect** pane, under the **To a File** section, select **Microsoft Excel**. Locate the GrainDemandProduction.xlsx file, select it to highlight it, and click on **Open**.

3.  The Tableau Desktop user interface will now take you to the **data source page**, as shown in *Figure 7.3*:

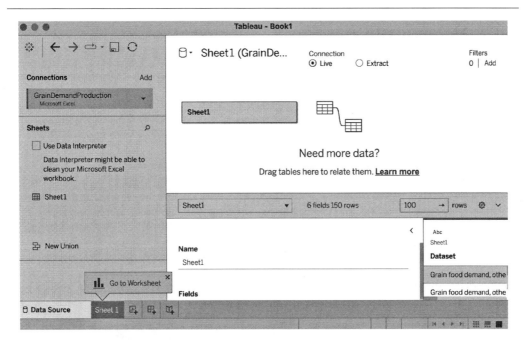

Figure 7.3 – Data source page in Tableau Desktop

4.  In the bottom-right section of the data source page, there are two grids. The left-hand grid is the **metadata grid**. This grid is shown in *Figure 7.4*. You can use the metadata grid to quickly see all the fields in your data model. You can see that Tableau automatically generated a field name for each of the columns in the Microsoft Excel sheet:

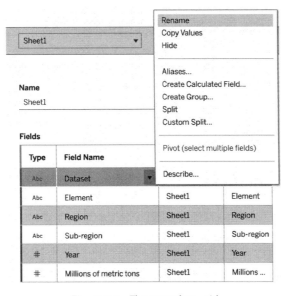

Figure 7.4 – The metadata grid

In the metadata grid, by clicking on the ▼ icon next to the **Dataset** field name, you can change the table name, field types, and field names. You can hide fields and create calculated fields, split fields, create groups, describe fields, and pivot data. Hiding fields will remove the field from our data model. In the cases of extracts, this means that Tableau will filter the column out of the data it imports. We will look at calculated fields, split fields, describing fields, and groups in *Chapter 10*. We will be looking at pivots later in this chapter when we look at the data interpreter feature. In our example, the spreadsheet table format imported metadata the way we want it, so we don't have to make any changes.

5.  The bottom-right section contains the **data grid** as shown in *Figure 7.5*. This allows us to preview the data in our model. Additionally, we can also perform all the same functions in the data grid that we could in the metadata grid. The advantage of performing these functions in the metadata grid is that we can see more fields on a single screen. The advantage of performing the functions in the data grid is that we can see the impact of our changes on the underlying data model immediately:

| Abc<br>Sheet1<br>**Dataset** | Abc<br>Sheet1<br>**Element** | Abc<br>Sheet1<br>**Region** | Abc<br>Sheet1<br>**Sub-region** | #<br>Sheet1<br>**Year** | #<br>Sheet1<br>**Millions of metric tons** |
|---|---|---|---|---|---|
| Grain food demand, other de... | Food grain demand | IFSA Countries | IFSA Countries, Total | 2021 | 694.52 |
| Grain food demand, other de... | Food grain demand | IFSA Countries | IFSA Countries, Total | 2031 | 911.28 |
| Grain food demand, other de... | Other grain demand | IFSA Countries | IFSA Countries, Total | 2021 | 348.98 |
| Grain food demand, other de... | Other grain demand | IFSA Countries | IFSA Countries, Total | 2031 | 465.26 |
| Grain food demand, other de... | Total grain demand | IFSA Countries | IFSA Countries, Total | 2021 | 1,043.50 |
| Grain food demand, other de... | Total grain demand | IFSA Countries | IFSA Countries, Total | 2031 | 1,376.54 |
| Grain food demand, other de... | Grain production | IFSA Countries | IFSA Countries, Total | 2021 | 770.00 |
| Grain food demand, other de... | Grain production | IFSA Countries | IFSA Countries, Total | 2031 | 982.02 |
| Grain food demand, other de... | Implied additional supply requ... | IFSA Countries | IFSA Countries, Total | 2021 | 273.50 |
| Grain food demand, other de... | Implied additional supply requ... | IFSA Countries | IFSA Countries, Total | 2031 | 394.52 |

Figure 7.5 – The data grid

6.  The top and right sections contain the **canvas**. We will be looking at the canvas in detail in *Chapter 8* and *Chapter 9*. For now, we will look at only the top rightmost section of the canvas where we see the radio button to choose between a **Live** or **Extract** connection and the ability to **Add** filters, as shown in *Figure 7.6*:

Figure 7.6 – The Live and Extract Add filters

We will be exploring the pros and cons of live connections versus extracts in *Chapter 10*. For now, it is a good practice to always extract data when working with files. Click on the **Extract** radio button to create an extract now. After clicking on **Extract**, you will notice that the **Edit** and **Refresh** links now also appear but nothing else appears to happen. We will look at these in the next step.

7.  To create our extract, click on `Sheet 1` in the bottom-left corner of Tableau Desktop. Now, Tableau will launch a dialog box that prompts you to name and save your extract as seen in *Figure 7.7*. Give your extract a name and location and press the **Save** button. For now, feel free to use the default name and location:

Figure 7.7 – The Tableau extract dialog

8.  Tableau will now extract your data into a Tableau **Hyper** file. Hyper is Tableau's high-performance database for analytical queries from Tableau. We will explore Hyper in more detail in *Chapter 10*.

9.  Now, we will add a filter to limit the number of rows in our data. Click on the **Data Source** tab in the bottom-left corner of the screen to go back to the data source page. Looking at the upper-right corner of the canvas, where we just created our extract, you will see three options (as shown in *Figure 7.6* after *step 6* in this section):

    •   **Edit** – This option allows you to control the data in your extract, including adding filters to limit the number of rows and hiding unused filters to limit the number of columns imported to the extract.

- **Refresh** – Clicking on this will manually load new data into your extract if it has been added to your source data.

- **Add** – This option allows you to add a data source filter that filters data coming from your data source.

It is important to understand the difference between extract and data source filters. In the case of live connections, it is straightforward: data source filters will filter your queries by eliminating filtered data from any analysis in Tableau while extracts filters and the refresh option are not visible as there is no extract. In the case of extracted data, the extract filters are performed before the data source filters. This means that the extract filter will filter out any data that goes into the extract. Then, the data source filter will further filter out any data in the extract and eliminate that data from any analysis in Tableau.

10. In our case, we have extracted data from Excel, so let's look at the **Edit** option. Click on **Edit** and you should see a dialog like the one in *Figure 7.8*. For now, we are only looking at the filters section. We will look at the other options in *Chapter 10* after learning about **logical tables** in *Chapter 8* and **physical tables** in *Chapter 9*. Click on the **Add** button to bring up the filter dialog box:

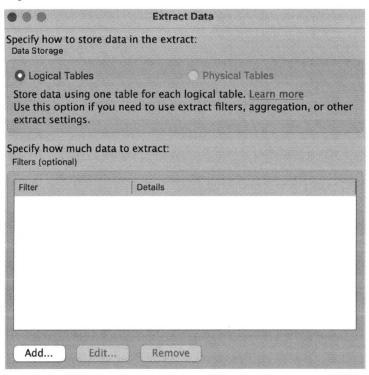

Figure 7.8 – The Extract dialog box

11. Now we can add our filter by first selecting a field, as shown in *Figure 7.9*. Let's filter down our data by limiting the number of years in the data. Highlight the `Year` field and click on **OK**:

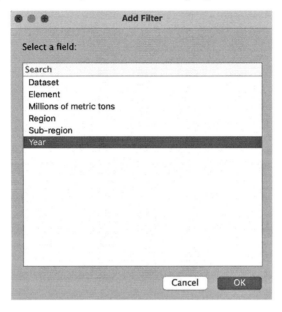

Figure 7.9 – The data extract filter dialog

12. Now we can limit the number of years we want in our data via the dialog box shown in *Figure 7.10*. For example, we could set the maximum range to 2026. For now, hit **Cancel** to dismiss the dialog box:

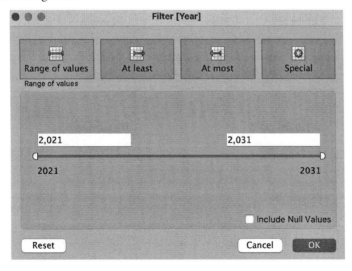

Figure 7.10 – The date filter dialog

13. The final pane of the data source page is simply called the *left pane*. It is on the left-hand side of the user interface, as shown in *Figure 7.11*:

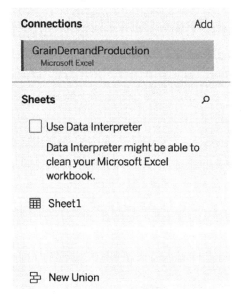

Figure 7.11 – The left pane of the data source page

It contains three sections, as follows:

- **Connections** – A single workbook can have multiple data models. To add another data model to the same workbook, we can click on the **Add** button to add the new data.

- **Sheets** – Each sheet in a Microsoft Excel workbook shows up in this section. When we connect to databases, this section will show the tables in the database. Tableau treats each sheet of a Microsoft Excel workbook as a unique table. **Use Data Interpreter** only appears for Microsoft Excel and delimited files. We will look at this feature later in this chapter.

- **New Union** – We can use this feature to add additional rows of data from another table(s) to our model through a union. We will look at unions in greater detail in *Chapter 8*.

14. For our final step, we are going to save our workbook to use later in this chapter. From the **File** menu, choose **Save** and then name the workbook `Chapter 7 Grain Data` in the default location.

In this section, we explored how to use Microsoft Excel as a data source for our Tableau data model. Often, Microsoft Excel is a source of data for both personal analysis and in organizations due to the ubiquitous nature of Microsoft Excel and the ease of use for storing and updating data.

In the next section, we will look at how to connect to delimited files. Tableau treats these files similarly to Microsoft Excel.

## Getting data from text (or delimited) files

Often, we get data for analysis in the form of delimited text files. Typically, the files are in the form of having the field names appear first, each separated by a character (or tab) to space or delimit them, followed by a carriage return. Then, the data itself comes next with that same character delimited by each value and a carriage return signifying the start of a new record. A common delimiter is a comma. Delimited files with a comma separator are called **comma-separated value (CSV)** files. If you open one of these files in Microsoft Excel or another spreadsheet application, they usually look like the file we saw in the previous section, that is, nicely arranged in a spreadsheet table format.

Often, we get delimited files, especially CSVs, as data exports from systems to which we do not have access. They might be available as public data such as our example from `https://data.gov/` or be data *dumped* from internal or partner databases where the database administrator doesn't allow us access. We will now bring in data from a CSV file to demonstrate this capability:

1.  Open Tableau Desktop. From the **Connect** pane, under the **To a File** section, select **Text file**. Locate and highlight the `Contribution_Amounts_for_Fiscal_Years_2002-03_to_2015-16.csv` file and click on **Open**.

2.  The metadata and data grids now look indistinguishable from how they would look if our data was in Microsoft Excel or any other data source that was structured this way. It should look like the screenshot in *Figure 7.12*:

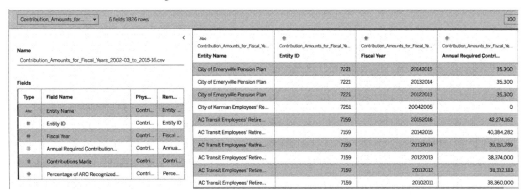

Figure 7.12 – Metadata and data grids for our CSV file

3.  The only significant difference you will see will be in the left-hand pane. The section that said **Sheets** when we connected to Microsoft Excel will now say **Files**, as shown in *Figure 7.13*. The list contains all the files that are in the same directory as the file we just added to our model. This makes it easier to combine files through unions and joins if you keep them in the same file location:

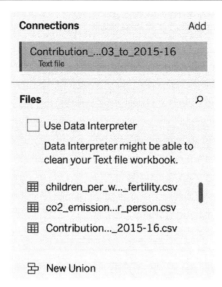

Figure 7.13 – The left-hand pane example with a CSV file

4.   We will conclude our exploration of connecting to delimited files here. Everything else about delimited files behaves like Microsoft Excel files.

In this section, we looked at delimited files (text files) in Tableau. We saw how they were the same as and different from Microsoft Excel files in terms of how Tableau handles them.

In the next section, we will look at spatial files. These allow for visual analysis with maps.

## Importing geospatial file types to allow for visual analysis with maps

Tableau allows for geospatial analysis, that is, performing visual analytics on top of maps. Tableau can plot any data on a map when it has the latitude and longitude (latitude/longitude) values for the point. In *Chapter 1*, we also looked at the built-in geospatial field types in Tableau. Sometimes, we want our analysis to go beyond latitude/longitude and the built-in Tableau functions to look at custom, specific geospatial analysis. At the time of writing, Tableau allows for the import of Esri, GeoJSON, KML, KMZ, MapInfo, and TopoJSON files. We will now follow the steps required to connect to a GeoJSON file:

1.   Open Tableau Desktop. From the **Connect** pane, under the **To a File** section, select **Spatial file**. Locate and select the DETROIT_BIKE_LANES.geojson file to highlight it and click on **Open**.

2.   Scroll to the bottom of the metadata grid and you should see a field named Geometry, as shown in *Figure 7.14*:

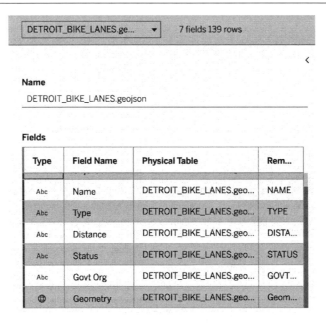

Figure 7.14 – Metadata grid for the Detroit bikes spatial file

3.  Let's see what the `Geometry` field does by by first clicking on **Sheet 1**. Then, double-click on **Geometry** in the data pane. Drag the `Name` field to the **Color** card of the **Marks** card and drop it, as shown in *Figure 7.15*:

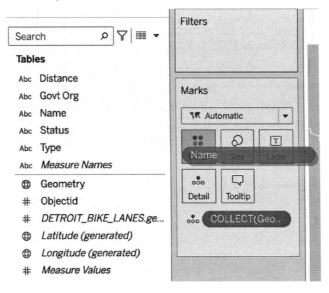

Figure 7.15 – Dragging the name and dropping it on the color card

4.    The resulting visualization should look like the screenshot in *Figure 7.16*:

Figure 7.16 – The resulting map

This is a simple example of a spatial file showing the bike lanes in Detroit, each colored uniquely based on its name. We could combine this data with other information about Detroit to create a compelling analysis. For example, combining population data by neighborhood could help us to understand whether the bike lanes are in highly populated areas.

In this section, we explored how to bring in spatial files to create map-based analysis in Tableau. In the next section, we will discuss how to import statistical files into Tableau.

## Creating data models from statistical files

Often, data is run through statistical models to have additional context added in the form of new columns. For example, you might have a file of customer comments collected via internal systems and through social media and review sites. Your organization might want to score custom sentiment over time by customer from this large amount of text. Tableau does not do this type of text analysis, but it could be done in commercial statistical software programs such as **SPSS** (**Statistical Package for the Social Sciences**) or **SAS** (**Statistical Analysis System**) or from open source programs such as **R**. These three programs have proprietary data export formats, although programmers will often export in CSV or other delimited exports.

Tableau can connect to SAS (`*.sas7bdat`), SPSS (`*.sav`), and R (`*.rdata`, `*.rda`) data files natively. To connect to these files, navigate to the **Connect** pane, under the **To a File** section, and select **Statistical file**. From this point, the experience is very similar to the experience of text (delimited) files.

In the next section, we will look at how to import JSON files. Typically, these files are generated from web applications and are worth future exploration due to their unique file format.

## Creating data models from JSON files

**JavaScript Object Notation** (**JSON**) files are text-based files that are typically used to transfer data in web applications, usually from a database to a web page to convert into HTML for viewing. Because JSON files are sources of data, they can be opened by other applications, such as Tableau. We will now connect to a JSON file containing information from the United Nations Educational, Scientific, and Cultural Organization (UNESCO):

1. Open Tableau Desktop. From the **Connect** pane, under the **To a File** section, select **JSON file**. Locate and select the `unece.json` file to highlight it and click on **Open**.

2. You will be presented with a dialog box to select schema levels from the JSON file, as shown in *Figure 7.17*:

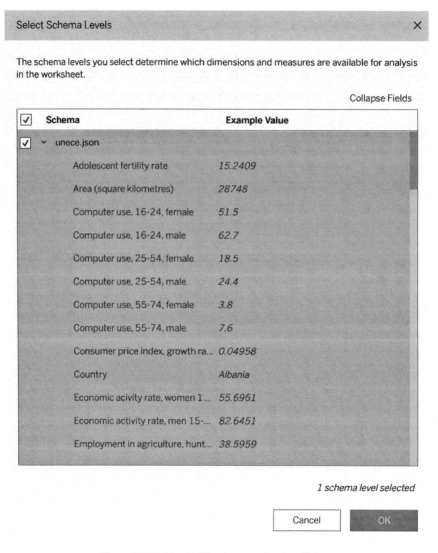

Figure 7.17 – The JSON schema selection dialog

Tableau works to flatten the schema to give us the spreadsheet table format that works best with Tableau. If the JSON file is organized into multiple schemas, you can select and deselect them at this point. In our example, the JSON file is organized into a single schema, which is selected by default. Click on **OK** to bring the JSON data into our data model.

3.   At this point, the data from the JSON file will behave like data from a delimited text file and Microsoft Excel.

In this section, we looked at connecting to JSON files. JSON files are a file format that is used to transfer data, typically in web applications. JSON files have a schema in them that Tableau helps *flatten* to get the file in the format of a spreadsheet table, making data modeling and analysis easy in Tableau.

In the next section, we will look at the last of the file options for Tableau: the **Portable Document Format** (**PDF**) from Adobe.

## Getting data from tables in PDF files

There are many use cases where it is helpful, or even necessary, to get data from tables contained in PDF documents. Financial data, including corporate filings and investment statements, can often only be found in PDFs. Another example is public policy data and other reports generated by governments. We will look at one of these examples next.

Before we begin this exercise, locate the `hcilicensed-daycare-center760narrative11-13-15.pdf` file from the location you saved it in on your computer. Open the document in your PDF reader of choice and take notice of the table found on *page 7*, as shown in *Figure 7.18*:

**Table 1. Number (N) of Licensed Daycare Center Slots per 1,000 Children, by Region, California, 2015**

| Region | Rate of Infant Center Slots | | | Rate of Day Care Center Slots | | |
| --- | --- | --- | --- | --- | --- | --- |
| | N | Pop (ages 0-2) | Rate | N | Pop (ages 2-5) | Rate |
| Bay Area | 11,465 | 266,632 | 43.0 | 137,485 | 362,283 | 379.5 |
| Butte | 443 | 7,322 | 60.5 | 2,984 | 9,973 | 299.2 |
| Central/Southeast Sierra | 165 | 5,021 | 32.9 | 2,094 | 7,075 | 296.0 |
| Monterey Bay | 770 | 30,784 | 25.0 | 9,858 | 41,730 | 236.2 |
| North Coast | 282 | 11,217 | 25.1 | 3,992 | 15,360 | 259.9 |
| Northeast Sierra | 222 | 5,975 | 37.2 | 2,543 | 8,166 | 311.4 |
| Northern Sacramento Valley | 232 | 4,992 | 46.5 | 1,376 | 6,774 | 203.1 |
| Sacramento Area | 4,277 | 92,513 | 46.2 | 36,493 | 128,775 | 283.4 |
| San Diego | 4,549 | 122,267 | 37.2 | 53,599 | 161,978 | 330.9 |
| San Joaquin Valley | 3,507 | 198,999 | 17.6 | 53,326 | 269,226 | 198.1 |
| San Luis Obispo | 205 | 7,845 | 26.1 | 3,512 | 10,991 | 319.5 |
| Santa Barbara | 446 | 16,335 | 27.3 | 6,425 | 22,120 | 290.5 |
| Shasta | 235 | 6,102 | 38.5 | 2,719 | 8,315 | 327.0 |
| Southern California | 18,679 | 731,810 | 25.5 | 275,405 | 991,930 | 277.6 |
| California | 45,477 | 1,507,814 | 30.2 | 591,811 | 2,044,696 | 289.4 |

Source: CDSS, Community Care Licensing Facility Search, June 21, 2015; U.S. Census Bureau, 2010 Census Summary File 2.

Figure 7.18 – Table 1 from page 7 of PDF

In the following steps, we will learn how to connect to the preceding table in Tableau Desktop:

1.  Open Tableau Desktop. From the **Connect** pane, select **PDF file**, locate `hcilicensed-daycare-center760narrative11-13-15.pdf`, and press **Open**.

2.  Tableau will now present a dialog box (*Figure 7.19*) where you can instruct Tableau to search the PDF document. In a long document, such as a corporate financial statement that might be over 100 pages in length, your PDF search will go much faster if you instruct Tableau which

page(s) the table or tables you want to model are in the document. In our case, the PDF is only 7 pages long, so leave the default option of **All** and press **OK**:

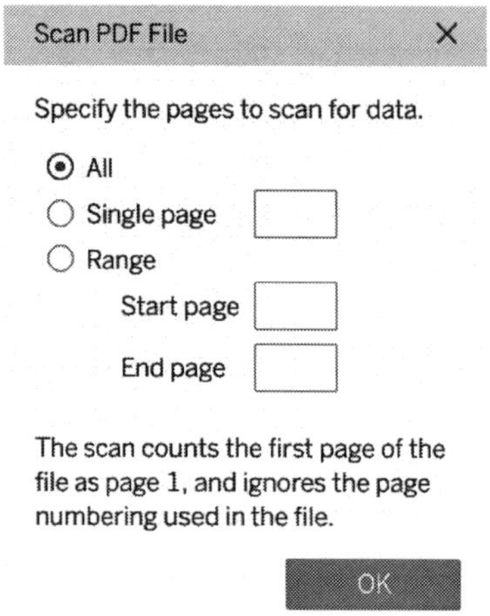

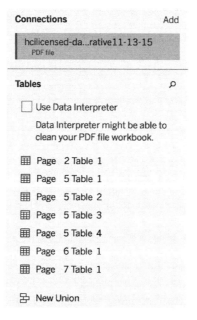

Figure 7.19 – The Scan PDF File dialog

3.  Tableau will now switch focus to the data source page and display all the tables that it found as per *Figure 7.20*:

Figure 7.20 – Tables found in the PDF

4. Tableau found a total of 7 data tables in the PDF. The first six tables are Tableau interpreting the data behind the charts in the first six pages of the PDF. We are looking to pull in the data from the table on *Page 7*. To bring this data into our data model, double-click on **Page 7 Table 1** to create the model.

5. Click on **Sheet 1**, and you will see all the fields from the table listed in the data pane. To recreate the basis of the table from *Page 7* of the PDF, click on the following fields in this order: **Region**, **N**, **Pop (ages 0-2)**, **Rate**, **N1**, **Pop (ages 2-5)**, and **Rate1**. You should now have a sheet that looks like *Figure 7.21*:

## Sheet 1

| Region | N | Pop (ages 0.. | Rate | N 1 | Pop (ages 2.. | Rate 1 | |
|---|---|---|---|---|---|---|---|
| Bay Area | 11,465 | 266,632 | 43.0 | 137,485 | 362,283 | 379.5 | Abc |
| Butte | 443 | 7,322 | 60.5 | 2,984 | 9,973 | 299.2 | Abc |
| California | 45,477 | 1,507,814 | 30.2 | 591,811 | 2,044,696 | 289.4 | Abc |
| Central/Southeast Sierra | 165 | 5,021 | 32.9 | 2,094 | 7,075 | 296.0 | Abc |
| Monterey Bay | 770 | 30,784 | 25.0 | 9,858 | 41,730 | 236.2 | Abc |
| North Coast | 282 | 11,217 | 25.1 | 3,992 | 15,360 | 259.9 | Abc |
| Northeast Sierra | 222 | 5,975 | 37.2 | 2,543 | 8,166 | 311.4 | Abc |
| Northern Sacramento Vall.. | 232 | 4,992 | 46.5 | 1,376 | 6,774 | 203.1 | Abc |
| Sacramento Area | 4,277 | 92,513 | 46.2 | 36,493 | 128,775 | 283.4 | Abc |
| San Diego | 4,549 | 122,267 | 37.2 | 53,599 | 161,978 | 330.9 | Abc |
| San Joaquin Valley | 3,507 | 198,999 | 17.6 | 53,326 | 269,226 | 198.1 | Abc |
| San Luis Obispo | 205 | 7,845 | 26.1 | 3,512 | 10,991 | 319.5 | Abc |
| Santa Barbara | 446 | 16,335 | 27.3 | 6,425 | 22,120 | 290.5 | Abc |
| Shasta | 235 | 6,102 | 38.5 | 2,719 | 8,315 | 327.0 | Abc |
| Southern California | 18,679 | 731,810 | 25.5 | 275,405 | 991,930 | 277.6 | Abc |

Figure 7.21 – The rebuilt PDF table in Tableau

In *Chapter 10*, we will explore how to extend our data model. This will contain the formatting techniques that will allow us to make the preceding data table look close to the presentation in the PDF.

Now that we know how to connect to data in PDF documents, we can use PDF documents from financial, government, and other sources to incorporate into our data models without first needing to move that data to a spreadsheet or database.

In this section, we looked at how to connect to files. We looked at Microsoft Excel, delimited files, spatial files, statistical files, JSON files, and PDF tables, including examples of use cases for each type. There are many cases in both personal and organizational analysis where we might use these file types. In the next section, we will look at a data interpreter that can help us to save data modeling time and effort in certain types of Microsoft Excel and delimited files.

# Dealing with preformatted reporting files with data interpreter and pivoting columns to rows

Often, data in Microsoft Excel and text fields comes with a few rows that act as headers to describe the data in the file. Looking at the SIPRI-Milex-data-1949-2021.xlsx file we downloaded from the GitHub repository, we can see that the data table doesn't start until row 6. The first four rows describe the dataset with a blank fifth row, as shown in *Figure 7.22*:

| | A | B | C | D | E | F | G | H | I | J | K |
|---|---|---|---|---|---|---|---|---|---|---|---|
| 1 | **Military expenditure by country as percentage of gross domestic product, 1949-2021** | | | | | | | | | **© SIPRI 2021** | |
| 2 | Countries are grouped by region and subregion | | | | | | | | | | |
| 3 | Figures in blue are SIPRI estimates. Figures in red indicate highly uncertain data. | | | | | | | | | | |
| 4 | ". ." = data unavailable. "xxx" = country did not exist or was not independent during all or part of the year in question. | | | | | | | | | | |
| 5 | | | | | | | | | | | |
| 6 | **Country** | **Notes** | **1949** | **1950** | **1951** | **1952** | **1953** | **1954** | **1955** | **1956** | **1957** |
| 167 | France | 101 | ... | 4.65% | 5.99% | 7.23% | 7.57% | 6.12% | 5.38% | 6.46% | 6.16% |
| 168 | Germany | | ... | ... | ... | ... | 3.97% | 3.74% | 3.84% | 3.41% | 3.90% |
| 169 | Greece | | 5.91% | 6.01% | 6.64% | 6.43% | 5.11% | 5.49% | 5.11% | 5.94% | 5.00% |
| 170 | Iceland | 86 | ... | ... | ... | ... | ... | ... | ... | ... | ... |
| 171 | Ireland | | ... | ... | ... | ... | ... | ... | ... | ... | ... |
| 172 | Italy | 87 | ... | ... | 3.78% | 3.99% | 3.33% | 3.53% | 3.25% | 3.17% | 3.09% |
| 173 | Luxembourg | 88 | ... | 1.21% | 1.41% | 2.14% | 2.61% | 2.94% | 2.92% | 1.71% | 1.76% |
| 174 | Malta | †‖ | xxx | xxx | xxx | xxx | xxx | xxx | xxx | xxx | xxx |
| 175 | Netherlands | | ... | ... | ... | ... | ... | ... | ... | 5.79% | 5.32% |
| 176 | Norway | | 2.71% | 2.37% | 3.05% | 4.01% | 5.08% | 5.00% | 3.93% | 3.52% | 3.59% |
| 177 | Portugal | | ... | 3.10% | ... | ... | 3.29% | 3.41% | 3.45% | 3.28% | 3.27% |
| 178 | Spain | 89 | ... | ... | ... | ... | ... | 2.29% | 2.31% | 2.26% | 2.23% |
| 179 | Sweden | | ... | ... | ... | ... | ... | ... | ... | ... | |
| 180 | Switzerland | †¶90 | ... | ... | ... | ... | ... | ... | ... | ... | 2.83% |
| 181 | United Kingdom | 91 | ... | 7.21% | 8.30% | 10.37% | 10.96% | 10.06% | 9.09% | 8.56% | 7.99% |

Figure 7.22 – Excel with header rows

Tableau is expecting the first row to be field names, one per column, and each of the other rows a record of data. Let's open Tableau Desktop and connect to the file to see how we can bring it into a well-structured data model:

1. Open Tableau Desktop. From the **Connect** pane, select **Microsoft Excel**, locate SIPRI-Milex-data-1949-2021.xlsx, and click on **Open**.

2. Tableau will now switch the focus to the data source page. Double-click on the Share of GDP table to bring that data into Tableau. In the data details section of the Tableau user interface, you will see that Tableau is not automatically able to create a useable data model (*Figure 7.23*):

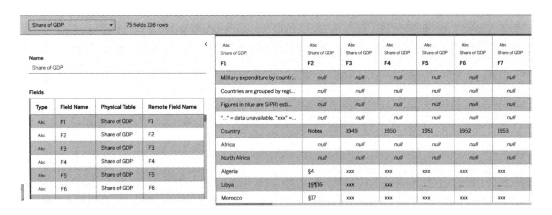

| | Abc Share of GDP F1 | Abc Share of GDP F2 | Abc Share of GDP F3 | Abc Share of GDP F4 | Abc Share of GDP F5 | Abc Share of GDP F6 | Abc Share of GDP F7 |
|---|---|---|---|---|---|---|---|
| Military expenditure by countr... | null | null | null | null | null | null | null |
| Countries are grouped by regi... | null | null | null | null | null | null | null |
| Figures in blue are SIPRI esti... | null | null | null | null | null | null | null |
| ".." = data unavailable. "xxx" =... | null | null | null | null | null | null | null |
| Country | Notes | 1949 | 1950 | 1951 | 1952 | 1953 |
| Africa | null | null | null | null | null | null |
| North Africa | null | null | null | null | null | null |
| Algeria | §4 | xxx | xxx | xxx | xxx | xxx |
| Libya | ‡§¶16 | xxx | xxx | .. | .. | .. |
| Morocco | §17 | xxx | xxx | xxx | xxx | xxx |

Figure 7.23 – Before the data interpreter

3.  To fix this issue, we could manually delete the first five rows in the Excel file. If we were doing this analysis only once, that might be fine but what if we want to automate the process? This is where the data interpreter feature comes in. Click the checkbox next to **Use Data Interpreter** under the **Sheets** section of the **Connections** pane. After clicking on the checkbox, the user interface will change to **Cleaned with Data Interpreter**, as shown in *Figure 7.24*:

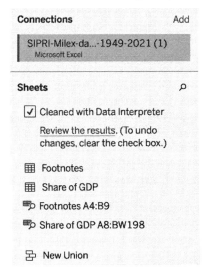

Figure 7.24 – Cleaned with Data Interpreter

4.  In addition, the data details now show a data model that is much closer to the one we want (*Figure 7.25*):

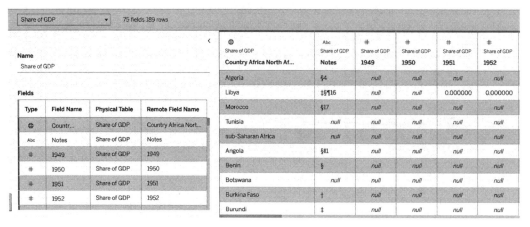

Figure 7.25 – Data details after Data Interpreter has been applied

5.  This almost gives us the right data model with one step remaining. As you can see, the years go across the first row of the model and we want these years in a `Date` field with the values in a `% of GDP` field, making three fields, along with `Country`. The `Notes` field is not one we need, so we can eliminate it from our data model.

6.  For our first step, we will rename the first field to just `Country`. Next to the first field, click on the ▼ symbol in the field header and click on **Rename** as per *Figure 7.26*. Type `Country` into the textbox that appears and hit *Enter/Return*:

Figure 7.26 – Renaming the field to Country

7.  Next, we want to hide the Notes field as we don't want it in our data model. Click on the ▼ symbol in the field header and select the **Hide** option, as shown in *Figure 7.27*:

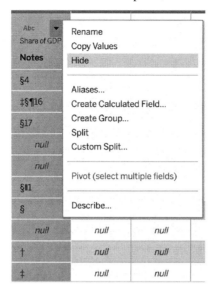

Figure 7.27 – Hiding the field

8.  Our next step is to pivot the years into a Date field. In *Chapter 4*, we explored the pivot columns to rows feature of Tableau Prep Builder. We can also pivot columns to rows in Tableau Desktop, although the user experience is different. To pivot columns to rows, click on the column header of the 1949 field. Holding down the shift key, scroll all the way to the left, and click on the 2021 field to select all the date fields. Next, click on the ▼ next to the 2021 field header and select **Pivot**, as shown in *Figure 7.28*:

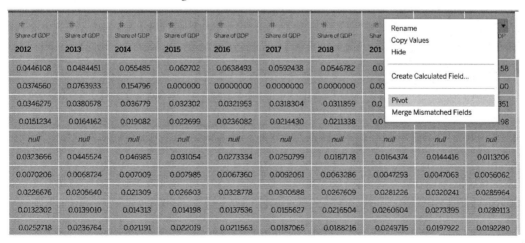

Figure 7.28 – Pivoting the dates

Note that both Tableau Desktop and Tableau Prep Builder can pivot columns to rows but only Tableau Prep Builder can pivot rows to columns. We will look at this and other differences between Tableau Desktop and Tableau Prep Builder in *Chapter 15*.

9. Our final step is to rename the `Pivot Field Names` field to `Date` and `Pivot Field Values` to `% of GDP` using the renaming technique in *step 5* of this section. When you are finished, your data details pane should look like *Figure 7.29*:

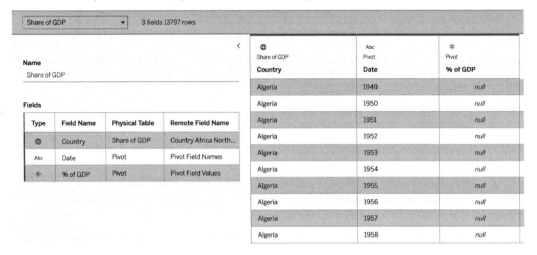

Figure 7.29 – Final renaming

In this section, we learned how to create data models from Microsoft Excel and delimited files that come in the structure of pre-formatted reports by using the data interpreter feature and pivot columns to rows feature of Tableau Desktop. This allows us to save time and resources to automatically create data models from these types of data sources without needing manual intervention for every new file.

In the next section, we will look at how to connect to enterprise database servers, both on-premises and in the cloud.

## Connecting to servers through installed connectors

Within an organizational setting, versus personal analysis, the data sources for Tableau data models are often contained in file stores, applications, and database servers. At the time of writing, using Tableau Desktop version 2022.2 on macOS. Tableau comes with 59 installed connectors for data servers. Installed connectors are connectors written and developed by Tableau and distributed with Tableau Desktop and Tableau Server and Cloud. Tableau Prep Builder also comes with installed connectors.

These connectors fall into the following general categories:

- On-premises database servers (for example, Oracle and Microsoft SQL Server)
- Cloud database servers (for example, Snowflake and Google BigQuery)

- Cloud applications (for example, Salesforce and ServiceNow)

- File shares (for example, Box and Google Drive)

Tableau maintains a list of current native connectors at `https://help.tableau.com/current/pro/desktop/en-us/exampleconnections_overview.htm`.

Connecting to these servers is beyond the scope of this book as it requires running servers that we would either need to set up, as in the case of cloud servers, or downloading and configuring, as in the case of on-premises servers.

Sometimes, connecting to these servers will require downloading database-specific drivers from the software vendor who creates the database. Tableau will direct you to the locations and instructions to download the necessary driver when you need it.

Once you have connected to the server, modeling in Tableau follows the same experience we used when exploring flat files.

Before leaving this section of the chapter, we will look at the two server connection experiences in Tableau. The first of these is via a dialog box within Tableau Desktop. An example of this style is Microsoft SQL Server:

1.  Open Tableau Desktop. Click on **Connect to Data**. Select **To a Server, More...** and then **Microsoft SQL Server**, as shown in *Figure 7.30*:

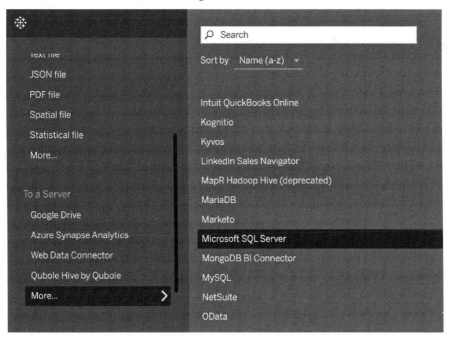

Figure 7.30 – Connecting to Microsoft SQL Server

2. If you have the driver already installed, which is typically the default on computers running the Microsoft Windows operating system, you should see a dialog box that looks like the screenshot in *Figure 7.31*:

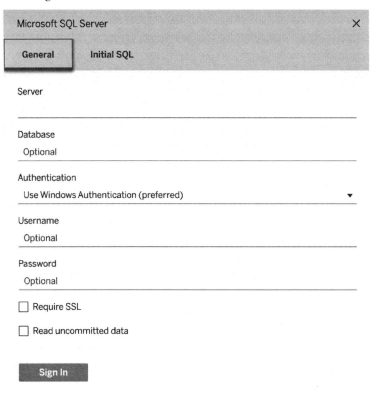

Figure 7.31 – The Microsoft SQL Server connection dialog

Once you enter the connection information in the dialog box, you will be taken to the data source page where you will be able to choose the tables just like choosing sheets from Microsoft Excel workbooks.

The other type of connection begins with authentication in a web browser. This is typical for data servers that use OAuth to manage user access. An example of a server that uses this style is Google Drive. If you connect to Google Drive, Tableau will open a browser window where you can connect using your Google account. At that point, Tableau will bring you back to the data source page where you can then start working with your data.

In this section, we explored the different types of installed data servers and how to connect to them. In the next section, we will look at how to connect to data via web data connectors, data server connectors created by Tableau partners, and generic connectors for data servers without native or partner connectors.

# Connecting to servers through other connectors

In the previous section, we looked at how to connect to data servers through connectors developed by Tableau. As there are hundreds to thousands of potential data servers, it isn't realistic for Tableau to develop connectors for all of them. In these cases, there are three other types of connectors:

- Additional connectors
- Web data connectors for connection to websites and web applications
- Generic ODBC and JDBC connectors

Let's look at each of these types in detail.

## Additional connectors

Additional connectors are listed in Tableau Desktop as **Additional Connectors** under **To a Server**. Typically, these connectors are developed by the Tableau software partner who also develops the data server they connect to, but they can be developed by Tableau and other third parties. At the time of writing, there are 21 additional connectors.

These connectors aren't installed by default. Let's look at how to install one of these connectors:

1.  Open Tableau Desktop. From the **Connect** pane, select **To a Server**, and then select **Qubole Hive by Qubole**.

2.  You should then see a dialog box like the screenshot in *Figure 7.32*. Note that there might be a newer version of the connector when you take this step, as additional connectors are updated regularly:

Figure 7.32 – The installation box for the Qubole connector

3.  Click on **Install and Restart Tableau**. You should be taken to the `https://extensiongallery.tableau.com/connectors` page where you can download and install the Qubole connector. If your Tableau Desktop started without taking you to the connectors page, go to the URL in your browser, find the **Qubole Hive** card, and click on it. From this page, you will get instructions on how to download both the connector and the necessary drivers. We are not going to go through these steps as we do not have a Qubole database that we can connect to.

4.  In Tableau Desktop, you should now see **Qubole for Qubole Hive** in the list of **To a Server** connectors, and your **Additional Connectors** should now have one less number. That is, after letting Tableau know you installed an additional connector, it behaves exactly like a regular server connector.

We have now looked at additional connectors. They behave the same as installed connectors except that they don't come pre-installed with Tableau Desktop.

Next up, we will look at web data connectors. These are often shortened to their acronym, WDC, in Tableau documentation.

## Web data connectors

**Web data connectors** (**WDCs**) are like additional connectors except that they pull data from the user interface layer of web applications, whereas server and additional connectors pull from the data layer of applications. In other words, you use WDCs to connect to data that is accessible over HTTP. A web data connector is an HTML file with JavaScript code. In all cases, Tableau will create an extract of the data it retrieves from the WDC.

Tableau makes it straightforward to create WDCs for web developers. Creating a WDC is beyond the scope of this book, so we will connect to an existing WDC.

We are going to use a WDC that accesses information from Tableau Public. Tableau Public is a free-to-use site to publish Tableau visualizations to share. This WDC was written by Andre de Vries:

1.  Open Tableau Desktop. Click on **Connect to Data**. Select **To a Server**, **More…**, and then select **Web Data Connector**.

2.  This will bring up a dialog, as shown in *Figure 7.33*. In the dialog, type in `https://tableau-public-api.wdc.dev/` and press *Enter*:

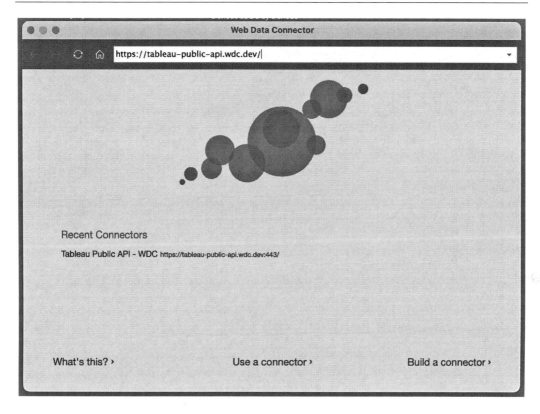

Figure 7.33 – Web data connector dialog

3.  After pressing *Enter*, the dialog box should change to look like the screenshot in *Figure 7.34*. If
    you have a Tableau Public profile, you can enter your username where it says to **Enter Username**.
    If not, you can enter `kirk.munroe` or your favorite Tableau Public author. After entering a
    username, press **Get Data**:

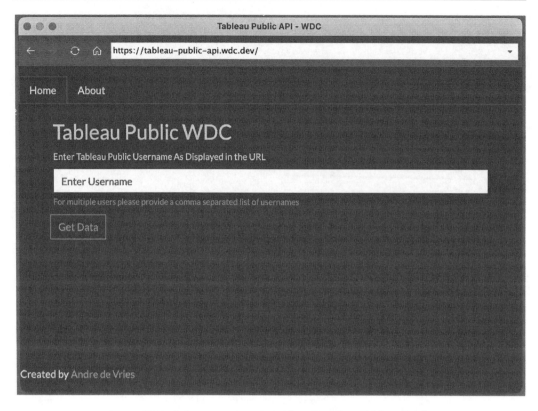

Figure 7.34 – Enter a username to retrieve stats from Tableau Public

4.  When the data comes back, you will be on the data source page. In the upper-right corner of the screen, you should notice that the only option is **Extract**. Tableau does not give the option to continually query the web application live as this type of query would be very slow.

In this section, we explored web data connectors to see how they allow us to get data from websites and web applications. We looked at one example of a WDC, one that allows us to retrieve data from http://public.tableau.com. In practice, we might need to get data from a web application that does not have a server connection. In these cases, we can write our own or get a web developer to write one for us. Creating a WDC is beyond the scope of this book. Instructions on how to build a WDC can be found via the link in the bottom-right corner of the WDC dialog box, as shown in *Figure 7.33* and *step 3* of this section.

Next, we will look at how to connect to databases that do not have native or additional connectors.

## Connecting to databases without a listed connection

As we discussed earlier in this chapter, Tableau provides many server connectors – both natively and through additional connectors. At the time of writing, Tableau has a total of 80 connectors for Tableau Desktop 2022.2. However, there are hundreds more databases available. If you are in a position where you need to retrieve data from one of these databases to build your data model, the generic **Other Databases (JDBC)** or **Other Databases (ODBC)** drivers might be your answer.

**ODBC** is an acronym for **Open Database Connectivity**. It is a standard that allows client software, such as Tableau, to query **database management systems** (**DBMS**). It is written for client software written in Microsoft technology (for example, C++ and C#). **JDBC** is an acronym for **Java Database Connectivity**. It serves the same purpose as ODBC except being written for clients written in Java.

In the case of Tableau Desktop (and Tableau Server and Cloud), the client can use both ODBC and JDBC, so the choice mostly comes down to the DBMS that is being accessed. How do we know which one to use? We should research the DBMS that we are connecting to and see whether they prefer one over the other. If this isn't a factor, it is worth trying both connectors to see which one offers better performance. We should always consider the type of connection we will keep when considering the connector, too. It could be that one of the connectors is faster for smaller query result sets and the other faster for fetching a larger bulk of records. In this example, the first choice is better for live connections, and the second is better if we know that we will be using a data extract.

In all cases where an installed or additional connector exists in Tableau, always choose the named connector. The purpose-built named connectors will yield faster query results and might offer additional features that aren't available in the generic ODBC and JDBC standards.

# Connecting to the Tableau data server

Typically, Tableau Server and Cloud are thought of as servers that provide web interfaces to create, share, and manage data analytics, typically in the form of dashboards. Tableau Server and Cloud also provide other capabilities including acting as a data server.

Tableau has two data server features. The first of these features is only available with the Data Management licensing and is called **virtual connections**. Virtual connections aren't data models but a method of accessing a database through Tableau Server and Cloud. We explored virtual connections in *Chapter 2*.

The more common feature is the **published data source** feature. Published data sources are the best practice for sharing data models with others in your organization. We will be looking at extending the metadata of published data sources in *Chapter 10*. We also created our first published data source from Tableau Prep Builder in the previous chapter, *Chapter 6*. Let's look at how we can create a published data source from Tableau Desktop, and then we will see how we can connect to our published data sources when we open Tableau Desktop:

1. Open Tableau Desktop. Open the `Chapter 7 Grain Data` workbook that we saved earlier in this chapter. This workbook can be opened from the home screen of Tableau Desktop or by navigating to the **File** menu and then clicking on **Open**.

2. Once the workbook is open, go to the **Server** menu, then **Publish Data Source**, then **Sheet1 (GrainDemandProduction)**, as shown in *Figure 7.35*. If you aren't signed into your Tableau Server or Cloud, you will need to do that first from the first menu option. Also, **Sheet1 (GrainDemandProduction)** is the default name of the data source. Additionally, you can change it from the data source page screen:

Figure 7.35 – The Publish Data Source menu

3. You will be presented with a dialog box, as shown in *Figure 7.36*. First, you need to pick a project from your Server or Tableau Cloud site. In this case, we will leave the project as **Default** as long as you have permission to publish to that project. If not, use the drop-down menu to choose a project that you do have permission to publish. In addition to the data source page, we have the option to rename the published data source here. For now, we will leave all the defaults and explore them in greater detail in *Chapter 10*:

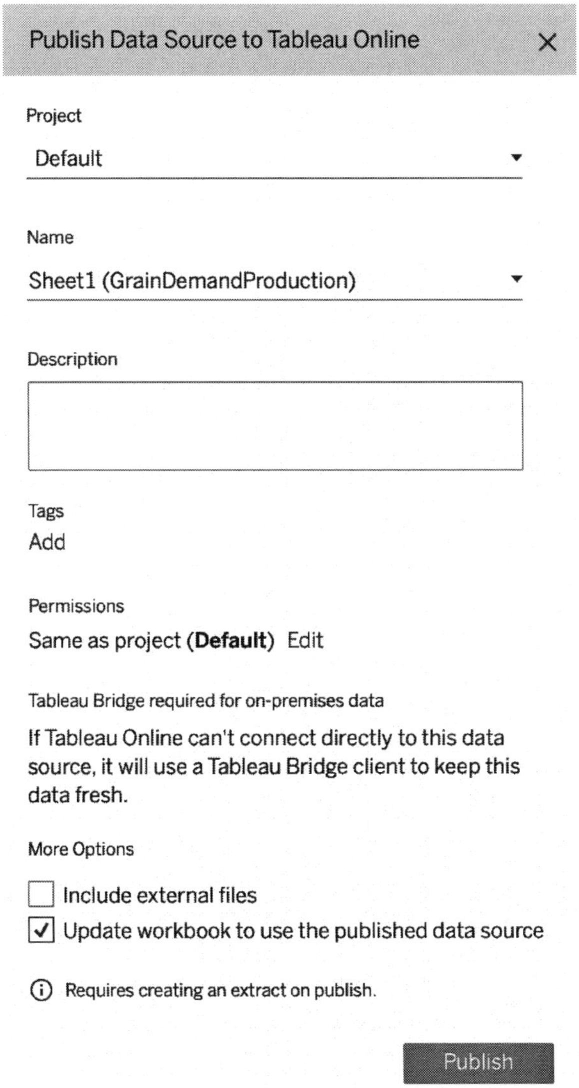

Figure 7.36 – The Publish Data Source dialog

4.   The data source page will show up in a browser window after being published as shown in *Figure 7.37*. If you are using Tableau cloud, you will see a warning about needing to use **Tableau Bridge**. We will explore Tableau Bridge in further detail in *Chapter 14*. For now, you can dismiss the browser window. Close Tableau Desktop without saving:

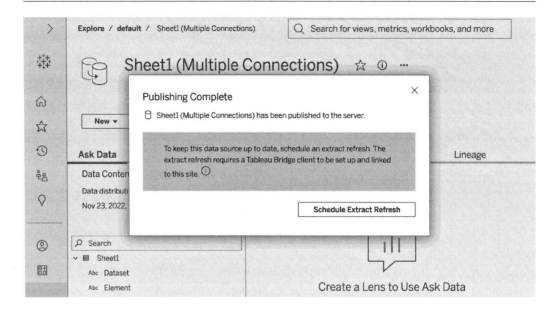

Figure 7.37 – Tableau data source page

5.  Open Tableau Desktop. From the **Connect** pane, select **Tableau Server** from the **Search for Data** section, as shown in *Figure 7.38*. You can make this selection whether you are using Tableau Server or Tableau Cloud:

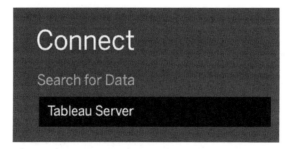

Figure 7.38 – Connecting to the Tableau published data source

6.  When the dialog comes up to connect, you should see the **AMER Sales Transactions** we created in *Chapter 6* as well as the **Sheet1 (GrainDemandProduction)** data source we created in *step 4* of this section, as shown in *Figure 7.39*. Select **Sheet1 (GrainDemandProduction)** and press **Connect**. You have now connected to your first published data source in Tableau Desktop:

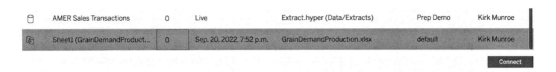

| | AMER Sales Transactions | 0 | Live | Extract.hyper (Data/Extracts) | Prep Demo | Kirk Munroe |
| | Sheet1 (GrainDemandProduct... | 0 | Sep. 20, 2022, 7:52 p.m. | GrainDemandProduction.xlsx | default | Kirk Munroe |

Connect

Figure 7.39 – Connecting to a published data source

In this section, we created our first published data source from Tableau Desktop and connected to our first published data source in Tableau Desktop. We will be exploring published data sources in more detail in the upcoming chapters. Published data sources are one of the key components of Tableau data modeling.

## Summary

In this chapter, we learned about the different data sources available to Tableau Desktop.

In the first section, we looked at the different file types that can be data sources for Tableau. We imported data to create data models from Microsoft Excel, CSV files, JSON files, spatial files, and tables from PDF files.

We looked at the different types of servers that Tableau connects to, including native connectors, additional connectors, and generic ODBC and JDBC connectors when our data server is not listed. Additionally, we looked at web data connectors for creating models from the data on web pages and web applications.

In the final section, we looked at creating and connecting to Tableau published data sources, one of the key components for data modeling at scale in Tableau.

This chapter focused on the building blocks of data modeling in Tableau – connecting to data. In the next three chapters, we will look at how to extend and scale our data models by combining multiple data sources into a single model and then securing and sharing that model. The next chapter will focus on extending data models through logical tables.

# 8

# Building Data Models Using Relationships

In the previous chapter, we explored the various data connections that can be made from Tableau Desktop. We will now look at how to combine multiple data sources into a single data model. Tableau has a way of combining data sources at the **logical layer** through a feature called **relationships**. This chapter will explore relationships, how to create them, and how they work with different levels of aggregation between tables. This chapter will also explore creating unions between data sources in Tableau Desktop.

In this chapter, we're going to cover the following topics:

- Using relationships to combine tables at the logical layer
- Understanding the difference between relationships and joins
- Setting performance options for relationships
- Creating unions in Tableau Desktop to add additional rows of data

> **Note**
>
> All the exercises and figures in this chapter will be described by using the Tableau Desktop client software except where noted. You can also recreate all the exercises in this chapter using the Tableau web client, which has a very similar experience to the Desktop client.

## Technical requirements

To view the complete list of requirements to run the practical examples in this chapter, please see the *Technical requirements* section in *Chapter 1*.

To run the exercises in this chapter, we will need the following files:

- `Superstore Sales Orders - US.xlsx`
- `Product Database.xlsx`
- `Sales Argentina.csv`
- `Sales Colombia.csv`
- `Sales Chile.csv`
- `Sales Targets.xlsx`

If you have not done so already, please download the files, save them to a directory, and make note of the directory name. Create a sub-directory and move the `Sales Argentina.csv`, `Sales Colombia.csv`, and `Sales Chile.csv` files into it.

The files we will be using are all based on the Superstore data, the sample data that Tableau uses in their products.

The files used in the exercises in this chapter can be found at `https://github.com/PacktPublishing/Data-Modeling-with-Tableau/`.

# Using relationships to combine tables at the logical layer

Tableau introduced a new data model in its 2020.2 release called relationships. Up until this release, the only way to expand your analysis to use additional fields from a secondary table in Tableau was to create a join at the **physical** layer of the data. Relationships offer advantages over physical joins. The advantages come down to quicker and easier data modeling. Just tell Tableau which fields are common between the different tables and let Tableau dynamically generate the right query based on the question asked by the analyst. This means no more pre-aggregation, complex join clauses, and custom SQL queries.

These advantages in modeling lead to two particularly compelling use cases:

- Supporting multiple use cases with a single data model
- Ability to handle different levels of aggregation

Let's start by exploring multiple use cases with a single data model.

## Many use cases with a single data model

We often have a case where an analysis might require two tables to be joined with a left join and another analysis might require a right join (or inner join or outer join). Also, thinking back to *Chapter 4*, when we joined the sales data with the product data, we had to consider if we wanted to see the following (with sales on the left and products on the right):

- All sales data, even if the product wasn't in the product database (left join)

- Only sales when a product was in the sales database (inner join)

- All products, even when they weren't part of a sale (right join)

Each of these leads to viable analyses. To answer all three types of questions in a single Tableau workbook, if you were using joins at the physical level, you would need to create three distinct data models. With relationships, this is not the case. We just let Tableau know that the field that is related between the two tables is `Product ID`; Tableau handles the rest for us dynamically. We'll look at each of the preceding three points in detail in the following sections.

### All sales data, even if the product wasn't in the product database (left join)

Let's use the aggregation of sales targets and the product and sales analyses as examples:

1.  Open Tableau Desktop. When you open Tableau Desktop, you will see the **Connect** pane on the left-hand side of the user interface. From the **Connect** pane, under the **To a File** section, select **Microsoft Excel**. Locate the `Superstore Sales Orders - US.xlsx` file, select it to highlight it, and click on **Open**. We should now be looking at the screen shown in *Figure 8.1*:

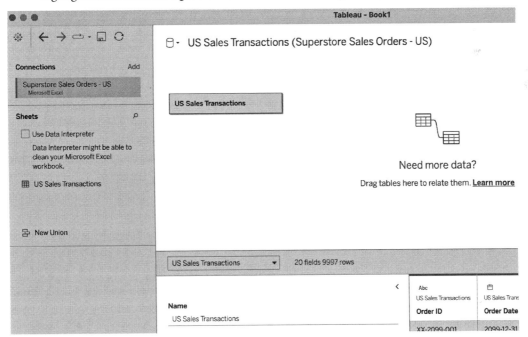

Figure 8.1 – Tableau data source page after connecting to US Sales Transactions

2.  The Superstore Sales Orders - US.xlsx file has a single sheet called US Sales Transactions, so Tableau automatically added that sheet to our canvas as a single table.

3.  The data in the table does not contain product information. To find out which products have sold and which products haven't sold, we need to create a relationship with our product database. Click on the **Add** link to the right of **Connections**. Under the **To a File** section, select **Microsoft Excel**. Locate the Product Database.xlsx file, select it to highlight it, and click on **Open**.

    Our screen should now look like *Figure 8.2*. We now have two data sources in our workbook, namely Superstore Sales Orders – US and Product Database. The Product Database.xlsx file also only has a single sheet. This sheet is called Product DB:

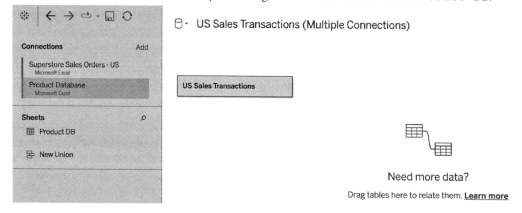

Figure 8.2 – Data source page with Product DB added

4.  To create our first relationship, drag the Product DB sheet onto the canvas. You should see a flexible line as you drag it to the canvas, as seen in *Figure 8.3*. This line is called a **noodle** and represents a relationship. Release the mouse button to form the relationship:

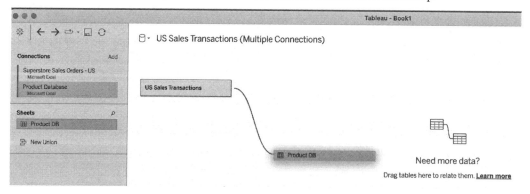

Figure 8.3 – Product DB with a noodle connection to US Sales Transactions

5.  To finish our relationship, click on the noodle line that connects the two tables and notice the area of the screen to the left of the data details pane, as seen in *Figure 8.4*:

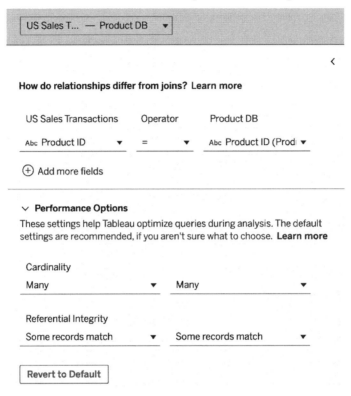

Figure 8.4 – Configuring the relationship fields

6.  The first thing we see is the area to instruct Tableau on how these tables relate to each other. Tableau picked up that there is a field named `Product ID` in both tables, so it creates that as a default. We will leave this default as it is correct for our use case. It is always good to check these fields, even when it looks like Tableau has found the right field. There are cases when the same field in two tables contains slightly different information. Notice that we could change these fields, add additional fields, and use operators other than =.

7.  The next section can be expanded to show **Performance Options**. Two options can be set here: **Cardinality** and **Referential Integrity**. We are going to look at how to optimize performance later in this chapter. For now, we are going to leave the default setting as-is in our example.

8.  Now, let's see how Tableau creates dynamic joins, depending on the question we want to ask. For our first question, let's see how we answer the question of, "*which products have we sold the most?*" Click on **Sheet 1** to begin. Let's look at our data pane to see how Tableau has arranged the metadata in our data model, as seen in *Figure 8.5*:

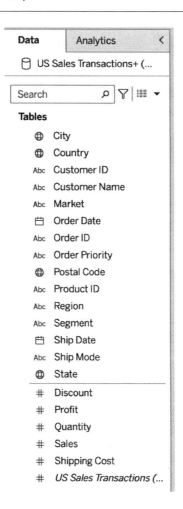

Figure 8.5 – The data pane after creating a relationship

9.  The first thing we notice is that Tableau organizes our data by source table. Toward the top of the data pane, we see all the fields from the `Product DB` table in a collapsible list. The discrete fields from the table show up at the top of the list, sorted alphabetically, with a line that separates the continuous fields, which are also sorted alphabetically. This process repeats itself for all tables; in our case, the only other table is `US Sales Transactions`. If we collapse these tables, we will see the fields that Tableau automatically generates, and could also be used across tables. These are listed at the bottom of the data pane, as seen in *Figure 8.6*:

**Tables**

> ⊞ **Product DB**

> ⊞ **US Sales Transactions**

Abc *Measure Names*
_____

⊕ *Latitude (generated)*

⊕ *Longitude (generated)*

\# *Measure Values*

Figure 8.6 – Fields generated by Tableau

10. With an understanding of our data, let's look at the answer to our question regarding products that have sold the most. Under the US Sales Transactions table, double-click **Sales** to bring it into the view. Under the Product DB table, double-click to bring **Product Name** into the view. Your screen should now look like what's shown in *Figure 8.7*:

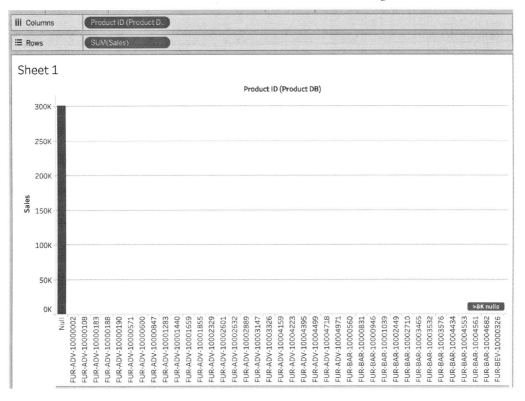

Figure 8.7 – Sales by Product Name

11. To make it easier to get to our answer of the product that sold the most, click on the **Swap Rows and Columns** icon in the toolbar below the menu bar, as seen in *Figure 8.8*:

Figure 8.8 – The Tableau Desktop toolbar

Click on the **Sort Descending** button, which is two icons to the right of the **Swaps Rows and Columns** icon. You should now have a view that looks like *Figure 8.9*:

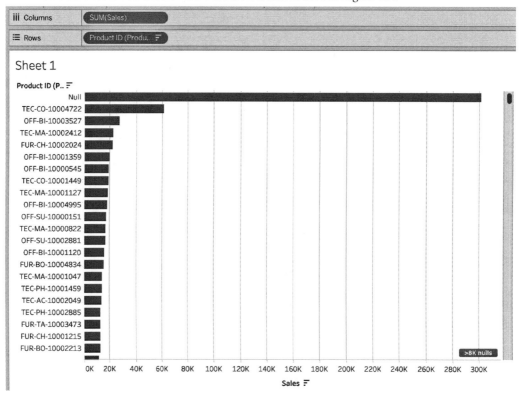

Figure 8.9 – Product names that have sold the most sorted descending

12. We notice two interesting pieces of information right away. The first is that we have a lot of sales where there is no product name attached to them. The second is that we have **1789** null records as well, which we can see if we hover over the **>2K nulls** icon at the bottom-right corner of the canvas, as seen in *Figure 8.10*:

Figure 8.10 – Hovering over the nulls indicator

13. First, let's look at all the sales where Product Name has a Null value. We told Tableau to create a relationship between these tables based on Product ID, so let's bring that into our view. Drag the Product ID (Product DB) field from the Product DB table and the Product ID field from the US Sales Transactions table onto the **Rows** shelf in the view. The result should look like what's shown in *Figure 8.11*. Leave Tableau Desktop open at this point. We will continue from this point in the next section:

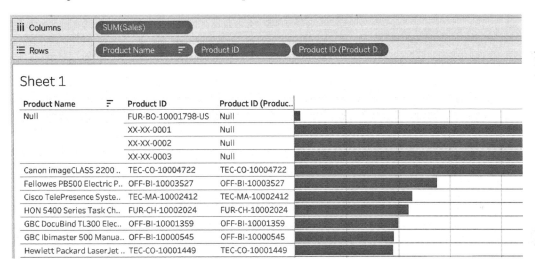

Figure 8.11 – Uncovering null product names

Now that we have the answer to our question of all sales, even if they do not have a Product ID associated with them, let's look at sales when there is only a Product ID on the sales record.

### Only sales when a product was in the sales database (inner join)

Let's begin:

1. We can see that there are two product IDs in the sales transactions that are not in our product database. Looking back to *Chapter 4*, we have already seen these and discovered how to clean and filter values like these in our data model. Right-click on the Null cell under Product Name and select **Exclude** to filter out these values, as seen in *Figure 8.12*:

## Sheet 1

| Product Name ⌐ | Product ID | Product ID (Produc.. |
|---|---|---|
| Null | FUR-BO-10001798-US | Null |
| | X-XX-0001 | Null |
| | X-XX-0002 | Null |
| | X-XX-0003 | Null |
| Canon i | C-CO-10004722 | TEC-CO-10004722 |
| Fellowe | F-BI-10003527 | OFF-BI-10003527 |
| Cisco Te | C-MA-10002412 | TEC-MA-10002412 |
| HON 54 | R-CH-10002024 | FUR-CH-10002024 |
| GBC Do | F-BI-10001359 | OFF-BI-10001359 |
| GBC Ibi | F-BI-10000545 | OFF-BI-10000545 |

Menu overlay:
Keep only
Exclude
Hide
Format...
Rotate Label
✓ Show Header
Edit Alias...
Split

Figure 8.12 – Exclude null values

2.  We now have the answer to our question. Canon imageCLASS 2200 Advanced Copier is our top-selling product with sales of $61,600. If we look at the **Filters** shelf, we will see the **Product Name** filter. Right-click on the **Product Name** filter in the **Filters** shelf and select **Edit Filter**, as seen in *Figure 8.13*:

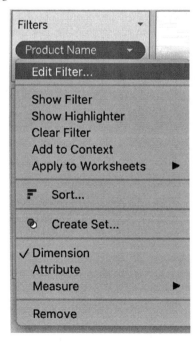

Figure 8.13 – Edit Filter…

3.  The result of our filter will come up as per *Figure 8.14*:

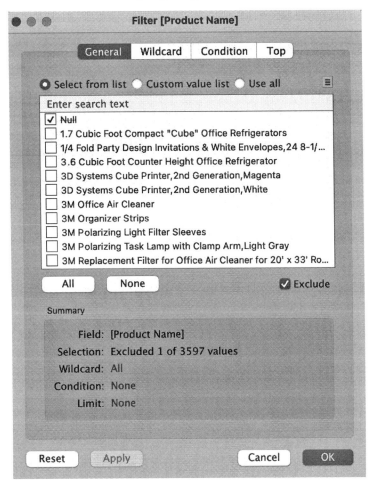

Figure 8.14 – Filter excluding nulls

Tableau created an exclude filter on null values based on the exclude gesture we made in *Step 15*. This filter is currently only applied in the analysis we are doing in **Sheet 1**. We could add a data source filter, as we explored in *Chapter 7*. Additionally, we can apply this filter to more than one sheet. Right-click on the filter and select **Apply to Worksheets** | **All Using This Data Source**, as seen in *Figure 8.15*. This is another way to create a data source filter. Leave Tableau Desktop open at this point. We will pick up from this step in the next section:

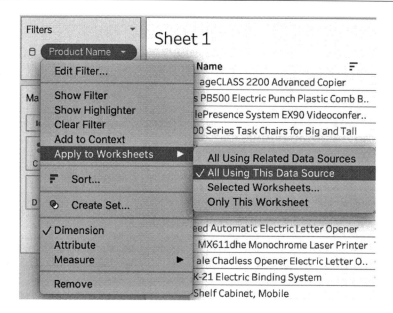

Figure 8.15 – Filtering to all using this data source

Now that we have the answer to the question of which product we have sold the most, let's answer the question, "*what percentage of all products in our catalog have not sold?*"

### All products even when they weren't part of a sale (right join)

Let's find out what percentage of all products in our catalog have not sold:

1.  To quickly see how many Product ID records are in each table, let's start by creating two new sheets. Click on the icon to the right of **Sheet 1** near the bottom left of the screen, as seen in *Figure 8.16*, to create a new sheet, which will be labeled **Sheet 2**. Repeat this to create **Sheet 3** as well:

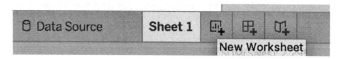

Figure 8.16 – Creating a new sheet

2.  Go to **Sheet 2**. Double-click on the Product ID field under the US Sales Transaction table. This will create a list of all the Product IDs that have sold. We know this because they are coming from the sales table. If you look at the bottom left of the screen, you will notice there are **1861 marks**, as per *Figure 8.17*. This means there are 1,861 products sold in our database table. If you click back on **Sheet 1**, you will notice the same number of records, as expected. To get these records, Tableau only had to query the US Sales Transaction table without creating a join to the Product DB table:

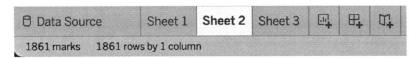

Figure 8.17 – 1,861 sold products

3.  Go to **Sheet 3**. This time, double-click on the Product ID (Product DB) field under the Product DB table. You will now see **10292 marks**. This means there are 10,292 total products in our product database. To get these records, Tableau only had to query the Product DB table without creating a join to the US Sales Transaction table. In other words, we have sold 1,861 products at least once while 8,431 products have never been sold. Let's validate these numbers to be sure.

4.  There are several ways to see which products have and have not sold in the same view. Before starting, click to create a new sheet, **Sheet 4**. For this exercise, let's do it using a **set**. Sets are specialized fields that define a subset of data based on the conditions you define. Go to the newly created **Sheet 4**. Right-click on the Product ID (Product DB) field and select **Create | Set**, as per *Figure 8.18*:

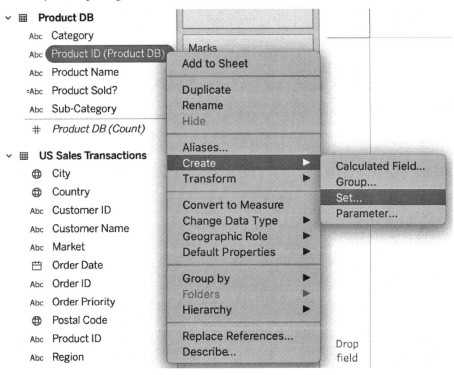

Figure 8.18 – Creating a set from Product ID (Product DB)

5.   Click on the **Condition** tab and select **By field**. Select **Sales** as the field, **Sum** as the aggregation, and then > as the operator and **0** as the value, as seen in *Figure 8.19*. This will create a new set with Product IDs that sold **IN** the set and those with no sales **OUT** of the set. Press **OK** to finish creating the set:

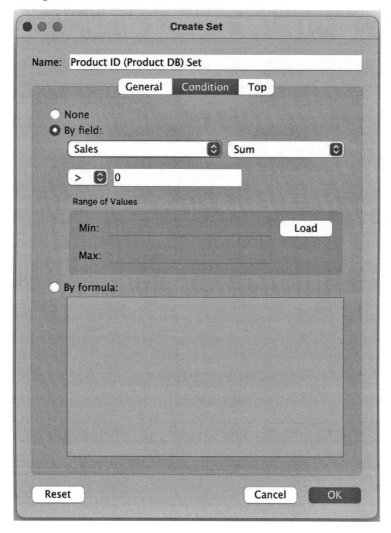

Figure 8.19 – Create Set

6.  To get the percentage of products from our product database that have not sold, drag the new
    `Product ID (Product DB) Set` field to the **Rows** shelf. You should now see `In` and
    `Out`, as seen in *Figure 8.20*:

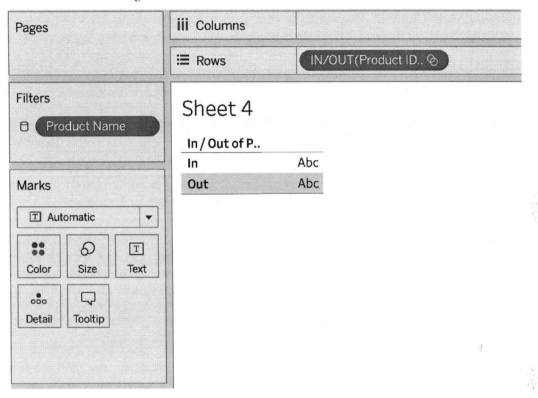

Figure 8.20 – Product ID set on the view

7.  Drag the `Product ID (Product DB)` field to the **Text** card. Right-click on `Product
    ID (Product DB)` in the **Marks** card and select **Measure | Count (Distinct)**, as seen in
    *Figure 8.21*. This will give us a count of unique Product IDs that have sold (IN) and have not
    sold (OUT):

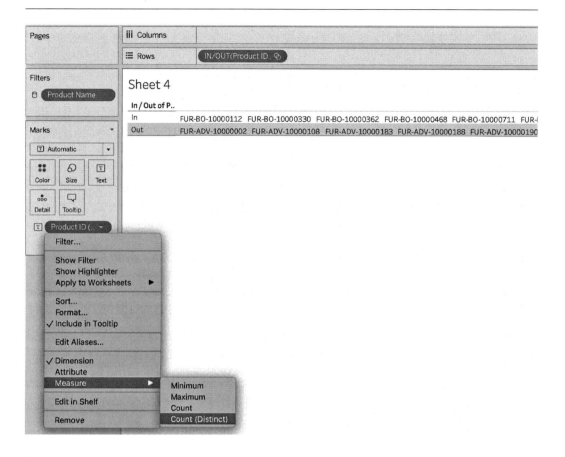

Figure 8.21 – Products that have sold and not sold

8.  As a final step, right-click on CNTD(Product ID (Product DB)) in the Marks card and select **Quick Table Calculation | Percent of Total**, as seen in *Figure 8.22*:

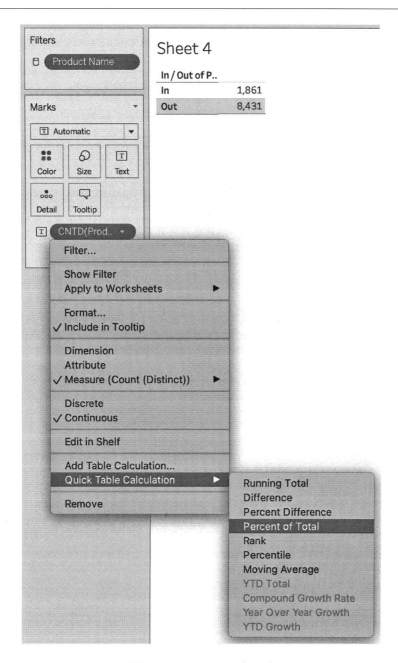

Figure 8.22 – Percent of Total

9. This will give us our answer that **81.92%** of the products in our product database have not been sold, as per *Figure 8.23*. This is the first query that we have looked at where Tableau needed to query both tables. Tableau has handled all of our queries and joins for us dynamically:

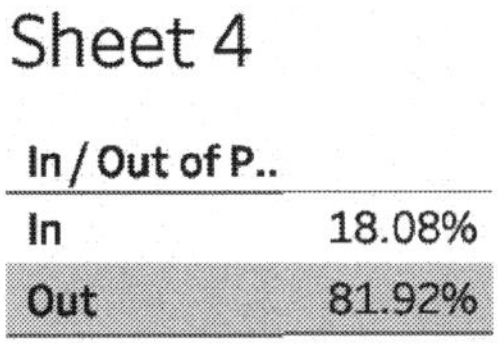

## Sheet 4

| In / Out of P.. | |
| --- | --- |
| In | 18.08% |
| Out | 81.92% |

Figure 8.23 – Our answer!

Now that we have explored how to support multiple use cases with a single data model using relationships, let's move on to creating relationships when the tables are at different levels of aggregation.

## Ability to handle tables at different levels of aggregation

When you join two tables together, Tableau will flatten the results into a single table. This means that all data needs to be at the same level of detail. With relationships, Tableau will know which table your field is in and will be able to handle it at the right level of detail. Looking back to *Chapter 4*, we had to aggregate our sales data source before we could join it to the monthly sales target in Tableau Prep Builder. We do not have to do this with relationships. We will now create a relationship between two tables at different levels of aggregation:

1. Open Tableau Desktop. From the **Connect** pane, under the **To a File** section, select **Microsoft Excel**. Locate the Sales Targets.xlsx file, select it to highlight it, and click on **Open**. This workbook has a single sheet with sales targets for 12 months for five countries in 2014.

2. We need to pivot our data before we can create a relationship with our sales transactions. Click on the 1/1/2014 field, hold down the *Shift* key, scroll to the right until you get to the end, and click on the 12/1/2014 field while still holding down *Shift*. Right-click on the 12/1/2014 field to bring up the ▼ and select **Pivot**, as seen in *Figure 8.24*:

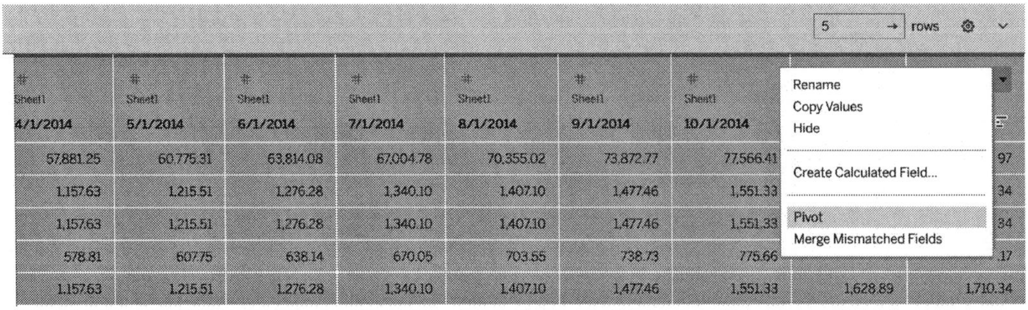

Figure 8.24 – First pivot date fields

3. After the pivot, rename `Pivot Field Names` to `Date` and change the field type to **Date**. Rename `Pivot Field Values` to `Sales Targets`. The result is seen in *Figure 8.25*:

| ⊕ Sheet1<br>**Country** | 🗓 Pivot<br>**Date** | # Pivot<br>**Sales Targets** |
|---|---|---|
| United States | 2014-01-01 | 50,000.00 |
| United States | 2014-10-01 | 77,566.41 |
| United States | 2014-11-01 | 81,444.73 |
| United States | 2014-12-01 | 85,516.97 |
| United States | 2014-02-01 | 52,500.00 |
| United States | 2014-03-01 | 55,125.00 |
| United States | 2014-04-01 | 57,881.25 |
| United States | 2014-05-01 | 60,775.31 |
| United States | 2014-06-01 | 63,814.08 |
| United States | 2014-07-01 | 67,004.78 |

Figure 8.25 – Renaming and changing the field type after the pivot

4. We can create a relationship with our sales data now that our sales targets are in the spreadsheet table format that works with Tableau. Click on the **Add** link to the right of **Connections**. Under the **To a File** section, select **Microsoft Excel**. Locate the `Superstore Sales Orders - US.xlsx` file, select it to highlight it, and click on **Open**.

5. Drag the `US Sales Transactions` sheet onto the canvas until the noodle appears. Release the left mouse button to drop the sheet onto the canvas and create a relationship, as seen in *Figure 8.26*:

Figure 8.26 – Relationship between sales targets and US Sales Transactions

6. We can see that Tableau thinks the relationship should be made on `Country`. This is partially true, but we also want to make sure that Tableau knows the relationship also occurs based on date. Under **How do relationships differ from joins?**, click on **Add more fields**, as seen in *Figure 8.27*:

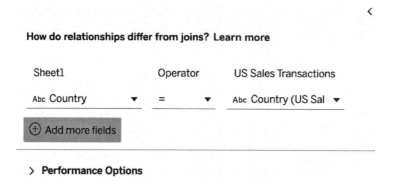

Figure 8.27 – Relationship field mapping

7.  On the `Sheet1` side, add `Date`. Keep the operator as = and select **Create Relationship Calculation…**, from under the **US Sales Transactions** side as seen in *Figure 8.28*. We need to create a relationship calculation because we do not want the sales targets to line up with the first sales date of the month. We need the sales targets to line up with monthly sales:

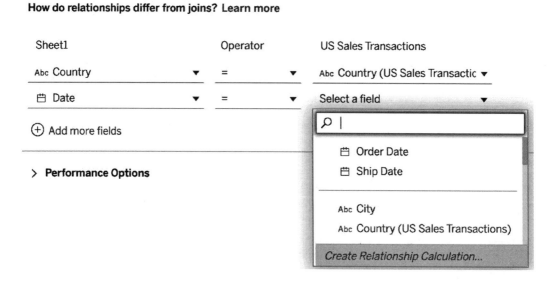

Figure 8.28 – Create Relationship Calculation…

8.  The relationship calculation we are going to create has the syntax of DATE(DATETRUNC('month', [Order Date])). Enter this in the calculation dialog and press **OK**, as per *Figure 8.29*:

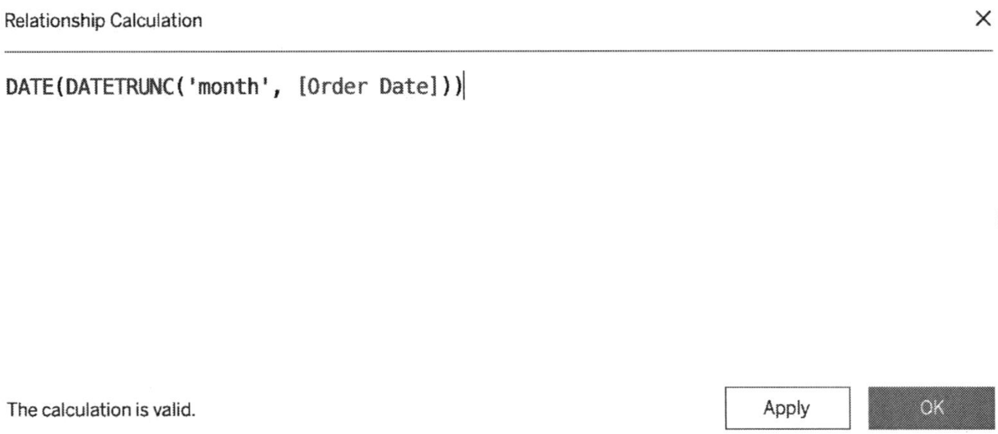

Relationship Calculation                                                                                                   ✕

```
DATE(DATETRUNC('month', [Order Date]))|
```

▶

The calculation is valid.                                                       Apply                  OK

Figure 8.29 – Relationship calculation

The reason for this calculation is we want all the sales for the month to map to the first day of the month as this is the way the monthly data is represented in the sales target table. The reason the calculation is wrapped in the DATE function is that Tableau will always make a DATETRUNC calculation of the Date/Time type, which would be a mismatch to Date in the sales targets sheet.

9.  To see how the relationship handled the difference in both levels of detail and having five countries when our sales data only had one country, click on Sheet 1. Drag and drop the Date field from the Sheet1 table to **Columns**. Right-click on the **YEAR(Date)** pill on the **Columns** shelf and change the aggregation to the top **Month** option, as seen in *Figure 8.30*:

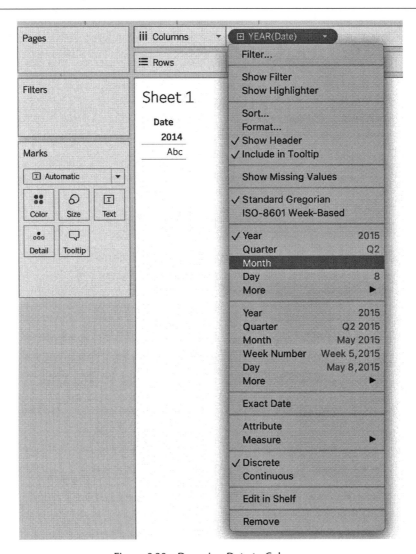

Figure 8.30 – Dragging Date to Columns

10.  From the Sheet1 table, drag and drop Country to the **Rows** shelf and drag and drop Sales Targets to the **Text** marks card. The result is shown in *Figure 8.31*:

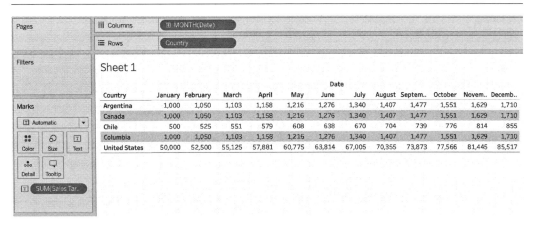

Figure 8.31 – Sales targets by county and month

11. Drag and drop `Country` from the `Sheet1` table to the **Filters** shelf and select only `United States`. Drag and drop `Date` from the `Sheet1` table to **Filters**, choose **Year**, and select only **2014** (the only available option). To see what percentage of the sales target has been achieved, we can create a field called `% Sales Target`. Click on the ▼ icon to the right of the search box and select **Create Calculated Field…**. Then, enter `SUM([Sales])/SUM([Sales Targets])` in the dialog box, as seen in *Figure 8.32*:

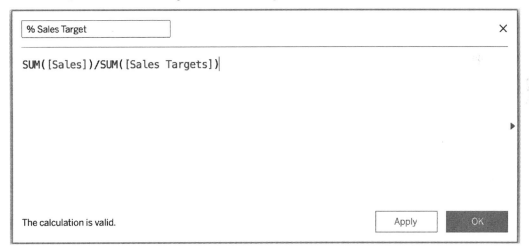

Figure 8.32 – % Sales Target achieved calculation

12. You will notice that the calculation falls in the data pane outside the area of either of the tables. The reason for this is to signify that Tableau needs to query both tables to create the calculation. Before adding this calculation to our view, right-click on the `% Sales Target` field, select **Default Properties | Number Format…**, as shown in *Figure 8.33*, and then pick a percentage with 2 decimal places:

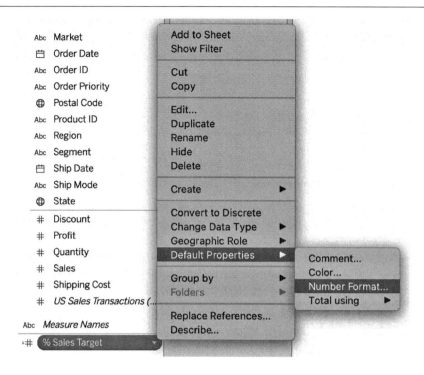

Figure 8.33 – Change number format

13. To complete our analysis, drag and drop the new `% Sales Target` on top of the `Sales Target` field in the **Marks** card to replace it in the view, as seen in *Figure 8.34*. The result is the answer to the question "*what percentage of the sales target was achieved in the US per month?*" and we answered it without needing to aggregate our sales transactions first:

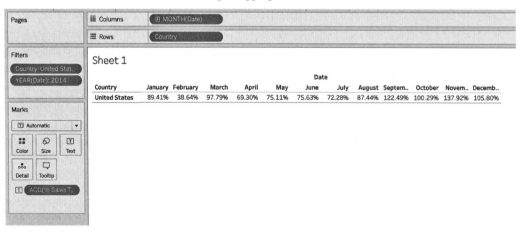

| Country | January | February | March | April | May | June | July | August | Septem.. | October | Novem.. | Decemb.. |
|---------|---------|----------|-------|-------|-----|------|------|--------|----------|---------|---------|----------|
| United States | 89.41% | 38.64% | 97.79% | 69.30% | 75.11% | 75.63% | 72.28% | 87.44% | 122.49% | 100.29% | 137.92% | 105.80% |

Figure 8.34 – Sales targets achieved per month

In this section, we looked at using relationships to deal with tables at different levels of aggregation. This saves a lot of time and complexity in data modeling. It also saves a lot of time in creating fewer data models and the need for less quality assurance by avoiding complicated joins.

In the next section, we will explore how relationships are different than joins.

## Understanding the differences between relationships and joins

It was a straightforward path to answering our question of which product had the highest sales using a relationship. If we had used a join, we could have made a left join with the US Sales Transactions table on the left and the Product DB table on the right and gotten the same answer. However, if we had created that join, it would have excluded all the products that did not sell from the product database, so we may not have been able to answer our question about the percentage of products that did not sell. We could have answered this question with a right join but then we wouldn't have been able to find the incorrect product IDs because they would not have been identified in our join. We could have created a full outer join, but this would have resulted in a lot of null values in our data, which would make analysis more difficult and caused an explosion of our data.

These limitations make relationships such a great choice. We just let Tableau know which field(s) are common across the tables and let Tableau handle the right queries and join types.

We will take a deeper dive into joins in *Chapter 9*, including use cases for joins over relationships.

## Setting performance options for relationships

In the previous two sections, we looked at relationships and how they differ from joins. As relationships are dynamic, they can sometimes create queries that could be better optimized by telling Tableau more about our data.

**Performance Options** is available in the user interface under the field mappings, as seen in *Figure 8.35*:

Figure 8.35 – Performance options

In most cases, the best practice is to leave the default options as-is unless we are 100% sure of our data. Let's look at these two settings and why the default is best:

- **Cardinality**: You can effectively use this to tell Tableau when a field is a unique key/index field. Using our example of product sales and the product catalog where product sales are on the left, we would want to leave **Many** on the left-hand side because a Product ID could be sold many times. If we were 100% sure we had no duplicates in our data – exactly one row per Product ID – we could set the right-hand side to One. Unless we are confident this is true, it is better to leave **Many** as-is; otherwise, there could be duplicate aggregate values in views created from the data model.

- **Referential Integrity**: Changing this from **Some records match** to **All records match** can speed up performance, but again only if you are confident. In our products example again, it seems like we should be able to have **All records match** on the left and **Some records match** on the right because only 80% or so of the records in the product database have a match in sales, but every record in the sales transactions should have a matching Product ID in the product database. If you remember, this wasn't true as we had one *bad* Product ID, along with a few records with a null Product ID. While setting the product database side to All records match would have resulted in more simple queries (which means faster queries in big data tables), we would have missed those records and might have ended up with confusing results.

In this section, we looked at optimizing the queries Tableau generates from relationships. We also learned how to change the default settings when we know exactly what is in our data to ensure we don't end up with confusing result sets in our analysis.

So far, we have looked at adding additional fields to our data model by using relationships. In the next section, we will explore the use of unions to add additional rows of data in Tableau Desktop.

# Creating manual and wildcard unions in Tableau Desktop to add additional rows of data

We use relationships to add additional fields to our data. For cases where we need to add additional rows from other tables or files, we use unions. We can union new data via **manual union** or **wildcard union**. We will look at both methods in the upcoming sections.

It is important to note that Tableau Desktop can create relationships and joins between tables, regardless of whether they are in the same database or across multiple databases (if the database supports cross-database joins). However, unions can only be created by tables in the same database. In the case of Microsoft Excel, this would mean the unions of multiple sheets within the same Excel workbook but not the ability to union across different workbooks.

Tableau Desktop can create unions across multiple text files. It is a common use case to get data dumps in the form of delimited files, which can then be joined together in Tableau Desktop. In our example, we will be using sample data representing Superstore sales from three South American countries, with each country represented in a unique file.

## Manual union

We perform a manual union by dragging an addition table to an existing connection on the canvas of the data source page. We will start with a union of Chile Sales data to Argentina Sales. Before we begin, make sure you have the following files copied from GitHub into the same folder on your computer:

- `Sales Argentina.csv`
- `Sales Colombia.csv`
- `Sales Chile.csv`

It will make your union easier if these three files are in a directory with no other files, although this isn't required. The reason is that the easiest and most manageable method of creating a union of text files is by having all those files and no other files in the same directory. As each of the files acts as a table, we will be using the terms files and tables interchangeably during this exercise:

1. Open Tableau Desktop. From the **Connect** pane, under the **To a File** section, select **Text file**. Locate the `Sales Argentina.csv` file, select it to highlight it, and click on **Open**. We should now be looking at a screen similar to the one shown in *Figure 8.36*:

Figure 8.36 – Tableau data source page after connecting to the Sales Argentina.csv file

2.  The easiest way to create a manual union is to take the table you want to union and drag it under the first table on the canvas. Put your mouse over Sales Chile.csv in the left pane, hold down the left mouse button, and drag the table under the Sales Argentina.csv card onto the canvas until the **Union** drop area appears, as shown in *Figure 8.37*:

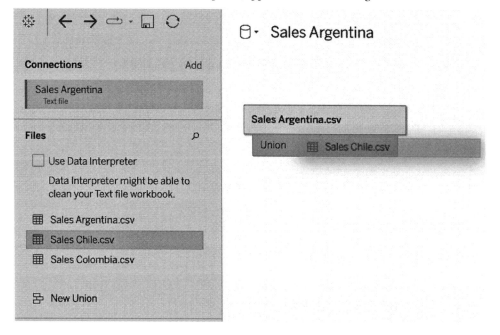

Figure 8.37 – Union drop zone

Tableau will show you a noodle, as per the relationships exercises from earlier in this chapter, until you find the **Union** drop zone. Release the left mouse button when you are over the **Union** drop zone.

3.  We will know if the union worked when the union icon of stacked building blocks appears in front of the `Sales Argentina.csv` card on the canvas, as seen in *Figure 8.38*:

Figure 8.38 – Union icon in front of Sales Argentina.csv

4.  To check the results of our union, you can hover to the right of the card with `Sales Argentina.csv` until the ▼ icon shows. Click on the down arrow to bring up the menu and select **Edit Union…**, as seen in *Figure 8.39*.

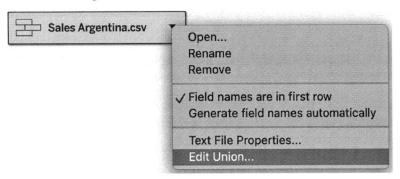

Figure 8.39 – Edit Union…

It is also worth noting that if you have a hard time finding the **Union** drop area, you can use this same menu to create a new union. If there isn't a previous union, the menu will say **Convert to Union**, which will bring up the union dialog box that we can see in the next step.

5.  We can now see the two tables that make up our union in the union dialog box, as seen in *Figure 8.40*:

Figure 8.40 – Union dialog box

6.  We want to add `Sales Colombia.csv` to our union as well. We can do this in one of two ways. The first method is by dragging and dropping the `Sales Columbia.csv` table below `Sales Chile.csv` in the union dialog, as per *Figure 8.41*. Do not press **OK** here as we are going to look at the second method in the next step:

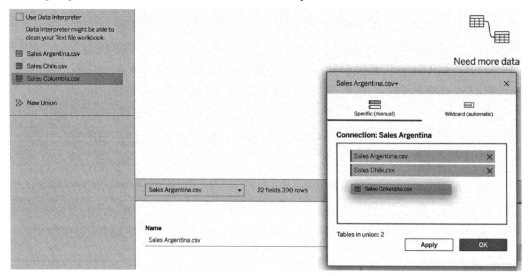

Figure 8.41 – Adding a union manually through drag and drop

7.  The other method is through a wildcard union. Click on the **Wildcard (automatic)** tab in the union dialog box. The result should look like what's shown in *Figure 8.42*:

Figure 8.42 – Wildcard union

8.  A wildcard union is a great option when you have a lot of files, especially if you are regularly getting new files. If the new files match the pattern you set in this dialog, Tableau will automatically add them to your union as they get added to the directory. The options in a wildcard union are as follows:

-   **Files**: Either include or exclude and then enter a pattern. For example, if you only want files with 2022 in the filename, you could leave **Include** and enter *2022* as a pattern. Tableau would ignore all the files in the directory or directories except those with 2022 in their filename.

-   **Expand search to subfolder**: This will tell Tableau to search in the folders below this one in the directory structure.

-   **Expand search to parent folder**: This will tell Tableau to look in the directory immediately above this directory.

9.    Leaving all these options blank tells Tableau to take all the files in the chosen directory, which is determined by the first file we added. If you have the three South American sales files in the same directory with nothing else in the directory, you can press **OK** now and Tableau will create a data model with these three files in a single union.

We can check to see if our wildcard union worked by clicking on **Sheet 1** and then double-clicking on the **Country** field in the data pane. The result should look like what's shown in *Figure 8.43*. We can see a dot for each of the countries from the three files of our union:

Sheet 1

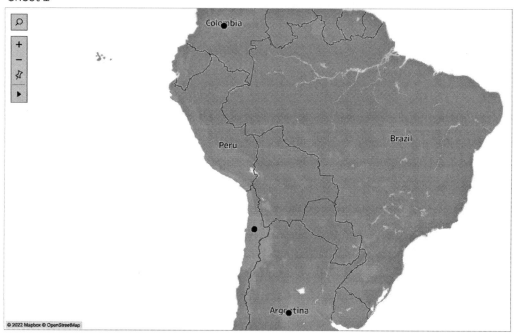

Figure 8.43 – Map showing a dot for each country in our union

If we replace our files with new data but keep the same filename, Tableau will automatically pull in the new data. For instance, if new data becomes available for Argentina and a new file overwrites our existing file for Argentina, Tableau will bring in the new data the next time you run the union without any manual intervention.

In this final section of this chapter, we learned about adding new rows of data to our data model through the use of manual and wildcard unions.

# Summary

In this chapter, we learned about adding additional fields to our data model through the relationship feature in Tableau. Relationships give us flexibility by allowing us to create relationships at the logical layer of databases. With relationships, we leave the mapping of joining data at the physical layer for Tableau to create dynamically, depending on the field we use in our analyses.

We looked at how relationships are different than joins and various use cases for relationships where joins would result in multiple data models. We also looked at how performance options are available to optimize relationship query performance.

In the final section, we looked at adding additional rows to our data model by using manual and wildcard unions.

The next chapter will focus on creating joins in Tableau Desktop at the physical database layer. We will also explore geospatial joins and custom SQL.

# 9

# Building Data Models at the Physical Level

Tableau relationships are the preferred way to bring multiple tables together in Tableau Desktop. We learned about relationships in *Chapter 8*. There are some cases where you, the data modeler, need to be one level deeper. For these use cases, we must go to the **physical layer** of the data source. We can get to this level by creating a join or using **custom SQL**.

When we create a join, Tableau creates a new table that results from the joining of the two tables. The structure of the new table depends on the type of join we use. We will be studying the four join options in this chapter. These are left join, right join, inner join, and full or outer join. In addition to joins, we will explore custom SQL statements and demonstrate the impact of using both versus using relationships.

In this chapter, we're going to cover the following topics:

- Opening relationships to join at the physical layer through database joins
- Geospatial joins and using the intersects operator with a BUFFER calculation
- Using joins to create a data model with row-level security
- Understanding custom SQL – when to use it and the pitfalls of using it

## Technical requirements

For the complete list of requirements to run the practical examples in this chapter, please see the *Technical requirements* section in *Chapter 1*.

All the exercises and images in this chapter will be described using the Tableau Desktop client software except where noted. You can also recreate all the exercises in this chapter using the Tableau web client, which has a very similar experience to the Desktop client.

To run the exercises in this chapter, we will need the following downloaded files:

- `Superstore Sales Orders - US.xlsx`
- `Product Database.xlsx`
- `Sales Argentina.csv`
- `Bicycle_Thefts.csv`
- `toronto_crs84.geojson`

The files we will be using are based on Superstore data, the sample data that Tableau uses in its products. The exception will be the bicycle thefts and Toronto neighborhood shapefiles. These files came from `https://data.torontopolice.on.ca/` and `https://www.toronto.ca/city-government/data-research-maps/open-data/` respectively.

The files used in the exercises in this chapter can be found at `https://github.com/PacktPublishing/Data-Modeling-with-Tableau/`.

# Opening relationships to join at the physical layer through database joins

Before Tableau released the relationships feature, the only way to expand your analysis to use additional fields from a secondary table in Tableau was to create a join at the **physical** layer of the data.

Although relationships are the preferred method of combining tables to get additional fields, joins still have their use cases.

Cases where you might use joins are as follows:

- When you know you are only supporting one use case in the Tableau workbook(s) that uses the model
- When you want to filter data through your join
- When you need to use an entity table for row-level security
- When you are making a geospatial join

Let's start by exploring the first two use cases, supporting a single use case and using the join for data filtering.

## Single use case and using the join for a filter

When exploring joins in *Chapter 8*, we looked back to *Chapter 4*, when we joined the sales data with the product data. We will continue to use these two tables in this join example.

Imagine that you have been tasked with providing analysis for the sales team. They want to know how sales have been affected by priority, product category and sub-category, shipping option, and other dimensions. They never need to ask the question, *"what didn't sell?"* That is a task they leave for the marketing team. They are also not concerned with the task of uncovering bad data. They only want facts on what sold over time.

Let's create our join for this use case:

1.  Open Tableau Desktop. When you open Tableau Desktop you will see the **Connect** pane on the left-hand side of the user interface. From the **Connect** pane, under the **To a File** section, select **Microsoft Excel**. Locate the `Superstore Sales Orders - US.xlsx` file, select it, and click on **Open**. We should now be looking at a screen as shown in *Figure 9.1*:

Figure 9.1 – Tableau data source page after connecting to US Sales

2.  Next, we need to join our product information. Click on the **Add** link to the right of **Connections**. Under the **To a File** section, select **Microsoft Excel**. Locate the `Product Database.xlsx` file, select it, and click on **Open**.

3.  Our screen should now look like the screenshot in *Figure 9.2*. We now have two data sources in our workbook, namely `Superstore Sales Orders – US` and `Product Database`. The `Product Database.xlsx` file also only has a single sheet. This sheet is called `Product DB`:

Figure 9.2 – Data source page with Product DB added

4.  This is where things get different from relationships. If we drag **Product DB** to the canvas, Tableau will show us the noodle and will try to create a relationship. To create a join, we first have to *open* our US Sales Transactions table. Hover on the right side of the US Sales Transactions card and when the ▼ symbol appears, click on it and choose **Open** as seen in *Figure 9.3*:

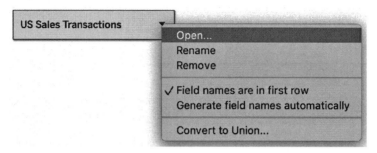

Figure 9.3 – Open on a table in the canvas

5.  Drag the Product DB table to the right of US Sales Transactions and release the left mouse button to drop the table. Your canvas should now look like the screenshot in *Figure 9.4*:

Figure 9.4 – US Sales Transactions joined to Product DB

6.  Instead of the noodle, we notice that we get a Venn diagram of two overlapping circles. This represents our join at the physical layer. The default is an inner join. Let's first look at this join type. Click on the Venn diagram and notice the join diagram as seen in *Figure 9.5*:

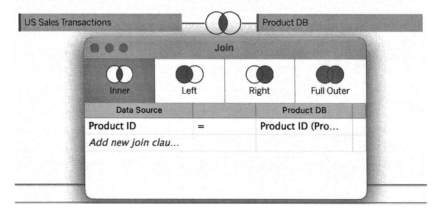

Figure 9.5 – Join diagram

We can see that we have four different join choices:

- **Inner** – This is a join where the resulting table will only contain records that exist in both the left and right table where the join fields/join clauses match

- **Left** – This is a join where the resulting table will contain all the records in the left table and only the records from the right table where the rows contain a matching record on the join fields/join clauses

- **Right** – This is a join where the resulting table will contain all the records in the right table and only the records from the left table where the rows contain a matching record on the join fields/join clauses

- **Full Outer** – This is a join where the resulting table will contain all the records of both tables

7.  Let's see what happens when we create an inner join between these tables. Leave the inner join selected and close the join dialog box. Click on **Sheet 1** to begin. Under the US Sales Transactions table, double-click **Sales** to bring it into the view. Under the Product DB table, double-click to bring **Product Name** into the view. To make it easier to get to our answer to which product sold the most, click on the **Swap Rows and Columns** icon in the toolbar then click on the **Sort Descending** button. Hover on the bar for the top item. You should now have a view that looks like *Figure 9.6*:

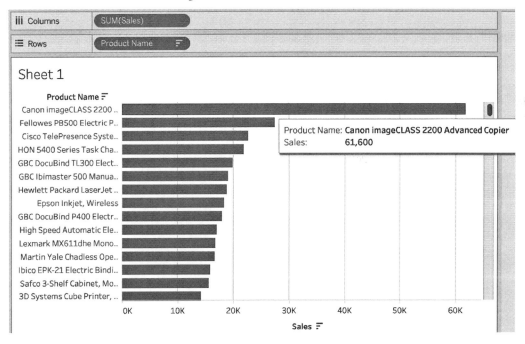

Figure 9.6 – Result of inner join of sales and product tables

8. The inner join worked to both apply the filter to eliminate the two *bad* product IDs from the sales table and answer the question of which products brought in the most sales. When we created a relationship between these tables in *Chapter 8*, we had to filter out the *bad* records. In addition to helping us find those records, it also allowed us to answer the question of which products did not sell. We can't get that answer from this inner join because products that did not sell are not in the new table that results from our join. To conclude with the inner join, it works well when you know you want to both filter out unmatched records and only need to answer questions that can be answered by records that match in both tables. It eliminates choice and flexibility in analysis, but there are cases where that is preferred. This inner join would work if we were building our data model for a sales team that is only concerned about sales of products from our product database. Less data also means faster queries, so it is a good idea to bring in only the data needed for analysis.

9. Let's now look at the left join of the same table. Click on the **Data Source** tab to go back to the data source page. Click on the Venn diagram for our join and then click on the icon for **Left join**. Your screen should now look like *Figure 9.7*:

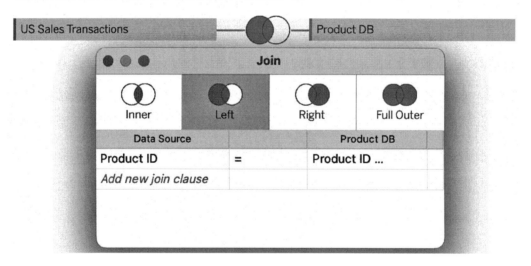

Figure 9.7 – Create a left join

10. Click to dismiss the join dialog. Click on `Sheet 1` and notice how the chart has changed. We now have a long bar, representing a lot of sales, associated with a `Null` product name. Drag and drop the `Product ID` field from the **US Sales Transactions** table to the right of `Product Name` on the `Rows` shelf. Your screen should now look like *Figure 9.8*:

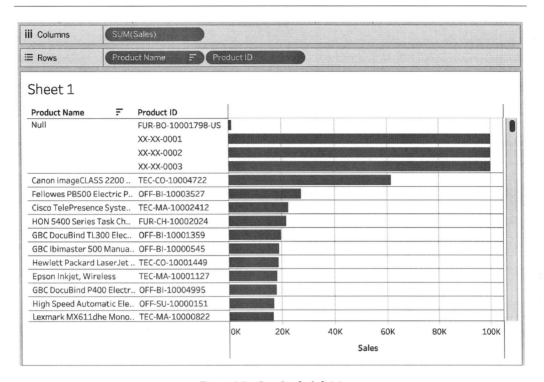

Figure 9.8 – Result of a left join

11. We notice that we have four product IDs that are in our sales (left) table but aren't in our product database (right) table. For this reason, the left join type kept the records from the sales table even though it couldn't find a match in the product database. Just like our similar exercise with relationships in *Chapter 8*, we could filter these out of our view by excluding them or by using a data source or extract filter. We can see how the inner join of *step 8* eliminates the need for these filters as it filters the data at the time of the join.

12. We will now look at the effect of a right join. Click on the **Data Source** tab to go back to the data source page. Click on the Venn diagram for our join and then click on the icon for **Right** join. Your screen should now look like *Figure 9.9*:

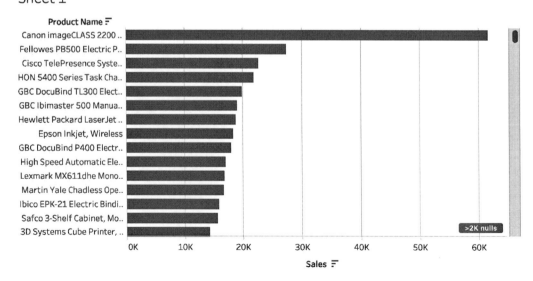

US Sales Transactions is made of 2 tables. ⓘ

Figure 9.9 – Create a right join

13. Click to dismiss the join dialog. Click on **Sheet 1**. Remove the **Product ID** field by dragging it off the view and releasing the mouse button. Notice how the chart is the same as the inner join result except we can see `>2K nulls` in the bottom right-hand corner of the chart as seen in *Figure 9.10*. This represents the product names that we haven't sold as we have gotten all those records from the product database (right) table. We don't see the null product names as they only existed in the sales (left) table. In this case, the right join gives us the answer to which products have and have not sold. It does not allow us to answer the question of which sales we had that did not have a product in our product database.

## Sheet 1

Figure 9.10 – Results of a right join

14. The final join type that we could do is a **Full Outer** join. This join type would bring in all records from both tables, joining on Product ID where it matched. It would also bring in all the records from both tables where there was no match for Product ID. This might seem the same as a relationship, but the big difference is that a relationship only queries the table or tables it needs to answer the question posed in Tableau. With a full outer join, the single table Tableau creates will be much larger than the combination of the two tables individually. In addition, the unmatched records will have null values for all the fields of the corresponding table as there were no rows to match. Having a lot of null values will lead to longer query response times and can make analysis difficult.

In this section, we looked at the four join types in Tableau and how they differed from relationships. We demonstrated each of the four and compared them to the results we saw with the same data tables with relationships in *Chapter 8*. In the next section, we will look at using geospatial joins.

## Geospatial join type to drive map-based analysis

Tableau has a lot of built-in capabilities for geospatial analysis. In addition to the built-in capabilities, it is possible to bring in geospatial files to enhance this type of analysis. We connected to a geospatial file in *Chapter 7*. In this section, we are going to join a geospatial file with a text file that contains information on bike thefts in the city of Toronto, Ontario, Canada.

The question we are going to answer is, *"which Toronto neighborhoods have the highest number of bicycle thefts?"*:

1. Open Tableau Desktop. When you open Tableau Desktop you will see the **Connect** pane on the left-hand side of the user interface. From the **Connect** pane, under the **To a File** section, select **Text file**, find the Bicycle_Thefts.csv file that you downloaded from GitHub, and click **OK**.

2. Click on **Sheet 1** and then double-click on **Latitude** followed by double-clicking on **Longitude**. Make sure you click on the **Latitude** and **Longitude** fields from the table and not the **Latitude** (**generated**) and **Longitude** (**generated**) fields that are in italics. You should now see a map that looks like *Figure 9.11*. This map shows a single value, which is the average latitude and longitude in our dataset:

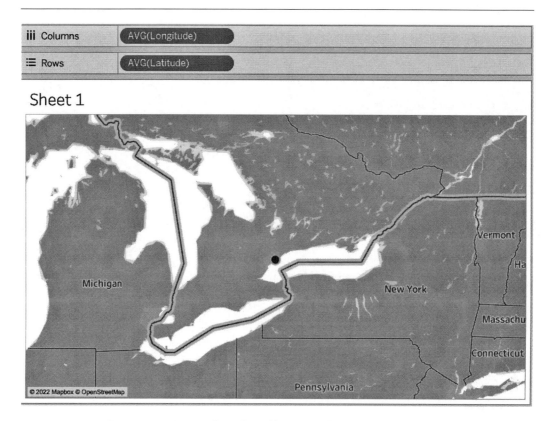

Figure 9.11 – Average latitude and longitude for bike thefts in Toronto

3.  To make this analysis meaningful, we need to add detail to our view. Drag and drop the Event Unique ID field on the **Details** mark card and drag and drop the Neighbourhood Name field on the **Color** mark card, as shown in *Figure 9.12*. Now we have a bit of an idea of which neighborhoods have the most bicycle thefts, but it isn't as clear as it could be. We can't realistically count all those dots!

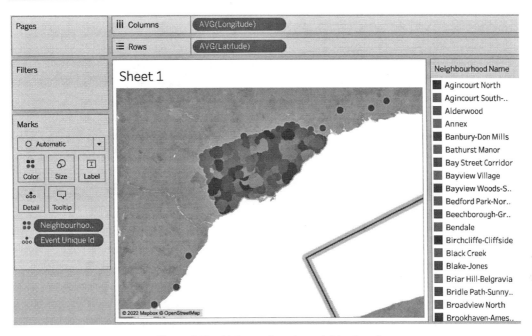

Figure 9.12 – Unique crimes by neighborhood

4.  To make the answer to our question clearer, we can use a geospatial file that has the shape of Toronto neighborhoods in it. Click on the **Data Source** tab. Click on **Add** in the connection pane. Choose **To a File | Spatial File**, select `toronto_crs84.geojson`, and click **OK**. Click on the ▼ symbol next to `Bicycle_Thefts.csv` in the canvas and choose **Open** for the table per *Figure 9.13*:

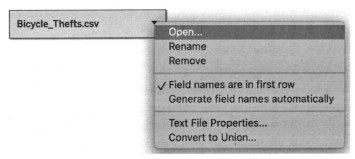

Figure 9.13 – Open bicycle thefts

5.  Drag the `toronto_crs84.geojson` table onto the canvas to create an **Inner** join. On the left side (bicycle thefts) of the join, click **Add new join clause** and then select **Create Join Calculation…** as seen in *Figure 9.14*:

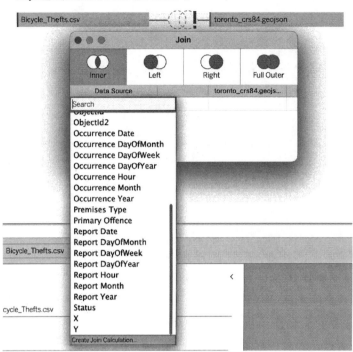

Figure 9.14 – Create Join calculation

6. In the calculation dialog box, enter MAKEPOINT([Latitude], [Longitude]) and click **OK** as in *Figure 9.15*. The reason for this calculation is that we need a single field for our join. MAKEPOINT allows us to do this with our latitude and longitude fields:

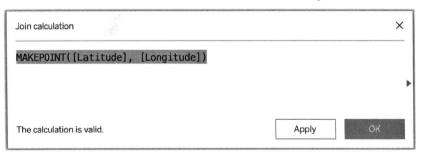

Figure 9.15 – MAKEPOINT calculation

7. To complete our join, click on the join clause on the right table (toronto_crs84.geojson) and choose the Geometry field. Choose Intersects for the join operator. Intersects is a unique join operator for geospatial joins. It tells Tableau to join records from the left table if

the latitude and longitude fall within the boundaries of the `Geometry` field of the right table. This option does not exist with relationships, which is why we need to use joins for combining geospatial files. We can see the join in *Figure 9.16*:

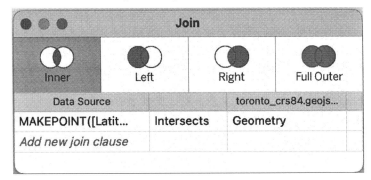

Figure 9.16 – Geospatial join

8.  To see how this enhances our analysis, click the new worksheet icon to the right of **Sheet 1** to create Sheet 2. From **Sheet 2**, double-click on the **Geometry** field under the `toronto_crs84.geojson` table in the data pane. Your screen should now look like *Figure 9.17*, showing the outlines of Toronto's neighborhoods:

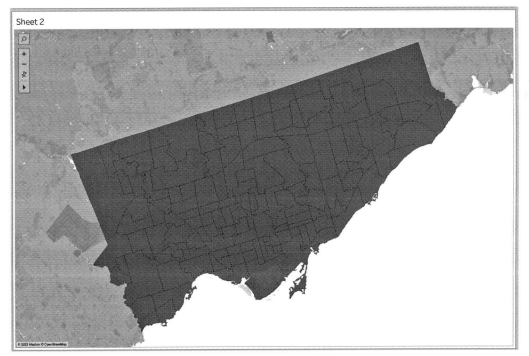

Figure 9.17 – Toronto neighborhoods

9.  To complete our viz, drag and drop the `Neighbourhood Name` field on the **Detail** marks card. Drag the `Event Unique ID` field on the **Color** marks card. This will result in a very colorful map but it doesn't help us with what we are looking to answer. Right-click on the `Event Unique ID` field in the cards shelf and select **Measure | Count (Distinct)** as per *Figure 9.18*:

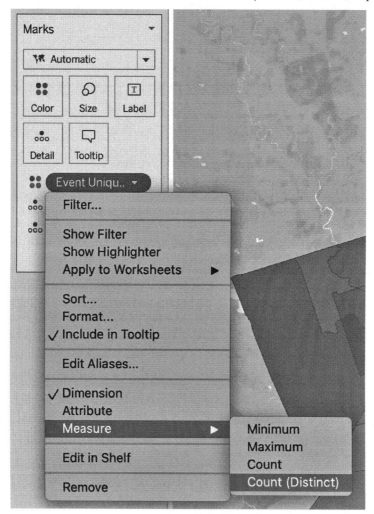

Figure 9.18 – Convert Event Unique ID to a measure

10. This now gives us the view showing where the most bicycle thefts occurred. The darker the color, the greater the number of thefts, as seen in *Figure 9.19*:

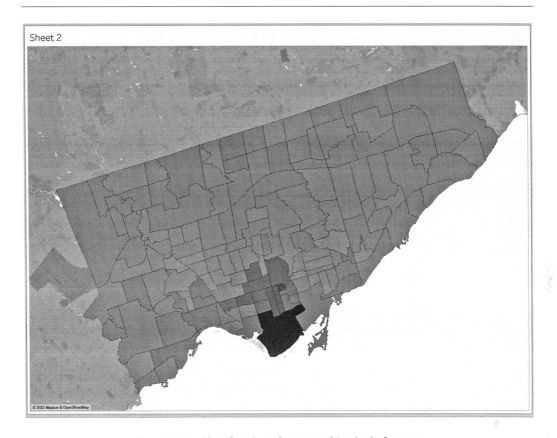

Figure 9.19 – Map showing where most bicycle thefts occur

In this section, we created a geospatial join to analyze data using maps. When we need to make a combination of fields to perform a geospatial analysis, we need to use a join as we can't use a relationship for this type of analysis. In the next section, we will discuss the use case of using joins with entity tables to achieve row-level security.

## Using joins to create a data model with row-level security

There are several ways to implement row-level security in our Tableau data model. We will be looking at these in detail in *Chapter 11*. For the purposes of this chapter, it is worth noting that one method is to have a separate table with usernames in it joined to the data table at the row level based on the user who is signed into Tableau Server or Cloud. We bring it up here as a use case for joins versus relationships. This technique only works with joins – your data would not be secure if you used a relationship, as this could be used to generate a query from the data table without joining to check entitlements to the data.

We will look at custom SQL in the next and final section of this chapter.

# Understanding custom SQL – when to use it and the pitfalls of using it

After we create our data models using relationships or joins, and analysts begin to interact with the data, Tableau dynamically creates SQL code to retrieve the data needed for the analyses. Tableau also goes beyond SQL with its proprietary query language called VizQL. VizQL adds additional features to SQL queries that also tells Tableau what chart type to use based on the data results from the query. Tableau does not expose the SQL and VizQL code it generates. It is all generated behind the scenes.

It is possible for us to write our own SQL in our data models using **custom SQL**. If we are connected to a data server that supports SQL queries, we will see a **New Custom SQL** option at the bottom of the tables from our database, as shown in *Figure 9.20*. Current versions of Tableau do not support custom SQL with Microsoft Excel:

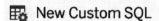

Figure 9.20 – New Custom SQL option

After double-clicking on **New Custom SQL**, you are able to type your SQL query into a Notepad-like textbox and save it. It will then appear on your canvas like any table you import, as shown in *Figure 9.21*. You can create relationships with it and joins within it as with any other table in Tableau:

Figure 9.21 – Canvas with a custom SQL query

The temptation to use custom SQL is high if we are comfortable writing SQL and new to Tableau. However, it is usually a good idea to avoid custom SQL whenever we can. The reason relates to the first paragraph of this section. Tableau dynamically creates VizQL, and the SQL associated with it. When we use custom SQL, Tableau always uses it as a sub-query. In other words, Tableau wraps the dynamic SQL it creates around the custom SQL query. This often has a negative impact on query performance and dashboard load time. If you have a use case that requires custom SQL, it is a better idea to create a table or view in the database and bring the resulting table into Tableau. Tableau can then create more efficient queries.

This does not mean it is never a good idea to use custom SQL. If you cannot get the database results you want from Tableau without creating a custom SQL statement, create the custom SQL statement and determine whether the load and query times for your data source and workbooks are fast enough. If performance is acceptable, you can continue to use the custom SQL tables without needing to create a new view or table in the database.

In this section, we discussed how Tableau dynamically creates SQL within its proprietary VizQL language. We learned that we can also create our own custom SQL queries to generate tables in Tableau. We also learned that we should avoid custom SQL when we can because Tableau always uses our custom SQL as subqueries, which can have a negative impact on performance.

## Summary

We explored building data models at the physical layer of our data sources in this chapter. We do this by creating joins between the tables in our data model.

We looked at left, right, inner, and full outer joins and how to create them by opening tables in the Tableau canvas. We created a geospatial join using the `Intersects` operator, something that is not possible with relationships.

Another use case for using joins over relationships that we covered is to create a data model with row-level security using a security table of usernames joined to the data that we want to secure.

In the final section of the chapter, we explored custom SQL within the scope of how Tableau dynamically creates SQL, concluding that we should use custom SQL sparingly.

In the next chapter, we will be looking at extending and sharing data models and when to use live connections versus extracts.

# 10

# Sharing and Extending Tableau Data Models

We discussed creating data models using Tableau Prep Builder in *Chapters 4* to *6* and using Tableau Desktop in *Chapters 7* to *9*. This chapter focuses on sharing and extending Tableau data models using published data sources and extending the model using hierarchies, folders, descriptions, grouping, and calculations. This chapter also explores the details and implications of live versus extracted data and embedded versus published data sources. Understanding the concepts in this chapter is key to being able to create data models that can be scaled and leveraged by the entire organization.

In this chapter, we're going to cover the following topics:

- Understanding live connections and extracts – scenarios of when to use each of them

- Creating extracts with the Tableau Hyper engine

- Understanding data sources and extract filters and their use

- Understanding the implications of an embedded data source versus a published data source

- Creating a published data source from the web interface of Tableau Server or Cloud

- Extending the Tableau data model with calculations, folders, hierarchies, grouping, and descriptions

## Technical requirements

To view the list of complete requirements needed to run the practical examples in this chapter, please see the *Technical requirements* section in *Chapter 1*.

The exercises and figures in this chapter will be described by using both the Tableau Desktop client software and the Tableau Server and Cloud web user interface.

To run the exercises in this chapter, we will need the following file:

- `Superstore Sales Orders - US.xlsx`
- `Superstore Sales 2022.csv`

The file we will be using is based on the Superstore data, the sample data that Tableau uses in their products.

The files used in the exercises in this chapter can be found at `https://github.com/PacktPublishing/Data-Modeling-with-Tableau/`.

## Understanding live connections and extracts – scenarios for using each

When you first connect to a data source in Tableau Desktop or via the Tableau web client, the default connection type is set to **live**. A live connection means that Tableau will use the query engine of the data source engine for every query from Tableau. This also means that the data in your Tableau workbooks will always be *fresh* or up to date with the information that is in the underlying data source.

The alternative to live connections is **extracts**. Extracts copy the data from the underlying data source and *extract* them to Tableau's high-performance analytic data engine, **Hyper**. We will be looking at extracts and the Hyper engine in the next section of this chapter.

Live connections might seem like the obvious choice as they ensure the data is up to date and they don't require the moving of data. Another good, and sometimes necessary, use case for live connections is when the data engine has user-based security embedded and security administrators want applications such as Tableau to respect and leverage those security models. However, live connections often perform slower when the data engine is under load from other applications, not optimized for read queries, or connected to Tableau Server or Cloud through a slow connection. The administrator of the data engine also might not want Tableau to run live queries against it.

Another case for extracts is file-based data connections as the files do not have a query engine to leverage. In fact, for some file types, such as JSON files, Tableau forces you to create an extract. For other flat files, Tableau will create a shadow extract, which is a temporary extract, even when you leave the connection set to live.

A quick reference for when to use live versus extract connections is seen in *Table 10.1*.

| Consider a live connection when: | Consider an extract when: |
|---|---|
| • Data needs to be up to the minute<br><br>• The data engine has row and/or column-based security embedded by the user<br><br>• The data source has an engine that is optimized for high-performance read queries | • The data source is a file<br><br>• The data source is not optimized for read queries (for example, a database running a transactional application)<br><br>• When the connection to the data engine is slow<br><br>• When the data engine vendor or internal department charges by the number of queries |

Table 10.1 – When to use live connections versus extracts

Now that we understand when to use live connections versus extracts, let's look at how we can create extracts with the Tableau Hyper engine.

# Creating extracts with the Tableau Hyper engine

On the top right-hand section of the canvas on the data source page, you can change your data connection from live to extract. This will cause Tableau to make a copy of your data and place it in a .hyper file to be managed and queried by the Tableau Hyper engine.

Hyper is a database engine that has been in the Tableau stack since version 10.5, in early 2018. Hyper is designed for high data throughput for both loading data and analytical queries. Tableau allows you to change many settings regarding how data is stored and queried in Hyper within Tableau Desktop and the web user interface. Let's look at these features and what they mean when it comes to creating data models:

1. Open Tableau Desktop. When you open Tableau Desktop, you will see the **connect pane** on the left-hand side of the user interface. From the connect pane, under the **To a File** section, select **Microsoft Excel**. Locate the Superstore Sales Orders - US.xlsx file, select it to highlight it, and click on **Open**.

2. You will now be on the data source page. On the top right-hand corner of the canvas, click on the **Extract** radio button, as seen in *Figure 10.1*:

Figure 10.1 – Converting a data source into an extract

3.   Click on **Edit** next to the **Extract** radio button; the dialog box shown in *Figure 10.2* will open:

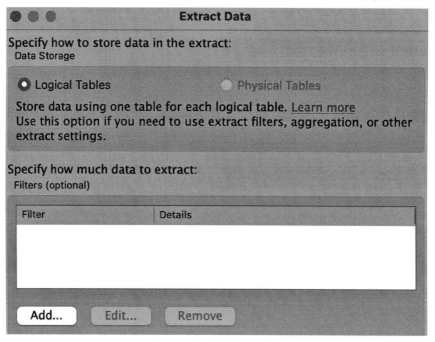

Figure 10.2 – The Extract Data dialog box

4.   The first setting is the choice between **Logical Tables** and **Physical Tables**. **Logical Tables** means that any tables in our data source will be extracted into Hyper as distinct tables. **Physical Tables** means that the tables will be joined into a single table. You will notice that **Physical Tables** is grayed out. **Logical Tables** is the only option when we have a single table and when we are using relationships. If we were using a data source with two or more tables connected

with join(s), the **Physical Tables** option would be available for selection. In this case, query performance can vary significantly between these options. As a rule of thumb, if one or more of the tables is much smaller than the other in terms of row count, logical tables will typically perform better; if the tables are of approximately the same length, physical tables will typically perform better. Because Tableau makes it so quick and easy to change options, it is always worth testing both options after we have built out analyses on our data source. We can test this using the **Performance recording** feature, which is native to the Tableau platform.

5.    The next section is where we can control the amount of data we will extract by using extract filters. To see how a filter works, click on **Add…**. Notice that the fields in our data source come up as an option, as seen in *Figure 10.3*:

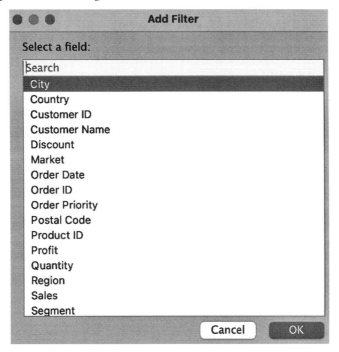

Figure 10.3 – The Add Filter dialog

6.    Click on the **Region** field and notice the additional dialog box in *Figure 10.4*. In our use case, we are building a data model for analysts who only work with teams from the East region. Click on the **East** region and click on **OK**. The next time the extract runs, only data from the East region will be moved to Hyper:

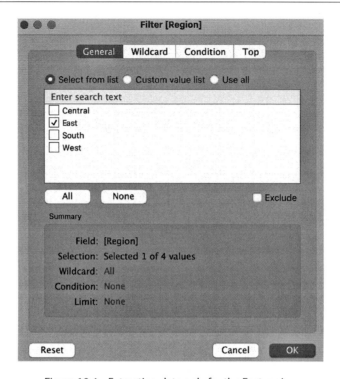

Figure 10.4 – Extracting data only for the East region

7.  Now, we will notice that the filter section of our extract dialog box will show our filter and allow us to either **Edit...** or **Remove** the filter, as seen in *Figure 10.5*:

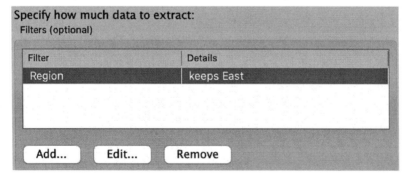

Figure 10.5 – Ability to edit and remove existing filters

8.  The next section allows us to aggregate our data. As an example, with the Superstore dataset, data is at the transactional level with one row for every product sold on each sale. If this was a real retailer, this would result in a lot of data. If the company only needed to analyze data at the level of the day, Tableau makes it easy to do this aggregation in an extract. Click on **Aggregate data for visible dimensions**, then **Roll up dates to**, and select **Day**, as seen in *Figure 10.6*:

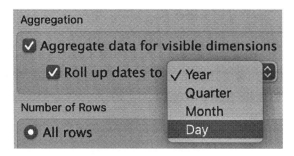

Figure 10.6 – Aggregation options

9.  Unclick the aggregate option as we do not want to aggregate in our exercise. We now have the option for an **Incremental refresh**. An incremental extract means that Tableau will only add additional rows based on a field we select. Looking at *Figure 10.7*, we can see a scenario where the US Sales Transactions table will refresh every time new dates are found in the Order Date field. In other words, the extract will look at Order Date from the last load and only load new rows if Order Date is more recent in the source data. Unselect **Incremental refresh** as we want to load all the data:

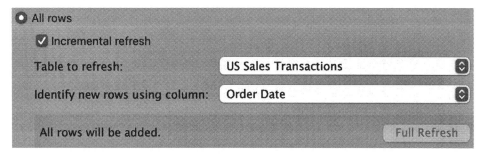

Figure 10.7 – Incremental refresh options

10. The next section is used for sampling large datasets before loading all the data. As shown in *Figure 10.8*, you can sample data based on the first number of rows or have Tableau create a random sample for you. As our data source does not contain many rows, we do not need to use the sample option:

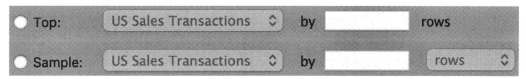

Figure 10.8 – Sampling data

11. The final section of the extract dialog box contains two buttons, **History…** and **Hide All Unused Fields**. Clicking on **History…** will show us the history of extract runs. The **Hide All Unused Fields** option is a way to ensure that all fields that aren't used in the analysis in the workbook aren't brought into the extract. This can help with both query performance and space on disk. However, only use this field after analysts have finished building out their analyses in the workbook; the fields are not available after the extract is run unless they unhide the fields and run the extract again. Click on **Cancel** to dismiss the dialog. Leave your screen on the data source page. We will pick up from this point in the next section.

In this section, we learned how to create an extract and when it should be used. In the next section, we will look at extract and data source filters and understand how and when to apply each.

## Understanding extracts and data source filters

In the previous two sections of this chapter, we learned about live and extract connections. We also looked at both data source and extract filters. In this section, we will look at how they work in more detail:

1. Continuing from the previous exercise, notice the top right-hand corner of the canvas, as seen in *Figure 10.9*:

Figure 10.9 – Extract and data source filters

2. When an extract is selected, we notice that Tableau will tell us when the extract was last run and if it includes all or some of the data from the underlying data source. Clicking on **Refresh** will load our extract based on the settings that we specify in the extract settings dialog. Clicking on **Edit** will take us to that dialog, as we detailed in the previous section. One of the options in the dialog box is to filter the rows in the extract based on one or more fields, as illustrated in *step 5* of the exercise in the previous section. In the case of an extract, these filters are applied before all other filters – that is, these filters work to control what comes into our newly extracted data source.

3. To the right of the **Connection** section is the data source **Filters** section. Click on **Add** to create a data source filter. You will then see a dialog as per *Figure 10.10*. This user experience is now the same as adding an extract filter:

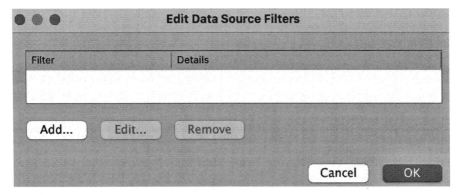

Figure 10.10 – The Edit Data Source Filters dialog

4.  Click on the **Add...** button and choose the Segment field. You should see a dialog that looks like *Figure 10.11*:

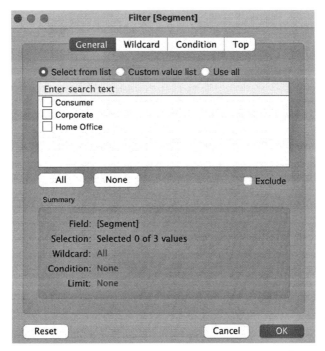

Figure 10.11 – Filter [Segment]

5.  You will be on the **General** tab, where you can manually select which values you want to filter from your data. By default, whichever values you select are included in the filter. You can select the values you want to exclude from your data by selecting values from the list and then selecting the **Exclude** option. In a large dataset, it might not be practical to manually select values, so Tableau also gives you the option to filter by **Wildcard**, **Condition**, and **Top**.

6.  As a final step, click **Cancel** to be taken back to the data source filter dialog, and then click **Cancel** from that dialog as well. Leave Tableau Desktop open here. We will continue from this point in the next section.

In this section, we explored two different types of Tableau filters, extract filters and data source filters. When we use extract filters, we are telling Tableau which data it doesn't need to move from the underlying data source to the Tableau extract. Extract filters play an important role in limiting the size of an extract, which saves query time, network traffic, and space on disk by storing smaller extracts.

Data source filters tell Tableau which data to not return in the queries generated by analysts and developers. In the case of live connections, data source filters are the first filters applied in the Tableau order of operations. In the case of extracts, data source filters are applied after extract filters. That is, Tableau first applies the extract filters to limit the size of the extract and then applies the data source filter to the data in the extract.

We will look at published and embedded data sources in the next section.

## Understanding the implications of an embedded data source versus a published data source

Tableau data models can be embedded in workbooks or accessible to many workbooks as published data sources.

We looked at the data model output options for Tableau Prep Builder in *Chapter 6*. We learned that Tableau Prep Builder can output to files, as well as output extracts as Tableau Hyper files, database tables, and published data sources. Most use cases of Tableau Prep Builder result in data models as published data sources to Tableau Server or Cloud.

In this section, we will look at publishing with embedded data sources and publishing data sources from Tableau Desktop:

1.  Picking up from our previous exercise, click on **Sheet 1** to get a blank sheet. At this point, you might be prompted to create an extract. You can follow the default options to create an extract or click cancel to return to a live connection. Either type will work for the rest of this exercise. If the sheet is not blank, click on the **Clear Sheet** icon (⊞) from the toolbar to ensure there is nothing on the sheet. Also, ensure there are no other sheets with information in the workbook, as per *Figure 10.12*:

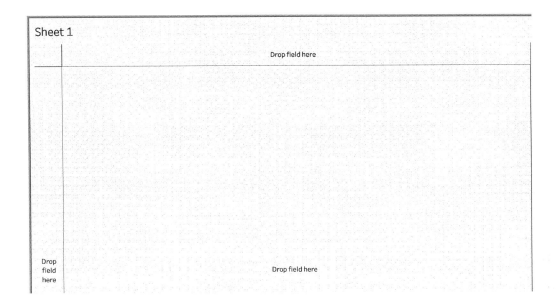

Figure 10.12 – Clean Sheet 1

2. Click on the **Server** option from the menu bar and notice that **Publish Workbook…** is grayed out and not available as an option, as per *Figure 10.13*. The reason is that none of the sheets have data on them, so the workbook is empty:

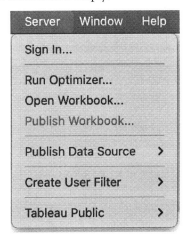

Figure 10.13 – Publish Workbook… grayed out

3. Let's add something to **Sheet 1** to populate our workbook. Double-click on **Sales** to bring it into the view and then double-click on **Segment** to break sales into segments in the view. Our sheet should now look like *Figure 10.14*:

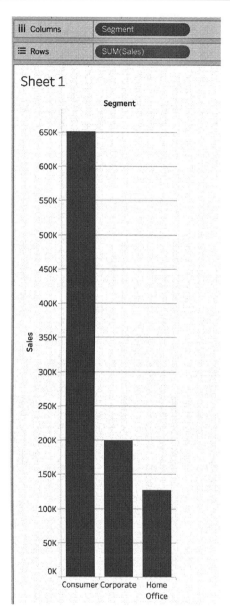

Figure 10.14 – Sales by Segment

4.  We should now be able to publish our workbook. Click on the **Server** menu item from the menu bar and then click on **Publish Workbook…**. If you are not signed in to Tableau Server or Cloud, you will be prompted to sign in. Please sign in to continue. You will then be presented with a dialog box that looks like *Figure 10.15*:

Figure 10.15 – The Publish Workbook to Tableau Online dialog

5.   There are several settings available when publishing a workbook. The setting we want to look at in this exercise is the **Data Sources** section. Click on the **Edit** link next to **1 embedded in the workbook**. This will bring up a dialog box like the one shown in *Figure 10.16*:

## Manage Data Sources

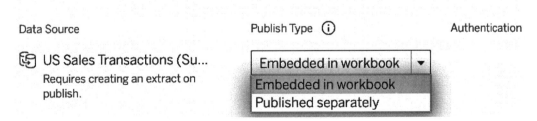

Figure 10.16 – The Manage Data Sources dialog

6. The first thing we notice in this dialog is that one workbook can have multiple data sources. In our case, we have a single data source. Next to each data source, there is a choice for **Embedded in workbook** or **Published separately**. There is also an option for **Authentication**. If the connection is to a data server, we can decide to embed credentials in the data source or prompt the user for their username and password combination. In our case, there is nothing under **Authentication** because we are connected to Microsoft Excel and not a data server. If we pick a **Project** where we can publish, give the workbook a **Name**, and keep the data source embedded, it will publish without any other prompts. This means the data source and associated data model are *embedded* in the workbook and cannot be used as a shared data model for other users.

7. Let's see what happens when we publish our workbook with **Publish Type** selected as **Embedded in workbook**. Make this change as per *Figure 10.17*:

Figure 10.17 – Publish with embedded connection

8. Select a **Project** to publish into and give the workbook a **Name**; then, click on **Publish**. Tableau will drop us into the workbook in the Tableau Server or Cloud user interface, as seen in *Figure 10.18*:

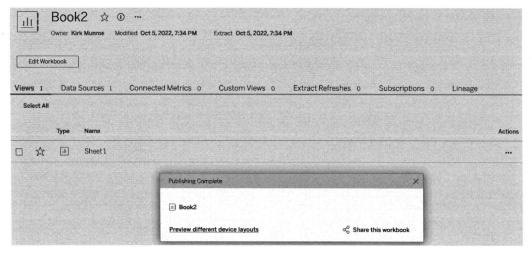

Figure 10.18 – Published workbook in the web user interface

You will see that there is one data source in our workbook. The option to embed a data source comes down to the type of use case. An embedded data source makes sense when the person responsible for the data model is the same as the person responsible for the analysis and dashboard development in the workbook and when the data model is not needed by other people in the organization. Embedded data sources are not available to other workbook authors. This does help manage content on Tableau Server and Cloud as analysts and dashboard developers who are looking for data models to start their analyses won't see these.

As this book is aimed primarily at data stewards who create data models for other people to use, the embedded data source option is not likely to be useful. When we are building data models for others to use, we need to use the published data source option. Let's continue this exercise to see how we share our data model as a published data source:

1.  Click on **Server** in the menu bar and select **Publish Data Source** this time. Select US Sales Transactions (Superstore Sales Orders - US), as per *Figure 10.19*:

Figure 10.19 – Publish Data Source

2.  The **Publish Data Source to Tableau Online** dialog will appear, as seen in *Figure 10.20*.

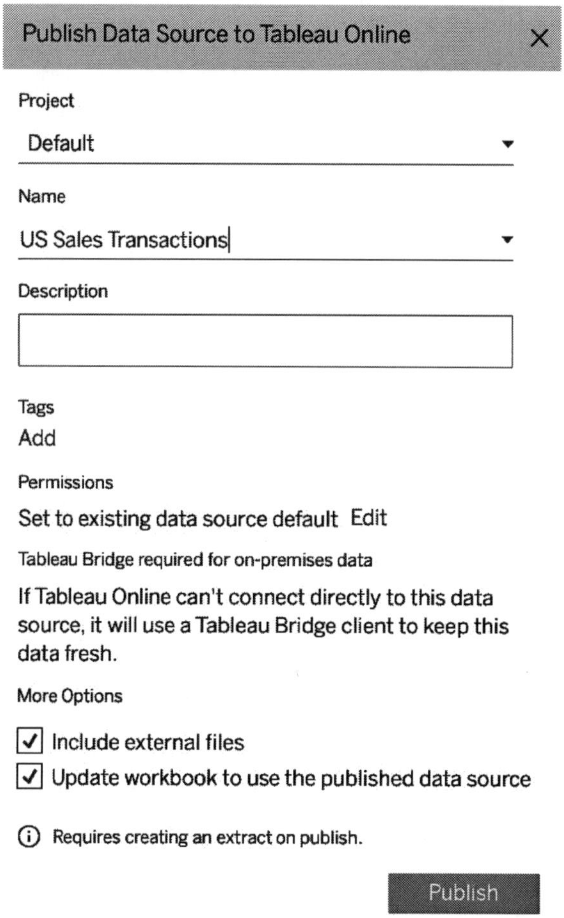

Figure 10.20 – Publish Data Source to Tableau Online

Choose a **Project** to publish into or leave the Default project as-is. Change **Name** to something shorter and more descriptive, such as US Sales Transactions. We can also give it a **Description** and add tags to make it easier to search for on Tableau Server or Cloud. Permissions can be set unless the permissions are locked to the project, which we will discuss in *Chapter 11*. When we are using Tableau Cloud, we will also get a warning about **Tableau Bridge** for on-premises data sources such as our Microsoft Excel file. We will discuss Tableau Bridge in detail in *Chapter 14*, so let's ignore this warning for now.

Finally, select the final two tick marks – that is, **Include external files** and **Update workbook to use the published data source**. If we don't tick this last box, any changes we make to our published data source will not be reflected in the workbook. Click **Publish** to publish our data source to Tableau Server or Cloud. Keep Tableau Desktop open at this point as we will pick up from this point in the final section of this chapter.

At this point, we will be taken to a new page in our browser. This is the data source page, as seen in *Figure 10.21*. People can now use **Ask Data** with our data source or connect to it from the web client, Tableau Desktop, or Tableau Prep Builder. We will look at extending our data model by creating a lens for use with Ask Data in *Chapter 12*.

Using published data sources is the best practices method of sharing data models in the organization to be used by people looking for a full-text search path to analysis with Ask Data, authors using Tableau Desktop and the web client, and other data modelers who want to use extend or model with Tableau Prep Builder.

In this section, we looked at embedded and published data sources, how to create each, and the use cases for each. Next, we are going to look at creating a published data source in the web client of Tableau Server or Cloud.

## Creating a published data source from the web interface of Tableau Server or Cloud

Tableau Desktop is the Tableau client for building both workbooks and published data sources. When using the Tableau web client, there are two distinct experiences for creating workbooks and published data sources. In this section, we will create a published data source from the web interface of Tableau Server or Cloud:

1.  From a web browser, sign in to your Tableau Server or Cloud. Navigate to **Home**. From the home screen, you should see a **New** icon. Click on the **New** icon to bring up the options shown in *Figure 10.21*:

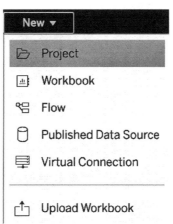

Figure 10.21 – New options in the Tableau web user interface

2.  If your Tableau Server or Cloud is not licensed for data management, you will not see the **Flow** and **Virtual Connection** options. For this exercise, we want to focus on the **Published Data Source** option. If you want to try this independently, you can click on the **Workbook** option, and you will be prompted to connect to data. You should see the published data source we created in the previous exercise, demonstrating the value of published data sources. The web client's **Workbook** experience is very similar to creating a workbook in Tableau Desktop. For now, we will create a new **Published Data Source** by clicking on that option. You will be prompted to connect to data. Select the **File** tab and upload the Superstore Sales Orders - US.xlsx file that we have been working with in this chapter. Your screen should now look like *Figure 10.22*:

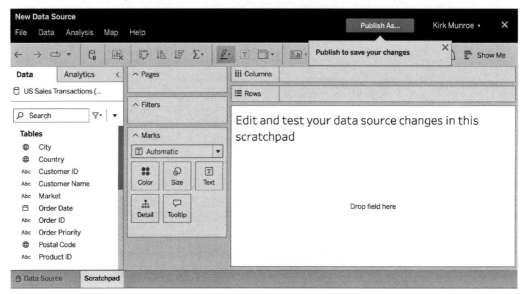

Figure 10.22 – Creating a published data source on the web

3.  Notice that there is no option to create sheets and dashboards like we would see if we created a new workbook. This interface allows us to test the data on a scratchpad, but it is intended only to create published data sources and not workbooks. To see it in action, click on the **Publish As...** button at the top-right of the screen. A dialog will come up, as seen in *Figure 10.23*:

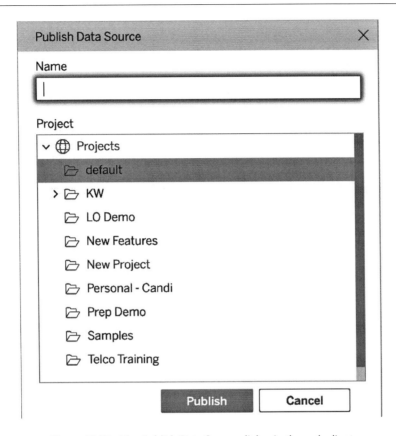

Figure 10.23 – The Publish Data Source dialog in the web client

4.   This dialog has fewer options than the publish data source option from Tableau Desktop. Just give your data source a **Name** and **Project** where it is to be published and we are good to go.

In this section, we learned about the web client option to publish data sources from Tableau Server and Cloud. This option is often a better option than using Tableau Desktop as it is custom-built for building published data sources.

Now that we have looked at how to build and publish data models, let's look at how to make them even more useful by enhancing the metadata in them and adding calculations.

# Extending the Tableau data model with calculations, folders, hierarchies, grouping, and descriptions

When creating data models, Tableau allows us to extend and enhance our models for easier and more robust analysis by adjusting the metadata in the model and adding calculations. Let's create a calculation for `Profit Margin %`:

1.  Open Tableau Desktop. From the connect pane, under the **To a File** section, select **Text file**. Locate the `Superstore Sales 2022.csv` file and click **Open**. Click on **Sheet 1**. Right-click on `Profit` and select **Create | Calculated Field** from the menu, as seen in *Figure 10.24*:

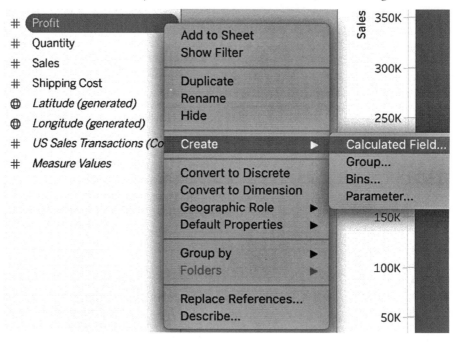

Figure 10.24 – Creating a calculated field

2.  In the calculation dialog box, give your calculation the name `Profit Margin %` and enter `SUM(Profit)/SUM(Sales)` as seen in *Figure 10.25*. Then, click **OK** to finish creating the calculated field:

Figure 10.25 – Calculated field

3.   Next, we will add a description to our calculated field via a **comment**. Right-click on the newly created Profit Margin % field and select **Default Properties | Comment** from the menu, as shown in *Figure 10.26*:

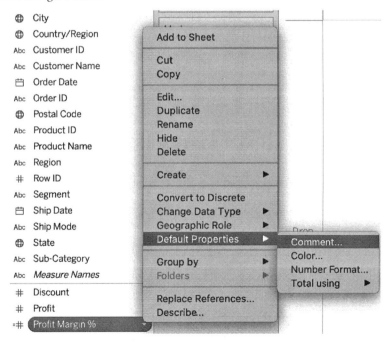

Figure 10.26 – Adding a comment to a field

4. In the text box, enter `This field is our official calculation for Profit Margin %, please use this in your analysis when presenting profit margin.` and click **OK**. When you hover and leave your pointer over **Profit Margin %** now, the text should appear in the tooltip.

5. Next, we will create a **hierarchy**. Creating a hierarchy allows analysts and data consumers to *drill down* into the data. To create our hierarchy, hold down your left mouse button as you click on the `Sub-Category` field in the data pane. Keeping the mouse button held down, drag `Sub-Category` on top of the `Category` field and release the mouse button. You should then be presented with what's shown in *Figure 10.27*:

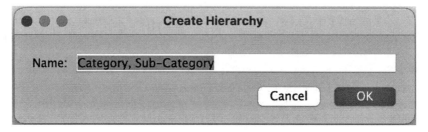

Figure 10.27 – Create Hierarchy

6. Enter `Product Hierarchy` over the `Category, Sub-Category` text and press **OK**. You should now be presented with the hierarchy seen in *Figure 10.29* in the data pane:

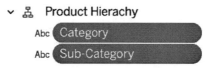

Figure 10.28 – Product Hierarchy

7. Continuing to add to the hierarchy, hold down the left mouse key and click and hold on `Product Name`. Drag the field under `Sub-Category` until you see the horizontal line appear and then release the mouse button. Your hierarchy should now be three levels with `Product Name` as the third and lowest level. If you happen to release the field into the incorrect level of the hierarchy, you can always drag and drop it into the correct order using the same technique.

8. To see the hierarchy in action, drag and drop `Product Hierarchy` to the **Columns** shelf and `Profit Margin %` to the rows shelf in the view, as seen in *Figure 10.29*. You will notice a bar chart with a bar and value for each of the three categories. You will also see that Tableau colors `Category` in blue because it is discrete and `Profit Margin %` in green because it is a continuous field. When these fields are in the view (for example, in columns and rows in this case), they are referred to as **pills** because of their shape:

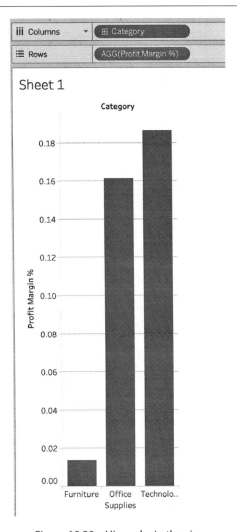

Figure 10.29 – Hierarchy in the view

9.  Next, let's click on the + symbol in front of the blue Category pill. Our view will drill down
    one level to show the Profit Margin % property of Sub-Category. If we click on the
    + symbol in front of Sub-Category, it will drill down to the next level of Product Name.
    You can see this in *Figure 10.30*:

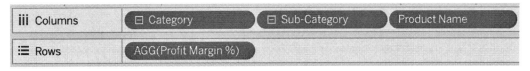

Figure 10.30 – Expanded hierarchy

10. One other thing you will notice in the view is that `Profit Margin %` is shown as a fraction with two decimal places. We can change this formatting so that it is ready for analysts to use. To do this, right-click on **Profit Margin %** in the data pane and select **Default Properties |** **Number Format**, as seen in *Figure 10.31*:

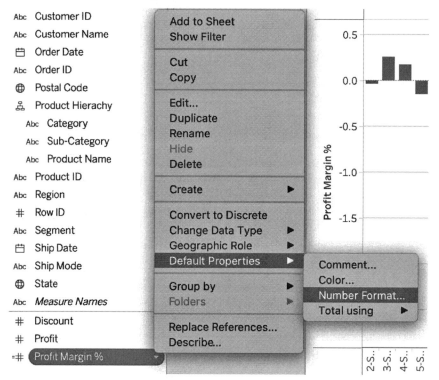

Figure 10.31 – Changing the number format

11. We now have a few choices available to use for formatting. Feel free to explore the different formatting options. In this case, we are going to select **Percentage** and set it to one decimal place. See how the view changes.

12. In addition to hierarchies, we can also make our data model easier to navigate by creating **folders** to group fields together. In the case of the relatively small number of fields in our sample data, this would likely not be necessary, but a lot of enterprise data models have many more fields. Let's create a logical grouping in a folder by right-clicking on the `Shipment Mode` field in the data pane. In the menu, select **Group by | Folder**, as seen in *Figure 10.32*. The default in Tableau is to group by table names. For many use cases where the primary analysts and consumers do not understand database structures, it is often more convenient and logical to change this to folders and group fields accordingly:

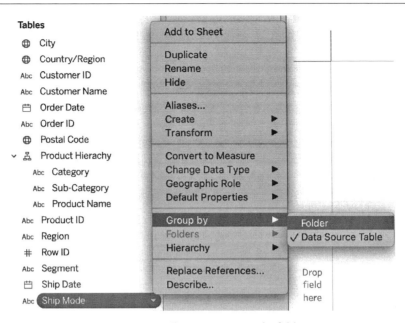

Figure 10.32 – Changing to group by folders

13. Now that we are set up to group by folder, right-click on `Ship Mode` again. Go to the **Folders** sub-menu and **Create Folder…** called `Shipping Information`, as seen in *Figure 10.33* and *Figure 10.34*:

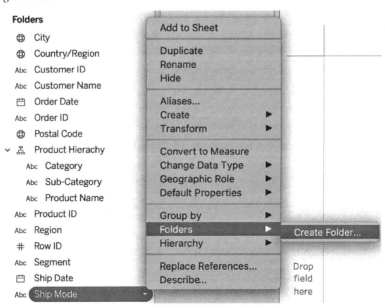

Figure 10.33 – Creating a new folder

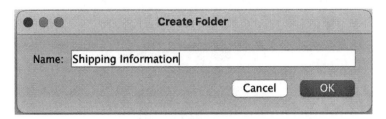

Figure 10.34 – Naming the folder

14. Right-click on Ship Date and select **Folders | Add to Folder | Shipping Information**, as seen in *Figure 10.35*:

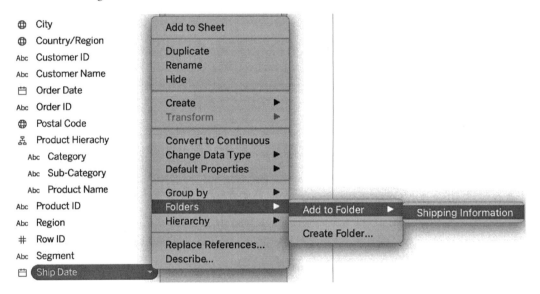

Figure 10.35 – Add to Folder

15. Now, we can see Ship Date in the same folder as Ship Mode, as seen in *Figure 10.36*:

Figure 10.36 – The Shipping Information folder

16. The last thing we will do before publishing our data model is look at the **Hide Fields** function. Hiding fields serves two purposes. First, it makes it easier for the analyst to find relevant fields and not waste time looking through fields that are in the data source but not relevant for analysis. Second, in the case of Tableau extracts, it tells Tableau to not bring those columns

into the extract. This saves a lot of physical space, the time queries take to run, and processing time on the server. In our data source, we might want to remove the **Customer Name** field for confidentiality reasons. To hide the **Customer Name** field, right-click on it in the data pane and click **Hide**, as seen in *Figure 10.37*:

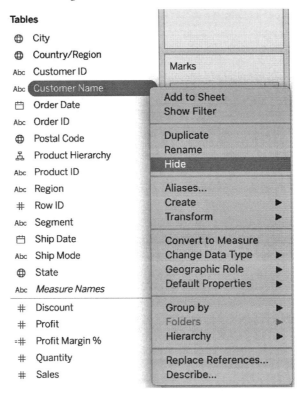

Figure 10.37 – Hiding fields from the data pane

In this section, we looked at enhancing our data model by creating hierarchies and folders, adding descriptions, creating calculations, and changing number formatting.

A final note on how published data sources behave after they are published is important to explore. If we are the owner of the published data source we want to make a change to, we can download the data source into Tableau Desktop, make our change, and republish it. All connected workbooks will see our change. We can also edit the published data source directly in the web client. It is important to note that only the data source owner can change it.

If other developers want to make additions to our published data source in their workbook by performing tasks such as creating calculations, they can do so, but these additions will only appear in their workbook. The changes will not be available to others using the published data source. Only the owner can make those changes.

## Summary

In this chapter, we took the time to understand live connections and extracts and when to use each. We looked at data source filters and extract filters and how each is used in the Tableau order or operations.

Then, we looked at both embedded data sources and published data sources. We created and published both types to our Tableau Server or Cloud and explored the use cases for each approach. We also created a published data source from the web interface of Tableau Server or Cloud.

In the last section of this chapter, we looked at extending the Tableau data model with calculations, folders, hierarchies, grouping, and descriptions. We also looked at how to update published data sources once they are already being used in others' workbooks and what an analyst can and can't do to extend the data model in their workbooks that use published data sources.

In the next chapter, we are going to look at the options available to us to secure our data models in terms of access to the model and the data we can see within the model.

# Part 4: Data Modeling with Tableau Server and Online

This final part of the book focuses on securing, sharing, and extending data models to get to a wider audience. It wraps up with a chapter that tells you which parts of the Tableau platform to use based on sample scenarios.

This part comprises the following chapters:

- *Chapter 11, Securing Data*
- *Chapter 12, Data Modeling Considerations for Ask Data and Explain Data*
- *Chapter 13, Data Management with Tableau Prep Conductor*
- *Chapter 14, Scheduling Extract Refreshes*
- *Chapter 15, Data Modeling Strategies by Audience and Use Case*

# 11

# Securing Data

This chapter focuses on governing and securing data at the data model level and the individual data elements within a data model. It covers considerations across the entire Tableau platform, from Tableau Desktop to managing data on Tableau Server and Tableau Cloud including the information architecture that is exposed through **projects**.

Some of the content in this chapter will cover items that are outside the typical scope of someone responsible for creating data models. We'll cover these topics while adding users and groups and setting project security since they are fundamental for understanding access and authorization to our data models and the data contained in them.

In this chapter, we're going to cover the following topics:

- Adding users and groups to Tableau Server and Cloud
- Using Tableau projects to manage data model security
- Adding user-based security using a user filter
- Adding user-based security inside a published data source using an entitlements table
- Using Tableau virtual connections to manage access and security
- Leveraging database security features for both row and column-level security

## Technical requirements

To view the complete list of requirements needed to run the practical examples in this chapter, please see the *Technical requirements* seciton in *Chapter 1*.

The files used in the exercises in this chapter can be found at `https://github.com/PacktPublishing/Data-Modeling-with-Tableau/`.

We will use the following files in this chapter:

- `Product Sales.csv`
- `Entitlements.csv`

## Adding users and groups to Tableau Server and Cloud

**Users** and **groups** are key to securing data and content on Tableau Server and Cloud. We will add users and groups directly to Tableau in this chapter. If you are following along using your organization's Tableau Server or Cloud and you have a role less than Server Administrator (Tableau Server) or Site Administrator, sign up for a trial Tableau site at the link provided in the *Technical requirements* section.

Before we start this exercise, it is important to note that users and groups are often maintained by a separate **identity provider** (**IdP**) in the Tableau environment. Microsoft Active Directory can be used as an IdP to manage users and groups with Tableau Server at install time. Tableau Cloud uses the **System for Cross-Domain Identity Management** (**SCIM**) standard to allow users and groups to be managed by an IdP outside Tableau. At the time of writing, Tableau supports Azure Directory Services, OKTA, and OneLogin as SCIM-enabled IdPs. In our exercise, we will be adding users and groups manually:

1.  Connect to your Tableau Server or Cloud instance. From the home page, click on the **Users** button in the sidebar on the left-hand side of the screen. If the sidebar is collapsed, you can find the button for users by hovering over the button shown in *Figure 11.1*:

Figure 11.1 – The Users navigation button

2.  We can see the number of users by the licenses they have been assigned at the top of the **Users** page. We can add new users by clicking on the **Add Users** button. We can add users manually by entering their email addresses. Here, we are going to import a list of users. Click on **Add Users | Import from File**, as shown in *Figure 11.2*:

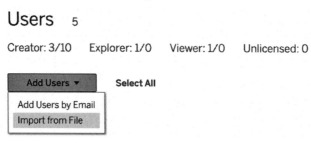

Figure 11.2 – Add Users

3.  We will now see the dialog for importing users from a file. In a production environment, it is always good to use **multi-factor authentication (MFA)** for better security. In our case, we want to keep our exercise straightforward, so select the **Tableau** radio button, click the **Choose a file** button, find the `Entitlements.csv` file we downloaded from GitHub, and click on **Open**. Our screen should now look like what's shown in *Figure 11.3*. Click on **Import Users** to bring in our users. Once the file has been uploaded, you will get a message saying that five users have been added to the site. Click **Done** to dismiss this dialog:

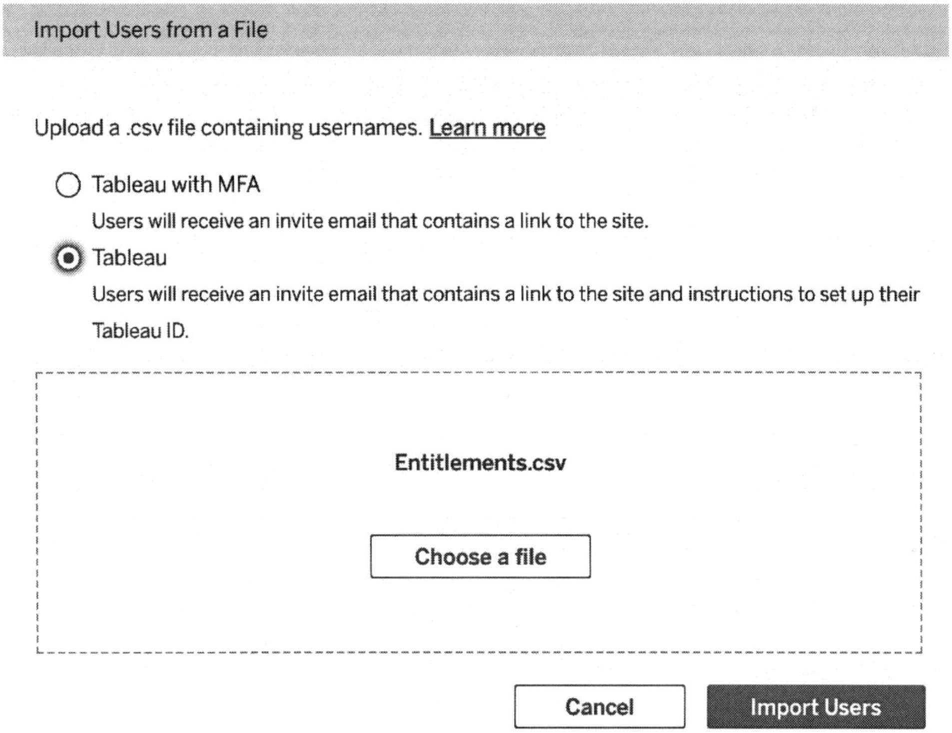

---

Import Users from a File

Upload a .csv file containing usernames. **Learn more**

○ Tableau with MFA
   Users will receive an invite email that contains a link to the site.

⦿ Tableau
   Users will receive an invite email that contains a link to the site and instructions to set up their Tableau ID.

> **Entitlements.csv**
>
> [ Choose a file ]

[ Cancel ]          [ **Import Users** ]

Figure 11.3 – The Import Users from a File dialog

4.  Our **Users** page will now show our five new users. Each of these users has a  . in front of their email. This signifies that the user has not signed into Tableau yet. You should also notice that the new users are **Unlicensed**, as seen in *Figure 11.4*. Click on **…** under the **Actions** column for **.argentina@company.com** and select the **Site Role…** option, also shown in *Figure 11.4*:

Figure 11.4 – New users

5.    We can now change the **site role** of the user by clicking ▼ next to **Unlicensed**, as seen in *Figure 11.5*:

Figure 11.5 – Assigning a site role

The different role options that we can see in the preceding screenshot are as follows:

- **Creator**:

  - **Site Administrator Creator**: This enables the user to use all the authoring capabilities of the Tableau platform and manage the site on Tableau Server or Cloud.

  - **Creator**: This enables the user to use all the authoring capabilities of the Tableau platform.

- **Explorer**:

  - **Site Administrator Explorer**: This enables the user to use the Explorer capabilities we explored in *Chapter 2*. It also allows the user to manage the site. If you are assigning someone to manage the site and they won't be creating content in Tableau Desktop or Tableau Prep Builder, assigning them this license is the best option as the Explorer license has a lower cost than the Creator one.

  - **Explorer (can publish)**: This enables the user to use the Explorer capabilities with the ability to publish to Server. This role is another great reason for using published data sources instead of embedded data sources. The primary difference between an Explorer and a Creator, in addition to cost, is that an Explorer does not have a license for Tableau Desktop and Tableau Prep Builder (nor for creating flows in the web client). They can use the web client to create and update workbooks, but they cannot connect to new data, except for files. If they are using a published data source, they have the same capabilities to create workbooks as Creators do while using the web client. If you aren't using published data sources, then the users would need the more expensive Creator license as they would need to connect to new data sources before they can create a workbook.

  - **Explorer**: This enables the user to use all the capabilities of Explorer, except that they cannot publish. Use this role for users who you want to enable to create their own analyses but not share them with others.

- **Viewer**:

  - **Viewers**: Can view and interact with content

- **Unlicensed**: A place to park users until they need access to the site. These users cannot connect to Tableau Server and Cloud until they are moved to one of the other roles, except for **Grant role on sign**, which we will discuss in *step 8* of this exercise.

If you are using Tableau Server, there will also be an option for **Server Administrator Creator**.

6. Select **Viewer** and click on **Change Site Role**, as shown in *Figure 11.6*. Repeat this step for each of the four remaining users we added:

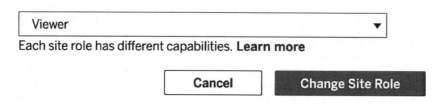

Figure 11.6 – Change Site Role

7.  We will now add these users to a new group called Sales. Adding users to groups makes managing access much easier as everyone within a group often has the same access to information. Click on the **Groups** icon. If the sidebar is collapsed, this icon will be below the **Users** icon, as shown in *Figure 11.1* in *step 1* of this section. After clicking on **Groups**, we will be taken to the **Groups** page. Click on **Add Group | Local Group**, as shown in *Figure 11.7*:

Figure 11.7 – Creating a local group

8.  We will be presented with a dialog to create a new group. Type Sales under **Group Name**, leave **Grant role on sign in** unchecked, and click on **Create**, as shown in *Figure 11.8*. The ability to grant a role upon signing in allows you to add members to a group without assigning a site role. When they sign in for the first time as an unlicensed user, they will be assigned the role you select here:

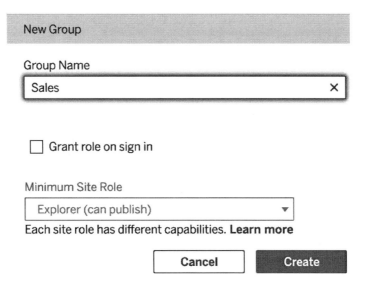

Figure 11.8 – Creating a new group

9.  We will now see our new group listed in the groups on our site. Click on the **Sales** group. The top left-hand side of our screen should now look like *Figure 11.9*:

Figure 11.9 – Sales group

10. Click on **Add Users** and check the names of all the @company.com users we added. Then, click **Add Users (5)**, as shown in *Figure 11.10*:

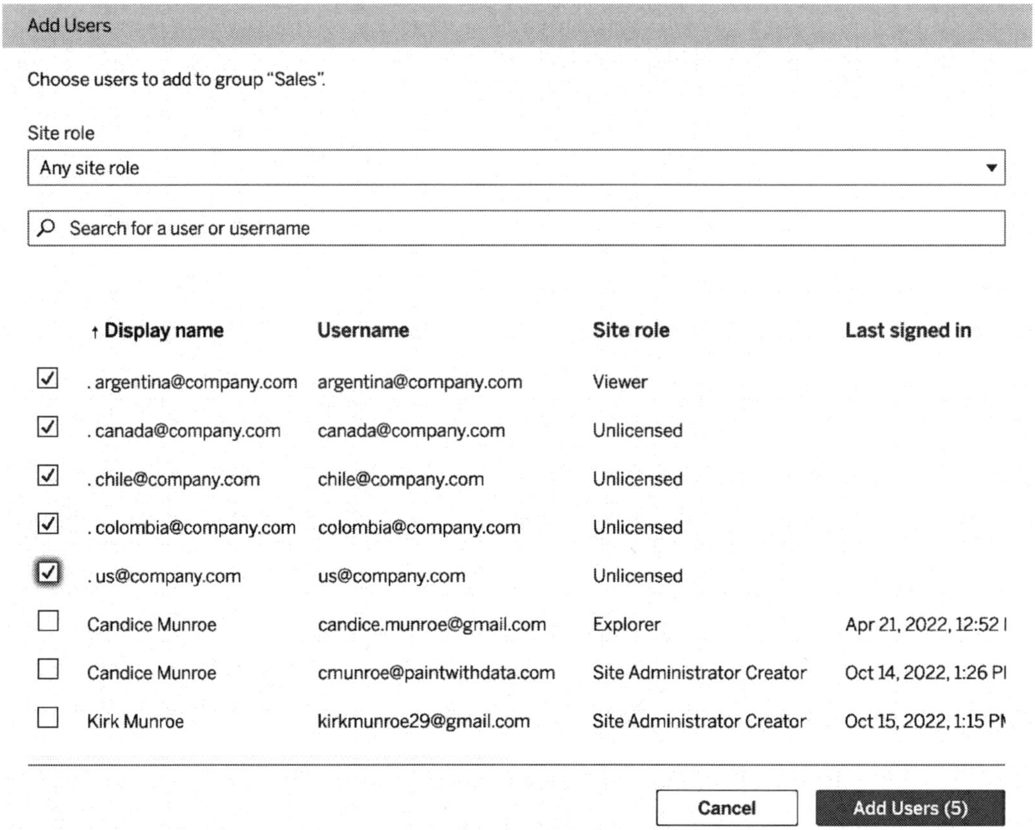

Figure 11.10 – Adding users to the Sales group

With that, we have created five new users, learned about site roles, assigned our users the Viewers role, and added them to a group. In the next section, we will learn how to use users and groups to secure our data models and other content.

## Using Tableau projects to manage data model security

Tableau Server and Cloud are intended to have content organized into **projects**. Projects act much like file folders on a network or cloud drive. When it comes to security and accessing content with projects, we can leave them unlocked and delegate access control to the individuals who create the content within the project. Alternatively, we can lock permissions to content within the project at the project level.

Locking permissions to the project level is the best practice for several reasons:

- It is easier to manage security as the number of projects will typically be much less than the number of workbooks, data sources, lenses, flows, and other objects that reside in projects.

- Projects often map very well to internal teams with shared data needs. These teams often map to groups in Tableau. Securing projects to groups, as opposed to individuals, makes the job of managing access control easier.

- Delegation can occur at the correct level. Instead of putting all the access control requirements on a site administrator, a site administrator can assign **project leaders** to manage individual projects. For example, if a project exists for the sales team in the company, a sales leader can determine who will manage access to content for their team and have a site administrator grant project leader status to this person.

- Projects can be nested within projects to make content management and access even easier. Nested projects can have their own access control or they can inherit it from parent projects.

- It takes the responsibility and potential for incorrect access away from content creators. Typically, content creators are responsible for creating their workbooks, data sources, flows, and other objects. It can put a lot of responsibility on them to determine who can and cannot see these objects at the time of publishing. When the projects they are publishing to are locked, they don't have to worry about this as access will be inherited from the project.

Let's learn how to set up a project and lock its permissions:

1. From the home page, navigate to the **Explore** page. If your sidebar is collapsed, you can find the **Explore** navigation button by hovering over the button shown seen in *Figure 11.11*:

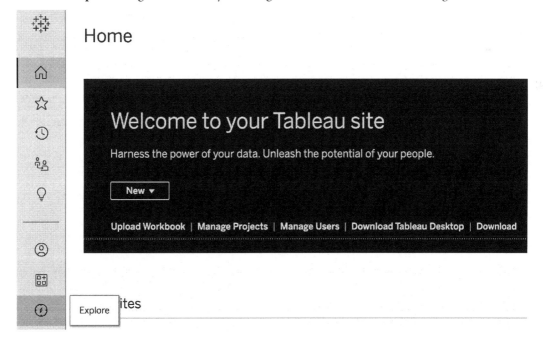

Figure 11.11 – The Explore page navigation

2.  We should now see all the top-level projects. If the view shows other objects, click on the drop-down menu next to **Explore** and select **Top-Level Projects**, as shown in *Figure 11.12*:

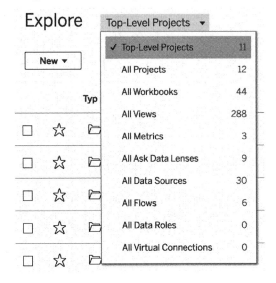

Figure 11.12 – The Explore page's drop-down

3.  Find the **default** project and click on the **...** icon in the **Actions** column and select **Permissions**, as shown in *Figure 11.13*. The **default** project is an important one because it acts as a template for all other projects – that is, the settings on **default** are inherited by all other projects when they are created. If we change the settings of **default**, this does not change the settings of existing projects:

| | | | Type | ↑ Name | Actions | Projects |
|---|---|---|---|---|---|---|
| ☐ | ☆ | 🗁 | | Data Modeling | ... | 0 |
| ☐ | ☆ | 🗁 | | default | ... | 0 |
| ☐ | ☆ | 🗁 | | KW | | |
| ☐ | ☆ | 🗁 | | LO Demo | | |
| ☐ | ☆ | 🗁 | | New Features | | |
| ☐ | ☆ | 🗁 | | New Project | | |
| ☐ | ☆ | 🗁 | | Personal | | |

Share...

Add to Collections...

Rename...
Move...
Permissions...
Change Owner...

Delete...

Figure 11.13 – Setting permissions on a project

4.  The set project permissions dialog box should now be visible, as per *Figure 11.14*. You will see that there is a group called **All Users** that has already been assigned permissions to this project. The **All Users** group includes all users on your Tableau Server or Cloud instance. This group cannot be deleted, so we need to think about which template to apply to this group as a default. Click on ▼ next to the **Template** option that corresponds to **All Users**, as per *Figure 11.14*:

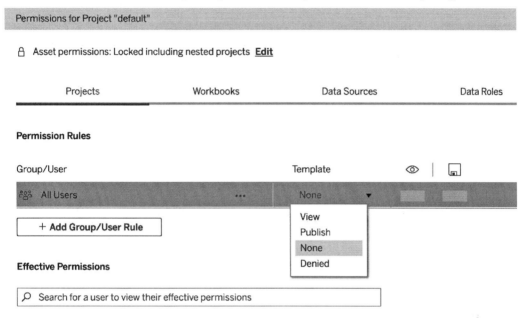

Figure 11.14 – Permissions dialog for projects

We can see the following four options in *Figure 11.14*:

- **View**: The user (or users within the group) will be able to see and interact with the content but will not be able to publish new content to the project.

- **Publish**: The user (or users within the group) will be able to see, interact, and publish (and edit) content to the project. It is important to note that the user will only be able to publish if they have this permission and have a site role of **Creator** or **Explorer (can publish)**.

- **None**: The user (or users within the group) will not be able to see or interact with content within the project. The exception to this are users who have the **Site Administrator** or **Server Administrator (Tableau Server only)** role.

- **Denied**: The user (or users within the group) are denied access to the content within the project. The exception to this is users who have the **Site Administrator** or **Server Administrator (Tableau Server only)** role.

**Denied** and **None** sound similar but serve different purposes. **None** means that the users or members of the group do not explicitly have access unless they are also in a group assigned with publish or view permissions. **Denied** means that they explicitly cannot see the project and content within. If they are also in a group with publish or view permissions, they will still not be able to see the project or its contents.

As an example, let's say we add the **Sales** group we created in the previous exercise as the only other group to a project and assign it **View** permission. If the **All Users** group is set to **None** on the same project, the people in the **Sales** group will be able to view all content in the project but no one else in the organization will have access. On the other hand, if the **All Users** group is set to **Denied**, the users in the **Sales** group will not be able to see content in the folder as **Denied** overrides other access.

With this background, the best practice is to set the **All Users** group on the **default** project to **None**. This will ensure users will not see content they should not see but will still be able to see the content if they are in a group added to a project.

As shown in *Figure 11.14*, select **None** and click on the **Save** button under **All Users** to make this change.

5.  To lock permissions on the **default** project, click on the **Edit** link next to **Asset permission: Customizable** in the project permissions dialog. We will now be taken to the **Asset Permissions** dialog box. Click on the **Locked** option and leave the **Apply to nested projects** checkbox selected so that any nested projects (projects created from within other projects) will inherit these permissions. We should see a screen that now looks like *Figure 11.15*. Click on **Save** to commit your changes.

> **Important note**
> All projects will now inherit whichever settings we have on our **default** project, except for the **Locked** option. We must set each new project to a locked state manually after creating it.

Dismiss the dialog box by clicking on the **x** button at the top right-hand corner:

Asset Permissions

⦿  🔒  **Locked:**  Assets inherit project permission rules. Asset-level permissions can't be modified. (Recommended)

☑ Apply to nested projects

> ⓘ  Project permissions will be applied to all assets and all nested projects in "default" when you save.

○  🔓  **Customizable:**  Assets starts with project permission rules. Permissions can be modified by users authorized to do so.

| Cancel | Save |
|---|---|

Figure 11.15 – The Asset Permissions dialog

6.   Now, let's create a new project for our sales team. Click on **New** | **Project**, as shown in *Figure 11.16*:

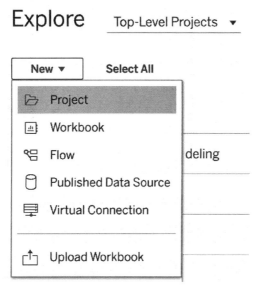

Figure 11.16 – Creating a new project

7.  Type `Sales` under **Enter a name for the new project:**, leave **Description** blank, and click on **Create**, as per *Figure 11.17*:

New Project

Enter a name for the new project:

Sales

Description

4,000 characters remaining

> Show formatting hints

Cancel        Create

Figure 11.17 – Sales project

8.  Find the **Sales** project in our list of projects and click on the **...** icon in the **Actions** column. Then, select **Permissions** in the same way we did in *step 3* of this exercise. You will notice that the **All Users** group has been assigned **None** because of the template we created from the **default** project. Click on the **+ Add Group/User Role** button and search for and select **Sales**. Set **Template** to **Publish**, as shown in *Figure 11.18*, and click **Save** to commit these permissions:

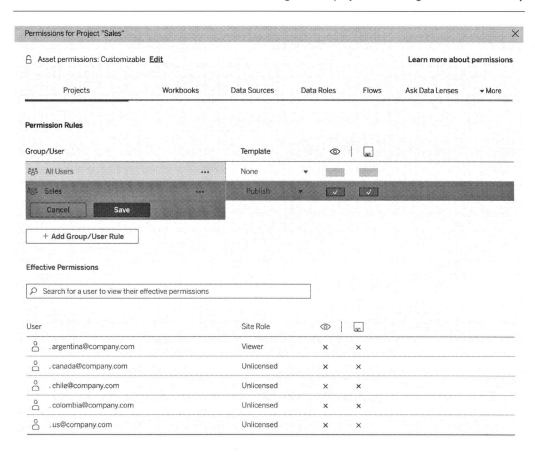

Figure 11.18 – Save sales permissions

9. As we can see in *Figure 11.18*, there are tabs to set permissions on many items – **Projects**, **Workbooks**, **Data Sources**, **Data Roles**, **Flows**, **Ask Data Lenses**, and **More**.

10. For our exercise, we will focus on the project level of permissions. In most cases, we can manage access to all content from the **Projects** permissions with a combination of the users' license roles. Let's use our example here. We have a sales department that has five people in a group called **Sales**. We want one of these people to be our developer to create data sources, workbooks, lenses, and flows. We want the other four people to only be able to view and interact with the content. The simplest way to manage this access is to give the developer the site role of Creator and leave the other four people with the site role of Viewer. Then, we can add the **Sales** group to the project and give it **Publish** permissions. Only our developer will be able to publish because the site role overrides the permission. Then, we only need to adjust permissions on other items if we have exceptions. For instance, we might want one developer to create data sources and flows and another to create workbooks and not vice versa. In this case, we could click on the corresponding tabs to limit access to these users as appropriate.

11. Next, we will set the project leader from the sales team to manage this project for us. Click on the + **Add Group/User Role** button. Select the **.argentina@company.com** user from the top of the list. Then, click on the **...** icon next to their email address and select **Set Project Leader...**, as shown in *Figure 11.19*:

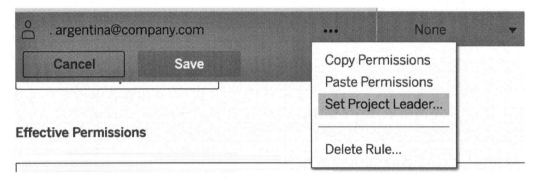

Figure 11.19 – Set Project Leader...

12. We will now see the message shown in *Figure 11.20*. This gives us a warning that we are granting this person administrative capabilities to this project that could be higher than their group permission. Click **Set Project Leader** to continue with the assignment:

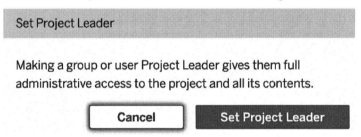

Figure 11.20 – Confirming the project leader

In this section, we learned how to use projects to control access to data sources. We learned how to assign permissions to a project and how we can delegate management to a project leader. Project-level access control determines who can see our published data sources and how people can interact with them. Projects do not control what data people can see within the published data source.

There are times when we might want to allow more general access to a data model than to the data contained within the model. Take, for example, human resources data, such as salaries. Many companies keep this information highly confidential. We don't want to create a data source for every manager in an organization, or maybe even every employee. That would not be scalable at all as it would be potentially a very long list of data sources and projects. In these cases, we want to add **row-level security** (**RLS**) so that we can share our models broadly while still ensuring people only see the data they are authorized to see.

In the rest of this chapter, we will be looking at four different ways to enable RLS in our Tableau data models. In the next section, we will look at enabling it by adding user-based security using a **user filter**.

## Adding user-based security using a user filter

We will begin our exploration of RLS options in Tableau by looking at how to create a **user filter** inside Tableau.

We will be creating our user filter in Tableau Desktop. Tableau Desktop will need to be connected to the Tableau Server or Cloud instance we used in the earlier exercises in this chapter. The user filter can only be created when Tableau Desktop is connected to retrieve a list of users:

1.  Open Tableau Desktop and connect to data to start. Select **To a File** | **Text file**, find the Product Sales.csv file that we downloaded from GitHub, and click **OK**. We should now be on the data source page, as shown in *Figure 11.21*:

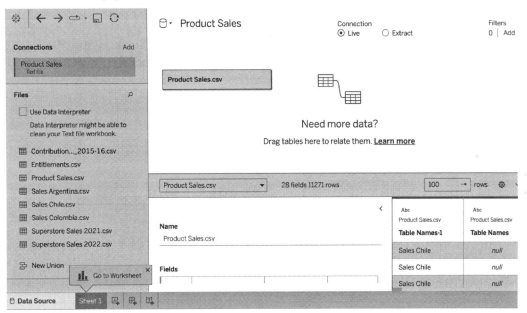

Figure 11.21 – Data source page connected to product sales

2.  If you aren't already signed into the appropriate Tableau Server or Cloud instance, from the menu bar, click on **Server** | **Sign in…**, as shown in *Figure 11.22*, and sign in. Once you have signed in, click on **Sheet 1** from the bottom left of the screen:

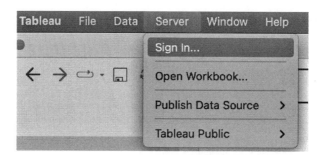

Figure 11.22 – Signing into Tableau Server or Cloud

3. Now, we want to create a user filter to ensure that each of the users we previously created can only see the data from the country for which they are responsible. From the menu bar, click on **Server | Create User Filter | Country…**, as shown in *Figure 11.23*:

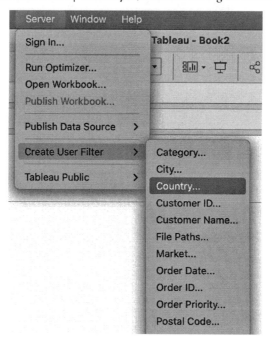

Figure 11.23 – Filtering by country

4. We will be taken to the user filter dialog box. Change **Name** to User Country Filter and click on .argentina@company.com in the **User/Group** column. Then, check the box in front of **Argentina** in the **Members for:** column, as shown in *Figure 11.24*:

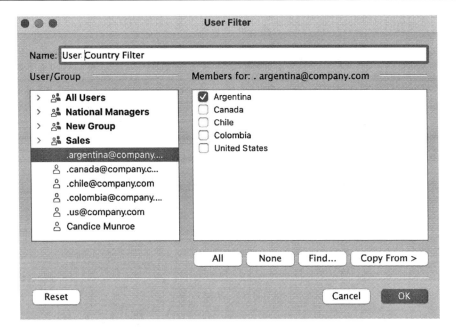

Figure 11.24 – The User Filter dialog

5.  Click on **.canada@company.com** and then check the box in front of **Canada**. Repeat this for the next three users and countries. Our screen should look like *Figure 11.25* once we have added the fifth user. Click **OK** to create the filter:

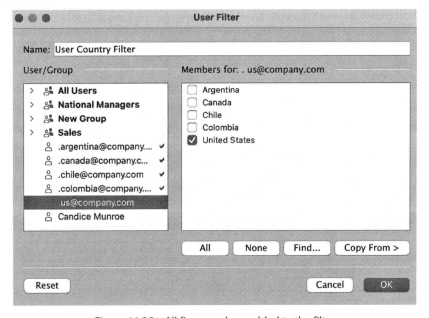

Figure 11.25 – All five members added to the filter

6.  We will now see our **User Country Filter** in our data pane. Drag and drop it to the **Filters** shelf, as shown in *Figure 11.26*. We will notice that the pill color changes to gray. This means it is a context filter and that it is applied before any other filters we add:

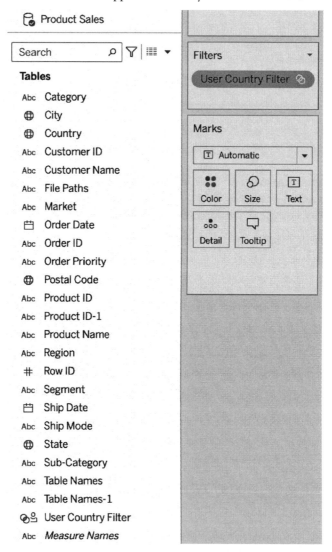

Figure 11.26 – User filter on the filters shelf

7.  At the very bottom of the Tableau Desktop user interface, toward the right-hand side, we can see the name we used to sign in to Tableau Server or Cloud. Click ▼ next to your name to bring up the **Filter as User** dialog box, as shown in *Figure 11.27*. This functionality allows us to see sheets, dashboards, and stories in Tableau as a given user or group would see them. Select .argentina@company.com:

Figure 11.27 – The Filter as User dialog

8.  To test our filter, double-click on **Country** in the data pane. We will now only see **Argentina** on the map, as shown in *Figure 11.28*. This is due to the combination of the user filter we created and the username we selected in **Filter as User**:

Figure 11.28 – Country seen by argentina@company.com

9.   We can continue to test by changing the user in the **Filter as User** dialog and watching which countries they see. Don't close Tableau Desktop at this point as we will continue from here in the next exercise.

In this section, we learned how to create user filters manually to achieve RLS. The advantage of this approach is that it is straightforward to create and easy to test if it works.

This approach to RLS does have downsides. The main three downsides are as follows:

- It cannot be used with a published data source as the user filter can only go on the filters shelf on a sheet and cannot be used as a data source filter.

- The addition and subtraction of new users and groups cannot be automated.

- Anyone who can edit the workbook can remove the user filter just by removing it from the filters shelf. When publishing a workbook with a user filter, the best practice is to ensure no one can download or use web edit by setting the appropriate project permissions.

In the next section, we will look at a more robust and scalable option: using an entitlements table.

## Adding user-based security inside a published data source using an entitlements table

An **entitlements table** is a table that identifies users and the data they are entitled to see.

Let's begin by opening the Entitlements.xlsx file that we previously downloaded from GitHub with Microsoft Excel or another program that opens Microsoft Excel files. This is the same file we used to add our users to Tableau Server or Cloud earlier in this chapter.

The file should look like what's shown in *Figure 11.29*:

| | A | B |
|---|---|---|
| 1 | Email | Countries can see |
| 2 | argentina@company.com | Argentina |
| 3 | colombia@company.com | Colombia |
| 4 | chile@company.com | Chile |
| 5 | canada@company.com | Canada |
| 6 | us@company.com | United States |

Figure 11.29 – Entitlements table

This is a simple version of an entitlement table but works well to create our use case. It has two columns. The first is the user's email, while the second is the countries they are entitled to see. We are going to take this table and join it to the Product Sales.csv table, which contains the Superstore sales data we have been using throughout this book.

Here are two important things to note before we start this exercise:

- First, as mentioned in *Chapter 9*, relationships will not work for this use case; we need to use joins.

- Second, we need to use a published data source as we will be building a filter. If we use this as a data source filter in a published data source, workbook authors will not be able to remove the filter. If the filter is in an embedded data source, a workbook developer could remove the filter, opening the rows for everyone to see.

We will pick up this from the exercise in the previous section:

1. Click on the **Data Source** tab to be taken to the data source page. Click on the ▼ icon next to the Product Sales.csv card and select **Open**, as shown in *Figure 11.30*:

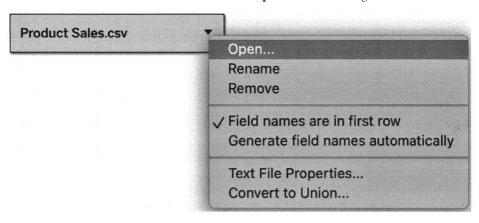

Figure 11.30 – Opening Product Sales.csv to create a join

2. Click on the **Add** link next to **Connections**. In the **To a File** section, select **Text file**, find the Entitlements.csv file, and select **OK**. Drag and drop the Entitlements.csv file to the right of Product Sales.csv in the canvas. Our screen should now look like *Figure 11.31*:

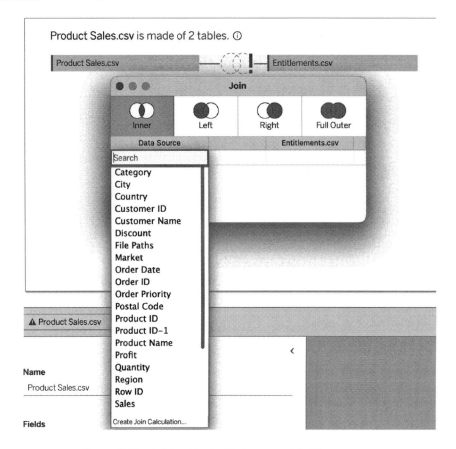

Figure 11.31 – Joining Product Sales.csv and Entitlements.csv

3.  Create an inner join by selecting **Country** from the **Product Sales** (left) table and **Countries can see** from the **Entitlements** (right) table, as shown in *Figure 11.32*:

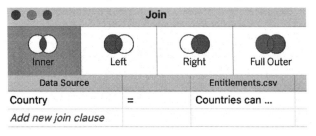

Figure 11.32 – Country joined to Countries can see

4.  Click on the red **x** button in the top left-hand corner to dismiss the join dialog box. Create a new sheet by clicking on the **New Worksheet** icon to the right of **Sheet 1**, as shown in *Figure 11.33*:

Figure 11.33 – New Worksheet

5.  From the menu bar, select **Analysis | Create Calculated Field…**, as shown in *Figure 11.34*:

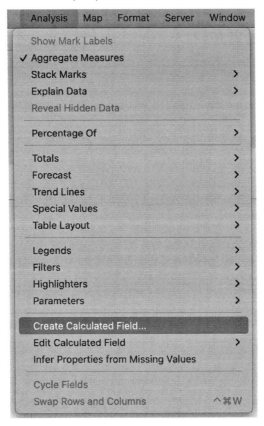

Figure 11.34 – Create Calculated Field…

6.  Type USERNAME() = [Email] in the calculated field dialog box and name the field User Filter, as shown in *Figure 11.35*; then, click **OK**. As we start typing, Tableau will autocomplete fields for us. This calculation will return a Boolean value of True or False. The USERNAME() function returns the email of the user signed into the session. As Email is a field in our data model on every row, we will get a True value returned when the row matches with the user who is signed in and a False value when the email field on the row does not match. If our entity table was set up to work on groups instead of users, Tableau has a function called ISMEMBEROF() to check the signed-in user against the groups to which they belong:

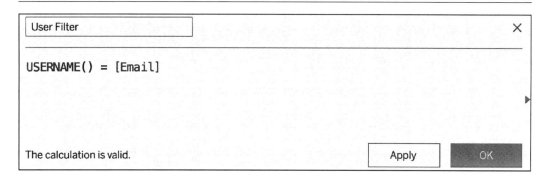

Figure 11.35 – Creating a user filter

7.  Set the **Filter as User** to **.argentina@company.com**. Click on the **Data Source** tab to be taken to the data source page. Click on the **Add** link in the top right-hand corner, as shown in *Figure 11.36*:

Figure 11.36 – Adding a data source filter

8.  This will bring up the data source dialog page. Click on **Add...**, which will bring up the **Add Filter** dialog box. Scroll to the bottom to find the **User Filter** field we created and press **OK**, as per *Figure 11.37*:

Figure 11.37 – Adding the User Filter field as a data source filter

9. We will now get the option to choose either **True** or **False**. If you only get the option to choose **False**, go back to **Sheet 1** and ensure the **Filter as User** is set to one of the @company.com users we created earlier in this chapter. Check the box in front of **True** and leave the box in front of **False** unchecked, as shown in *Figure 11.38*. Click **OK** to commit this change:

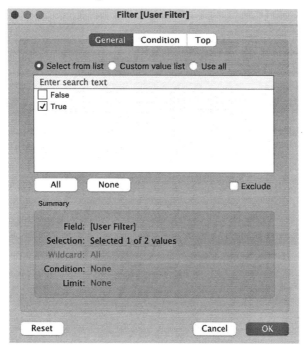

Figure 11.38 – Keeping True checked

10. This will leave us on the **Edit Data Source Filters** dialog. Press **OK** to accept this filter, as shown in *Figure 11.39*:

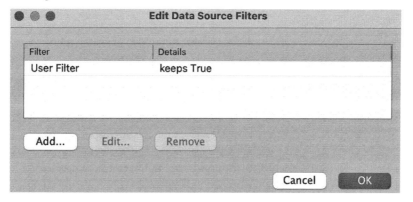

Figure 11.39 – All data source filters

11. Click on **Sheet 2** so that we can test our filter. Ensure that we are filtered to the **.argentina@ company.com** user and then double-click on **Country** in the data pane. Our screen should now look like what's shown in *Figure 11.40*. Notice that the user can only see Argentina and that the filter shelf is empty. The data source filter is working. If we want to see the filter continue to work, change the **Filter as User** value and watch the map change:

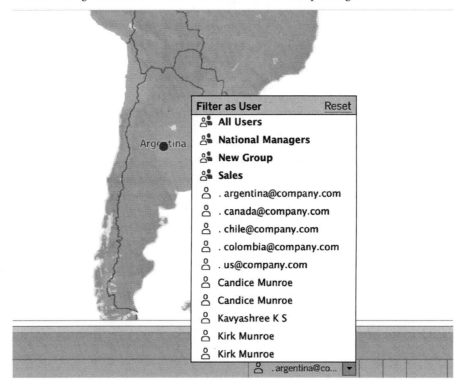

Figure 11.40 – The Argentina user can only see Argentina data

With that, we've learned about a second way to create RLS in Tableau by using an entitlement table. The advantages of this approach over the manual approach we learned about in the previous section are as follows:

- It can be used with a published data source, so it stays secure if others create workbooks from the data model

- The addition and subtraction of new users and groups can be automated by updating the table without any manual work required in Tableau

In the next section, we will discuss how RLS can be implemented in virtual data connections.

# Using Tableau virtual connections to manage access and security

We were introduced to Tableau virtual connections in *Chapter 2*. **Virtual connections** are enabled in Tableau Server and Cloud with Data Management. Virtual connections allow us to create an additional layer between our database(s) and Tableau data models. This feature makes sense when an organization delegates the building of data models to individuals who understand data in organizational content but may not understand database structures. The person who creates the virtual connection can perform tasks such as hiding and renaming columns in the database. The data modeler from the organization can then create a published or embedded data source of the virtual connection.

One of the other features of virtual connections is **data policies**. Data policies work in a very similar manner to the ones we described in the previous section on entitlement tables. Using a virtual connection in this manner also moves security closer to the database. For example, if someone in the human resources department is responsible for creating a data model for all human resources, they could protect salary information by using entitlement table(s). In this approach, this person would still see salaries. Using data policies within a virtual connection and then allowing the human resources data modeler to connect to the virtual connection would protect salary information from the data modeler.

Virtual connections can only be used with data servers and cloud drives. Installing and configuring a data server is beyond the scope of this book, so we will leave this section as-is. In the next section, we will explore leveraging the native capabilities of data servers for row and column-level security.

# Leveraging database security features for both row and column-level security

We often don't need to create RLS for users in Tableau as user security is already handled by database servers. Some database servers also have column-based security. As an example, you might want to let the human resources department see everything about employees except the data contained in the salary column.

If security is already set in the database, Tableau will respect the security in the database. However, the default behavior is to prompt the user inside Tableau. This is not the best user experience. To enable a better user experience, we want to enable Tableau to pass the user credentials they used to sign in to Tableau to the database so that they don't have to sign in a second time.

Tableau allows for **single sign-on** (**SSO**) with some databases. There are a few techniques for SSO, depending on the database technology, including impersonation, initial SQL and Kerberos, and constrained delegation.

As mentioned in the previous section regarding virtual connections, installing and configuring a data server is beyond the scope of this book, so we will leave this section as-is as well.

# Summary

In this chapter, we explored data access and data security on the Tableau platform. We began by adding users and groups to Tableau Server or Cloud.

We spent time creating and using Tableau projects to manage data models and content access and capabilities. We learned that locked projects are the best practice for managing access to data models across an organization.

Then, we looked at managing access to the data inside models using RLS. We saw how RLS works using manual user filters and adding users by using entitlements tables. Then, we discussed the pros and cons of each approach.

In the final two sections of this chapter, we looked at Tableau virtual connections and native database security to manage secure user access to the data within our data models.

We will look at data modeling considerations for Ask Data and Explain Data in the next chapter. These are machine learning capabilities for casual users that work best when our data models are tailored for each of them.

# Data Modeling Considerations for Ask Data and Explain Data

Tableau **Ask Data** and **Explain Data** are powerful machine learning features that put analysis in the hands of casual users – those who would struggle to create their own analysis through the drag-and-drop features of Tableau Desktop and web authoring. For these casual users to get answers to their questions, the data models and available fields supporting them must be well thought-out; otherwise, the users may end up frustrated with answers that don't make sense. This chapter explores these considerations.

In this chapter, we're going to cover the following topics:

- Visual analytics through natural language search with Ask Data

- Creating a lens for Ask Data, including field exclusions, renaming, and creating aliases

- Uncovering outliers in your data with Explain Data

- Curating data sources for Explain Data by telling the model which columns to use and ignore

## Technical requirements

To view the complete list of requirements needed to run the practical examples in this chapter, please see the *Technical requirements* section in *Chapter 1*.

In this chapter, we will be using the Tableau Desktop client software and the web interface of Tableau Server or Cloud. We are going to be working with the published data source we created in *Chapter 6*.

The screenshots and descriptions in this chapter are based on Tableau Cloud version 2022.3. They might be different in your version of Tableau Server or Cloud if you are working with a different version.

The published data source we will be using is based on the Superstore data, the sample data that Tableau uses in their products. This published data source contains sales from the US, Canada, Colombia, Chile, and Argentina, which we joined to a product database.

The name suggested for the published data source was `Product Sales`. If you did not publish the data source or no longer have access to it, you can rebuild the published data source from the following file in our GitHub repository:

- `Product Sales.csv`

The files used in the exercises in this chapter can be found at `https://github.com/PacktPublishing/Data-Modeling-with-Tableau/`.

## Visual analytics through natural language search with Ask Data

Ask Data is a natural language search interface from Tableau Server and Cloud. It allows users to perform visual analysis without needing to have the technical skills that are associated with traditional business intelligence products. If a person can type out a business question in natural text, they can get an answer. This is true if the answer is in their data, of course!

Data modeling strategies are essential for a seamless experience with Ask Data.

First, Ask Data only works with published data sources. That is, data models that are embedded in workbooks are not available for Ask Data.

Second, at least one **lens** needs to be created on your published data source to use Ask Data. Lenses allow data modelers to further refine published data sources to hide fields, rename fields, add synonyms, and create view recommendations. All these options can be very valuable to the natural language question experience.

In the next section, we will look at building our first lens to enable Ask Data.

## Creating a lens for Ask Data, including field exclusions, renaming, and creating aliases

To create our first lens, we are going to access the `Product Sales` published data source that we published to our Tableau Server or Cloud in *Chapter 6*. If you did not publish the data source at that step, or it is no longer on your Tableau Server or Cloud, download the `Product Sales.csv` file from GitHub, connect to it from Tableau Desktop or the Tableau web client, and publish it to your Tableau Server or Cloud. Take note of the project where you published the data source:

1.  Navigate to the project where you published the `Product Sales` data source. Click on the `Product Sales` data source to be taken to the data source page, as shown in *Figure 12.1*:

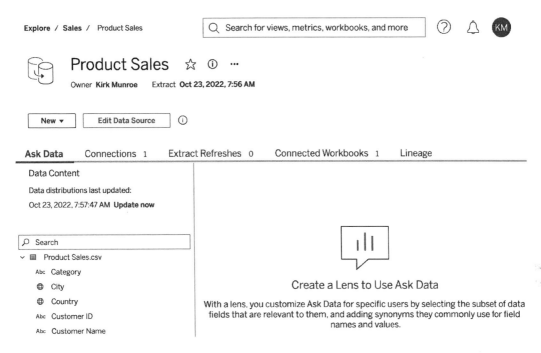

Figure 12.1 – Product Sales data source page

2.  You will notice that Tableau prompts you to create a lens before using Ask Data. Click on **Create New Lens** to begin. Tableau will prompt you to select the fields you want in your lens, as shown in *Figure 12.2*. This is an important first step as it makes sense to remove fields that can be searched through Ask Data, even though the fields might make sense to an analyst. For our example, de-select the following fields:

    *   Customer ID

    *   File Paths

    *   Order ID

    *   Product ID

    *   Product ID-1

    *   Row ID

    *   Table Names

    *   Table Names-1

    After de-selecting these fields, click **Submit**:

Figure 12.2 – Selecting fields for the lens

3.  We now have a lens and can begin to test Ask Data. Before we begin, let's look at some of the other features available in a lens. First, if we ever want to remove additional fields or add fields back into the lens, we can click on the pencil icon to the right of the **Data** label below the **Ask Data** tab, as shown in *Figure 12.3*:

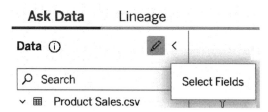

Figure 12.3 – Select Fields

4.  The next option available to us is creating **synonyms**. Synonyms are additional words or terms people might use in a search for field names or data elements within a field. To create a synonym, hover over a field until the pencil icon appears next to it. Hover over the **Postal Code** field until **Edit Field Details** appears, as shown in *Figure 12.4*. Left-click to bring up the **Field Details** dialog:

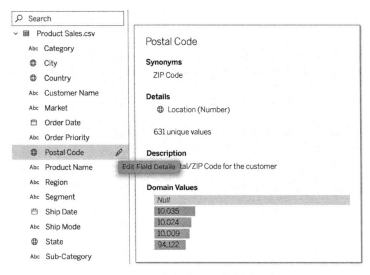

Figure 12.4 – Bringing up field details

5.  You will now be in the **Field Details** dialog. Type ZIP Code in the **Synonyms** field and enter The Postal/Zip Code for the customer in the **Description** field, as it appears in *Figure 12.5*. Click the **x** icon in the top-right corner of the dialog to dismiss the dialog box. This also saves our changes:

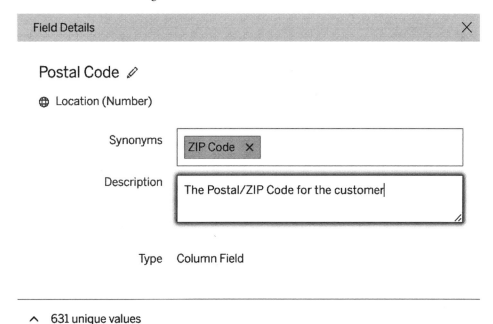

Figure 12.5 – Edit field dialog

6.  We can also create synonyms for data elements within a field. Click on the pencil icon next to the **Sub-Category** field to edit field details. At the bottom of the dialog, we can see **17 unique values**. Click on this section of the dialog box to expand the dialog to see these 17 values. For our exercise, we know that people within our organization often refer to binders as folders. To make their questions easier to answer, click in the **Synonyms** column next to the **Binders** row and enter Folders, as shown in *Figure 12.6*. Click on the **x** icon in the top-right corner to save our changes and dismiss the dialog box:

Figure 12.6 – Adding a synonym to a data element

7.  To test our synonyms, type Sales of folders by zip code in the **Search fields or values to create a visualization** box. Your screen should now look like *Figure 12.7*. Notice that Tableau mapped the fields and values to ones in our model in a manner that makes it clear to the person creating the search. Tableau also gives us information on the searches people are using in Ask Data. We can use that data to continually refine the synonyms in our lens:

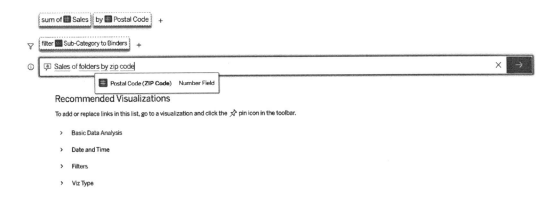

Figure 12.7 – Mapping the synonyms in the search area

8.   We do not want to ask this question because there could be a lot of postal codes! Clear the text in the search box and type Sales by Ship Mode. Press *Enter* or click on the white arrow on the blue background (-->) to issue the search query. Tableau will now run the query and, using its proprietary VizQL language, will return the answer in a bar chart, as shown in *Figure 12.8*:

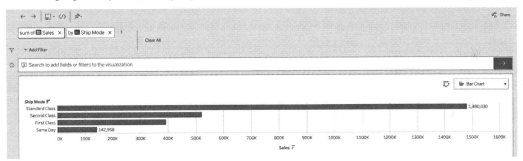

Figure 12.8 – Result of our search as a bar chart

9.   Tableau returns a bar chart as it is the best practice for comparing values. As lens authors, we can decide whether another chart type makes more sense by using a **view recommendation**. To the right of our chart, click on the drop-down that mentions **Bar Chart**. Select **Treemap** to get the visualization shown in *Figure 12.9*:

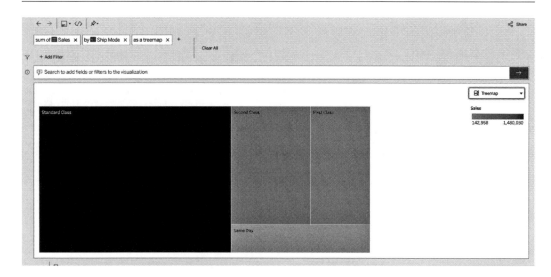

Figure 12.9 – Search results as a treemap

10. As our final step, we can create **recommendation visualizations** that appear when people search to help direct them to visualizations that we think work best for specific types of searches. Click on the recommendations pin on the Ask Data menu, as shown in *Figure 12.10*. We can use **Replace Recommendation…** to update existing recommendations. Since we haven't created a recommendation yet, let's look at the first option – that is, to **Pin to Recommended Visualizations…**:

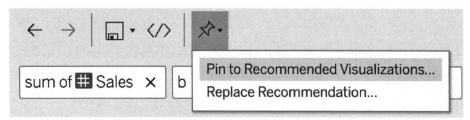

Figure 12.10 – Recommended visualizations

11. We can give our recommendation a name and a section to appear, as shown in *Figure 12.11*. For now, click on **Cancel** as we will end finish modeling the lens for Ask Data here:

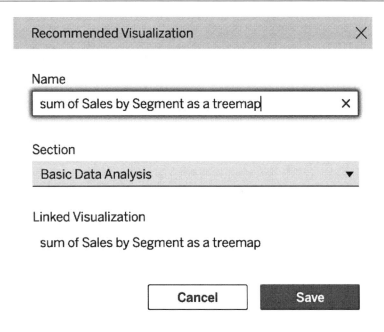

Figure 12.11 – Saving the recommended visualization

In this section, we learned about Tableau's natural language query interface, Ask Data. We also learned that Ask Data needs a lens to be added to an existing published data source. A lens makes a published data source easier to query for casual users using natural language. A lens allows us to remove fields from our model, rename fields, add synonyms, and create recommendation visualizations without disrupting our data model for analysts using Tableau Desktop or web edit to create dashboards and other analyses.

Tableau also provides reports on how people are using Ask Data. These reports can be invaluable to us to refine our data model. If people are asking questions with different terms, we can update our synonyms; if they are asking for information that's not in our data model, we can go back to our source data and add it to our published data source.

In the next section, we will look at Explain Data and the implications it has on data modeling.

## Uncovering outliers in your data with Explain Data

Explain Data is a feature in Tableau that allows users to find outliers in their data through the automatic creation of potential explanations presented visually. When you use Explain Data on an individual mark in a Tableau visualization, Tableau builds these potential answers using statistical models that include data from the data source that isn't in the current view.

Unless you instruct it otherwise, Explain Data will use all the columns in your data source to try to find explanations. Unlike Ask Data, the additional data modeling for Explain Data occurs in the workbook. This means Explain Data works with both published and embedded data sources.

In the next section, we will see Explain Data in action and control how it works by deciding which columns (fields) we want to exclude from the analysis.

## Curating data sources for Explain Data by telling the model which columns to use and ignore

Let's look at Explain Data in action. We will begin by connecting to our Product Sales published data source. We can do this in Tableau Desktop or by creating a workbook from the web client of Tableau Server or Cloud. As we have been using Tableau Desktop in *Chapter 8*, *Chapter 9*, and *Chapter 10*, the examples in this section will use the web client. If you prefer, you can follow along using Tableau Desktop:

1.  From the home page on Tableau Server or Cloud, click on **New** | **Workbook**, as shown in *Figure 12.12*:

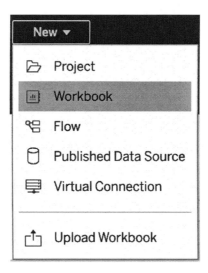

Figure 12.12 – New workbook

2.  You will be presented with a **Connect to Data** dialog. On the **On This Site** tab, select our **Product Sales** data source and click **Connect**. We are now in the workbook. Double-click on **Sales** in the data pane and then double-click on the **Ship Mode** field. Your screen should now look like *Figure 12.13*:

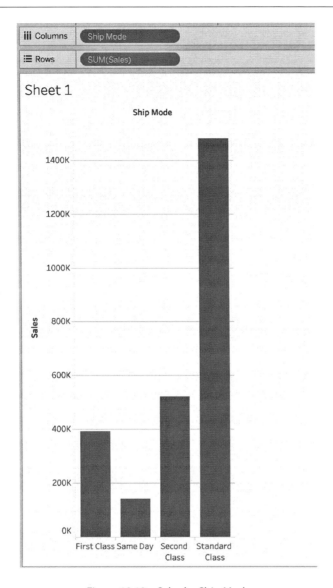

Figure 12.13 – Sales by Ship Mode

3.  Click on the blue bar associated with **Same Day** sales. Wait for the tooltip to appear and notice the lightbulb icon. Hover on the lightbulb icon (💡) until it shows **Explain Data…**, as shown in *Figure 12.14*, then click to activate the feature:

Figure 12.14 – Explain Data

4.  An Explain Data panel will appear to the right of the chart, as shown in *Figure 12.15*. Explain Data will make suggestions to best explain the mark you selected. In this case, it will explain why **Same Day** sales is 142,958. You will see that SUM(**Sales**) is **Slightly lower than expected for this viz**. Click on this card for further explanation:

Figure 12.15 – Explanation for SUM(Sales) of Same Day

5.  Tableau is now telling us that one potential explanation is that **Number of Records** is lower than expected but within normal limits, as shown in *Figure 12.16*. This makes sense. Since we have sold fewer items with **Same Day** delivery, the volume of sales in dollars is also lower than other **Ship Mode** types. If this finding was more insightful, we could click on the **Open in worksheet** (🖼) icon to explore it further. In our case, we are not likely to find true insights because our sample data is structured for easy demonstration and does not have the variance often seen in real-world data. For now, click on the < icon at the top left of the card to return to all explanations:

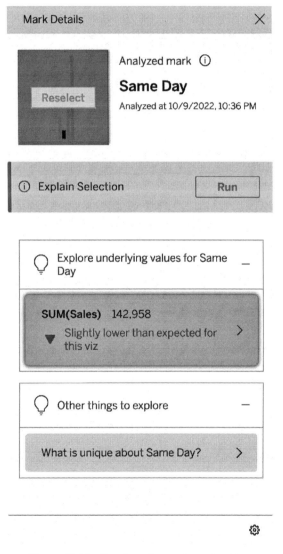

Figure 12.16 – Number of records explanation

6.  If we click on **What is unique about Same Day?**, we can see that Explain Data is suggesting that six dimensions might be having an impact on our selected mark, as shown in *Figure 12.17*. This is where our data modeling for Explain Data becomes important. The **File Paths** dimension contains the location where our source files came from. This cannot be related to why a sales number could be low:

Figure 12.17 – Potential dimensions

7.  Click on the settings icon in the bottom-right corner of the dialog, to the right of **11 of 23 fields**, as shown in *Figure 12.17*. This will bring up the **Explain Data Settings** dialog, as per *Figure 12.18*. We see that we can decide which fields we want to exclude from the Explain Data algorithms by selecting **Never Include** next to the fields that we don't want to be evaluated. Change **File Paths** to **Never Include** and then click on **OK**:

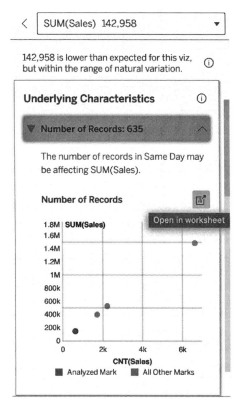

Figure 12.18 – The Explain Data Settings dialog

In this section, we learned about Explain Data, Tableau's feature that uses statistical models to uncover the reason for outliers in our data. We also learned how to remove dimensions from consideration in the statistical models. It is key to remove these fields; otherwise, business users are unlikely to trust the suggestions from Explain Data.

## Summary

In this chapter, we looked at Ask Data and Explain Data. These machine learning features put analysis in the hands of casual users if the data is modeled properly for each feature.

Ask Data requires us to first create a published data source. Next, we must create a lens on our published data source. A lens allows us to hide fields, rename fields, add synonyms, and create view recommendations. If we create a better lens, analysis by casual users through full-text search will provide much better answers.

By default, Explain Data runs statistical models that evaluate all the dimensions in our data model. We often know that some of these dimensions might appear in determining outliers but have no business value in the analysis. In these cases, we can remove dimensions from the analysis Tableau performs, increasing trust in the results of Explain Data.

In the next chapter, we will be looking at the role Tableau Prep Conductor plays in data modeling in the Tableau platform and exploring scheduling for extract refreshes.

# 13

# Data Management with Tableau Prep Conductor

With Data Management from Tableau, Tableau Prep has another component – Tableau Prep Conductor. This chapter will explore how to set up and use Prep Conductor.

This chapter will also explore the additional features of Data Management that enhance our data models. These features are the data catalog, data lineage, and data quality warnings. We will also look at certified data models, which are a standard feature of Tableau Server and Cloud.

In this chapter, we're going to cover the following topics:

- Scheduling Tableau Prep flows from Tableau Prep Conductor
- Data catalog, lineage, data quality warnings, and certified data sources

## Technical requirements

To view the complete set of requirements to run the practical examples in this chapter, please see the *Technical requirements* section in *Chapter 1*.

We will be using the following files in the exercises in this chapter:

- `Superstore Sales Orders - Canada.xlsx`
- `Product Database.xls`

The files that will be used in the exercises in this chapter can be found at `https://github.com/PacktPublishing/Data-Modeling-with-Tableau/`.

# Scheduling Tableau Prep flows from Tableau Prep Conductor

We looked at Tableau Prep Builder in *Chapter 4*, *Chapter 5*, and *Chapter 6*. When we use the Tableau Prep Builder client software, we can save our flows to our filesystem as Tableau Prep flows (the .tfl file extension) or Tableau Prep packaged files (the .tflx file extension). Tableau Prep flow files contain information on data server connections and the instructions we create in the flow. Tableau Prep packaged flow files contain the same information, plus the data from any file-based sources that have been embedded. In addition to saving flow files locally, Tableau Prep flows can be published to Tableau Server or Cloud.

When we use the Tableau Prep Builder web client, we only have the option to publish our flows to Tableau Server or Cloud. From both the installed client and web client, we can run our flows manually. When we run flows, Tableau performs all the data transformation steps we created and runs any outputs in the flow. All these capabilities are available to users with Creator licenses.

To automate the process of running our flows on a schedule or off a trigger when the underlying data changes, we need to use Tableau Prep Conductor. This is a feature of Tableau Server and Cloud and is only available with Data Management. We will now look at creating a new flow from the web client, publishing it, and scheduling it with Tableau Prep Conductor:

1.  Sign into your Tableau Server or Cloud instance. Click on **New** | **Flow** from any page, as shown in *Figure 13.1*:

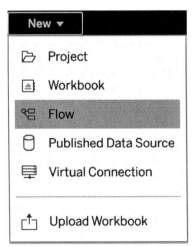

Figure 13.1 – Creating a new flow in the web client

2.  Click on the **Connect to Data** button in the middle of the screen, as shown in *Figure 13.2*. Choose **File** | **Microsoft Excel**, locate the Superstore Sales Orders - Canada.xlsx file from your computer, and click on **Open**:

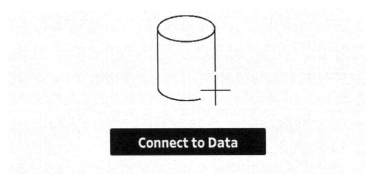

Figure 13.2 – The Connect to Data button

3.  We will now see our Canadian sales data. Click on the **+** symbol to the right of **Connections** in the **Connections** pane to **add a connection**, as per *Figure 13.3*:

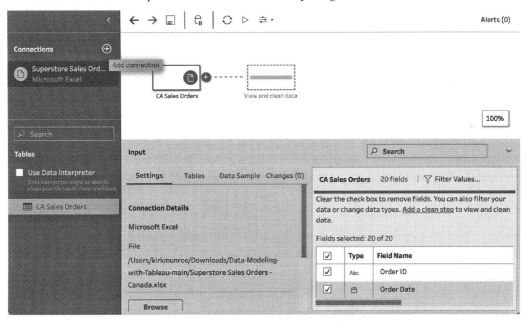

Figure 13.3 – Adding a new connection

4.  Choose **File | Microsoft Excel**, locate the Product Database.xls file from your computer, and click on **Open**. Click and hold the left mouse button on the **+** symbol to the right of Product DB, drag it over the **+** symbol to the right of CA Sales Orders, and release it to create a join, as shown in *Figure 13.4*:

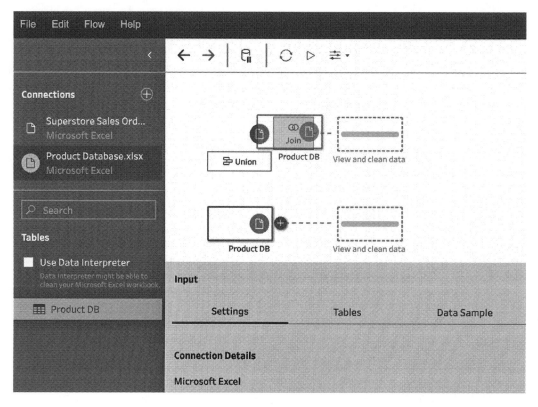

Figure 13.4 – Creating a join between the tables

5.  Notice that Tableau will create an inner join on the `Product ID` field. This is the join we want for our exercise so that we can add an output step. Click on the + symbol to the right of `Join 1` and choose **Output**, as shown in *Figure 13.5*:

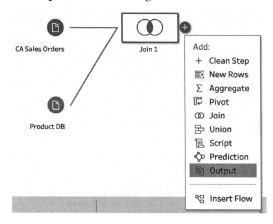

Figure 13.5 – Adding an output step

6.  Now, we can configure our output in the area below our flow pane. Leave **Save output to** set to **Published data source**. Change **Project** to the Sales project we created in *Chapter 11* and change the name from Output to Canada Sales. Our screen should now look like what's shown in *Figure 13.6*:

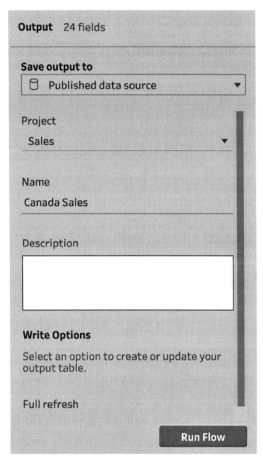

Figure 13.6 – Output step

7.  We will now publish our flow. Click on the **Publish** button in the top right-hand corner of the screen. This will bring up the **Publish Flow** dialog box. Change the **Name** to Canada Sales Flow and select **Sales** for **Project**. Then, click on **Publish**, as shown in *Figure 13.7*:

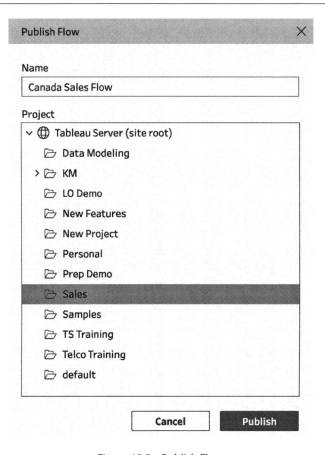

Figure 13.7 – Publish Flow

8.    After clicking **Publish**, Tableau gives us a notification at the top of the screen that our flow has been published. Click on the **View flow** link, as shown in *Figure 13.8*:

Figure 13.8 – Published flow notification

9.    We will now be taken to a page that gives us additional information and allows us to perform actions on our flow, as shown in *Figure 13.9*. We can go back in and edit our flow by clicking on the **Edit Flow** button. We can also manually run our flow, which would generate our Canada Sales published data source. Both options are available to us as a Creator, even if we don't have Data Management. We also have a tab to view the **Connections** properties in our flow. The other four tabs are only available with Tableau Prep Conductor:

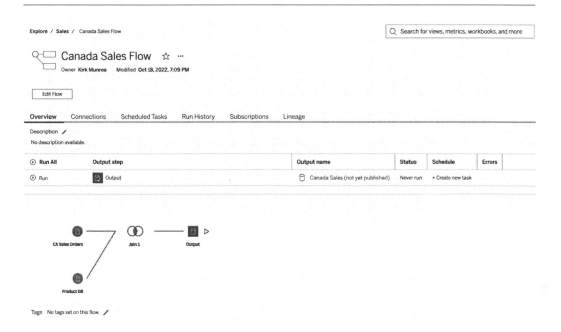

Figure 13.9 – The flow page on Tableau Cloud

10. Now, let's create a new task using Tableau Prep Conductor. Click on the + **Create new task** link in the **Schedule** column. This will bring up the new task dialog, as shown in *Figure 13.10*. There are a few things we can do on the **Single Task** tab, as follows (see *Figure 13.10*):

- **Select a schedule**: We can select a schedule of when we want the task to run. If we are using Tableau Cloud, there is a long list of options to choose from. If we are using Tableau Server, these schedules are created by the Server Admin.

- **Output steps**: We can choose to include all the steps from our flow or select output steps individually. Since our flow only has one step, both options have the same result. If we have multiple steps, we could select individual ones in the task.

- **Refresh Type**: If our connection contains data server connections, we have the option of a full or partial refresh. As our connections are Microsoft Excel, only the **Full refresh** option is available.

- **Send email when done**: By clicking on this option, we can configure an email to be sent to people when the task runs, including a custom message:

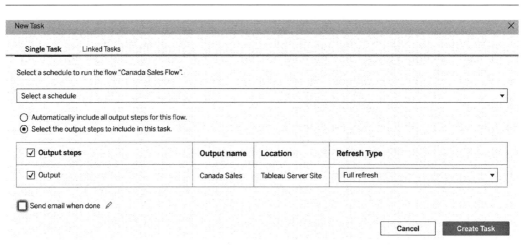

Figure 13.10 – New Prep Conductor task

11. Click on the **Linked Tasks** tab to see the options to create linked tasks, as shown in *Figure 13.11*. This tab allows us to link multiple flows together. Linked tasks make sense when one flow is dependent on another. We can send emails when each step is complete, stop the next task if one task fails, and add a data quality warning if a task fails. We will look at data quality warnings in the next section of this chapter. We do have linked tasks in our exercise, so click on the **Single Task** tab. Select any schedule to enable the **Create Tasks** button, leave all the other options as-is, and click **Create Tasks**:

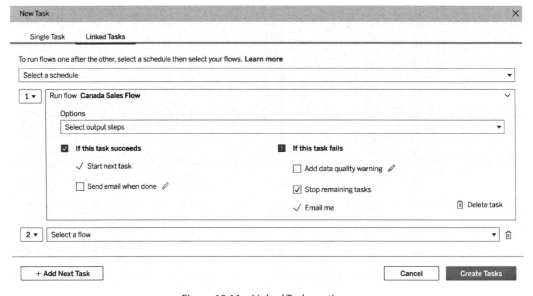

Figure 13.11 – Linked Tasks options

12. We will now be taken back to the page that provides an overview of our flow. We will see whatever schedule we picked in the **Schedule** column. We don't want to wait for our schedule's date and time, so click on the **Run Flow** link, as shown in *Figure 13.12*:

Figure 13.12 – Running the flow

We will get a dialog box asking us to confirm that we want to run the flow now, as shown in *Figure 13.13*. Click on **Run Now** to confirm:

Figure 13.13 – Run Now confirmation

13. Wait until the **Status** column returns a message that the run was successful. Once we see the success message, we can click on the **Run History** tab, as shown in *Figure 13.14*. Here, we will see details about our successful run. We can always come back to this tab to diagnose the state of scheduled tasks:

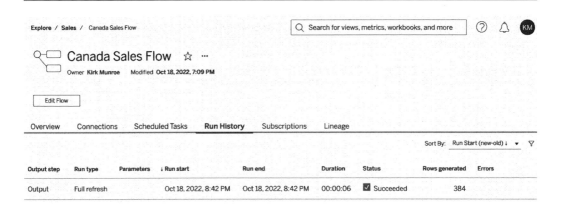

Figure 13.14 – The Run History tab

14. As our last step of exploring Tableau Prep Conductor, click on the **Subscriptions** tab and then click the **Subscribe** button. We will now see a screen like the one shown in *Figure 13.15*. Subscriptions are a way to send people, including ourselves, a message every time a task runs. Subscriptions give us a few options:

- **Frequency**: We can pick from the list of tasks for which we want to create a subscription. In our example, we only have the one we created in *Step 11* of this exercise.

- **Send to**: The list of users or groups to receive the notification.

- **Send to me**: An optional checkbox to send the email to ourselves.

- **Subject**: The subject of the email.

- **Email message**: The optional body of the email.

- **Include link to published data source**: Embeds a link in the email to make it easy for the recipient to click through to the published data source page:

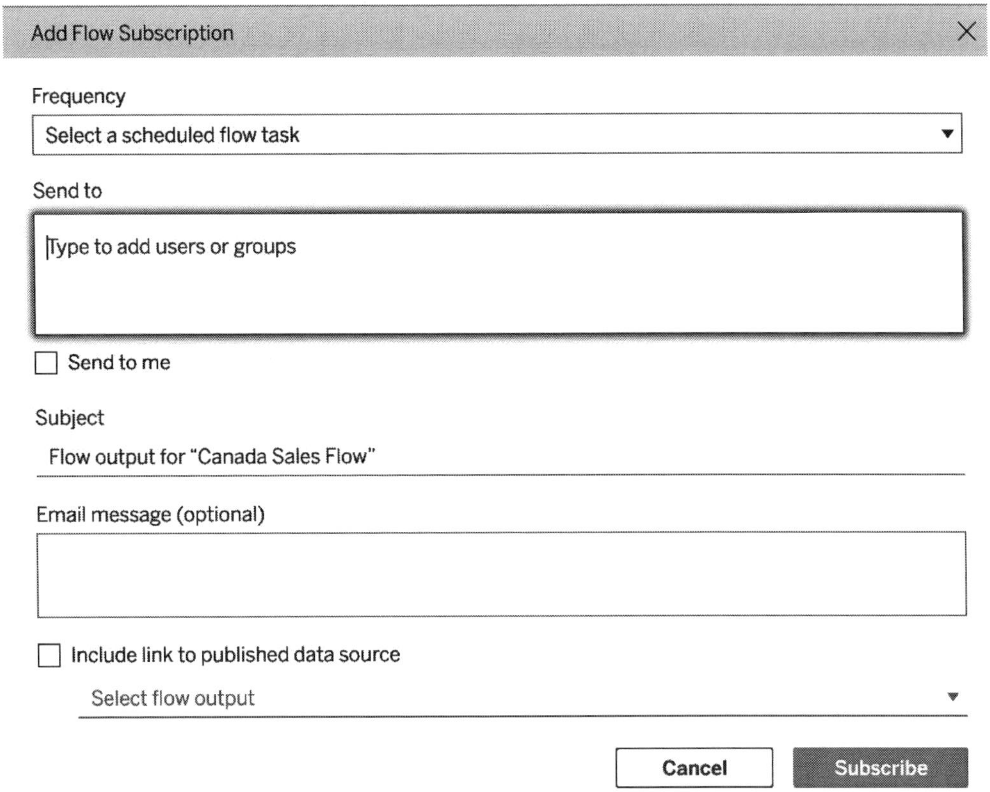

Figure 13.15 – Subscription options

In this section, we learned about Tableau Prep Conductor. This is a capability that allows people to scale flows to automate the maintenance of the data models that are created in Tableau Prep Builder.

Next, we will talk about three other features that are enabled with Data Management that enhance our data models.

# Data catalog, data lineage, data quality warnings, and certified data sources

In addition to Tableau Prep Conductor, Tableau Data Management also enables three other features, namely, **data catalog**, **lineage**, and **data quality warnings**. In this section, we will look at each of these features:

1.  From the same Tableau Server or Cloud instance we used in the previous exercise, click on the **Explore** navigation button on the left-hand side panel. If the side panel is collapsed, the **Explore** button will look similar to what's shown in *Figure 13.16*:

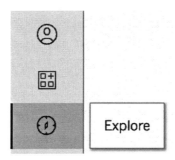

Figure 13.16 – The Explore button

2.   Click on the link for the **Sales** project. You should now see the **Canada Sales** published data source and **Canada Sales Flow**, which we created in the previous exercise, as shown in *Figure 13.17*:

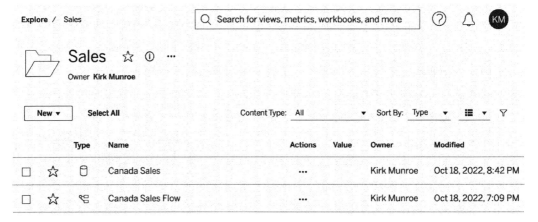

Figure 13.17 – Sales project contents

3.   Click on the **Canada Sales** published data source link. Once we are on the data source page, click the **Lineage** tab, as shown in *Figure 13.18*:

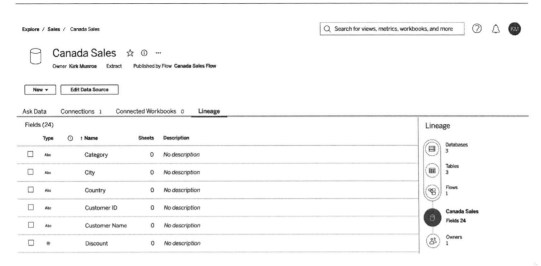

Figure 13.18 – The Lineage tab of the Canada Sales data source

4.   On the right-hand side of the page, you will see the **Lineage** property of the **Canada Sales** data source. If you click on any of the links, you will get more details about that stage of the lineage. If one or more workbooks are created from this data source, the count of **Workbooks** and **Sheets** will be listed between **Fields** and **Owners**; fields are hyperlinks that take us to the required content. This is the lineage feature of Data Management.

5.   We will now look at how the data catalog works. Click on the link for the **Category** field (see *Figure 13.18*) – it is the top field in our list. We will be taken to a dialog that gives us metadata about our field. We can also add a description to this field. To do this, click on the pencil icon, as shown in *Figure 13.19*:

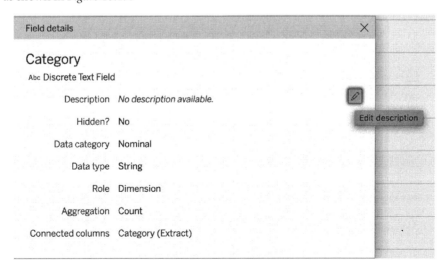

Figure 13.19 – Edit description

6.  After clicking the **Edit description** pencil icon, enter The categories of products we sell in the textbox and click on **Save** to commit our changes, as shown in *Figure 13.20*:

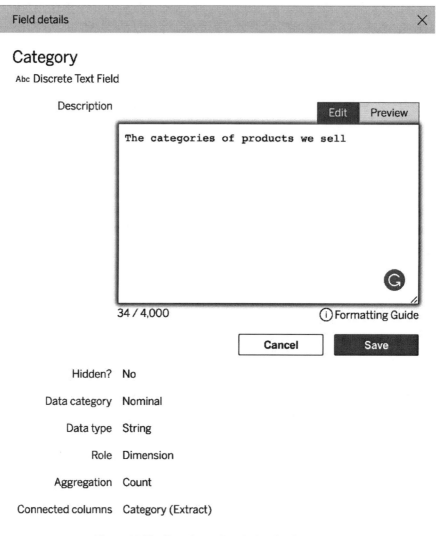

Figure 13.20 – Entering a description for Category

7.  Click on the **X** button at the top right-hand corner to dismiss the dialog. We will now be on our data source page and will see the description for the Category field, as shown in *Figure 13.21*. This description will now also be available to viewers who are exploring dashboards on Tableau Server and Cloud. This allows you to build trust in your data model with these users:

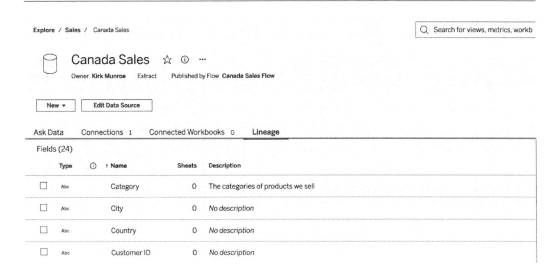

Figure 13.21 – Description of Category

8.  Click on the **…** icon to the right of the `Canada Sales` title again. This time, select **Quality Warning | Quality Warning…**, as shown in *Figure 13.22*. Data quality warnings are features that are only available with Data Management:

Figure 13.22 – Quality warning

9. We can enter a quality warning if we click on the toggle next to **Show warning**, as shown in *Figure 13.23*. For example, if we know the data has a minor problem, we can set our warning to **Standard visibility** and enter a message. People viewing any workbooks associated with this data source would then need to open **Data Details** to see this message. We can also set the warning to **High visibility** when we have an important data quality issue. For instance, perhaps the issue is large enough that we might be concerned about people making a bad decision with the data. In this case, the message will appear as an alert any time someone views a workbook with our data source. Now that we have seen how data quality warnings work, we can click on **Cancel** to dismiss the dialog box:

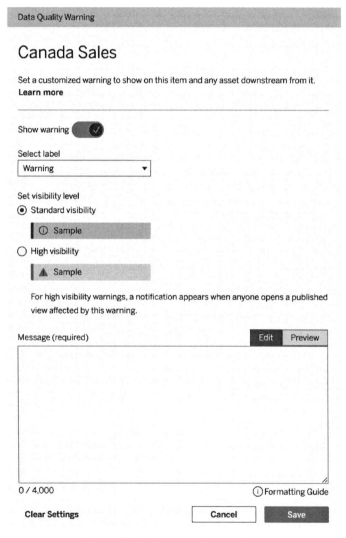

Figure 13.23 – Data quality warnings

10. For our final step in this exercise, click on the **...** icon to the right of the title again. This time, select **Quality Warning | Extract Refresh Monitoring....** This will bring up the **Extract Refresh Monitoring** dialog, as shown in *Figure 13.24*. This functionality acts in the same manner as the data quantity warning we explored in the previous step. The difference with this option is that the warning occurs automatically when an extract refresh fails. Click on **Cancel** to dismiss the dialog:

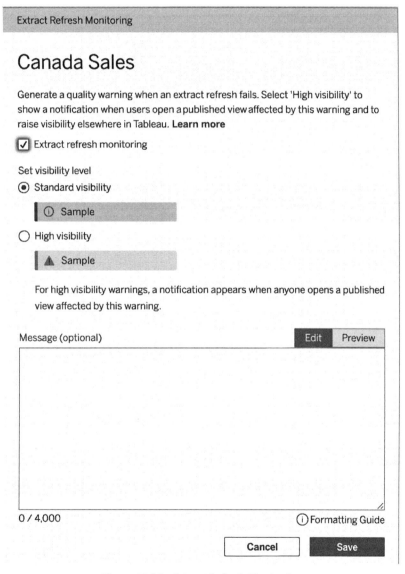

Figure 13.24 – Extract Refresh Monitoring

11. Now, we will look at **certified data sources**. Click on the **…** icon to the right of the Canada Sales title on the data source page. Click on the **Edit Certification…** option to bring up the certification dialog box, as shown in *Figure 13.25*:

Explore / **Sales** / Canada Sales

Figure 13.25 – Edit Certification…

12. Click on the **This data is certified** checkbox and enter This data source is the one source of truth for Canadian product sales. in the textbox, as shown in *Figure 13.26*. Click on **Save** to commit our changes:

Figure 13.26 – Data certification dialog box

13. We will see that there is a clear indication that this data source has been certified by the **Certified** logo on the data source page, as shown in *Figure 13.27*. This data source will now go to the top of the list when dashboard creators select **To a Server** as their connection type. This builds confidence in the data source for both authors and consumers of content. Certifying data sources is available to all Tableau deployments – that is, we do not need Data Management to certify data sources:

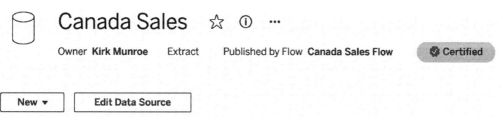

Figure 13.27 – Certified logo

In this section, we learned about additional data modeling features of the Tableau platform. The data catalog, lineage, quality warnings, and certified data sources features of Tableau all work together to help us build confidence in our data models.

## Summary

In this chapter, we explored Tableau Prep Conductor. This capability allows us to schedule the flows we create in Tableau Prep Builder and the web client. We can schedule our flows to run as single or linked tasks, we can subscribe to flows, automate messages when our flow fails, and check the status of our flows when they have run.

We learned that the data catalog and data lineage allow for building trust in our data source, allowing the people who view and interact with Tableau visualizations to see data definitions, where data originates, and where the data is being used in the organization.

Data quality warnings allow us to alert users when we have issues with the data in our data models. These warnings can be created manually or created to trigger when data extracts fail.

We also learned that certifying data sources signals to authors and consumers using published data sources that they can be used with confidence.

In the next chapter, we will be looking at the Tableau scheduling service and using Tableau Bridge to keep on-premises data sources fresh on Tableau Cloud.

# Scheduling Extract Refreshes

In the previous chapter, we discussed keeping data fresh for our data flow outputs using Tableau Prep Conductor. We are going to explore keeping data extracts created in Tableau Desktop and in the web client up to date using the scheduling service of Tableau Server and Cloud. We will also look at the role Tableau Bridge plays in making on-premises data available on Tableau Cloud.

In this chapter, we're going to cover the following topics:

- How to set up and run schedules

- Using schedules with subscriptions

- Tableau Bridge – what it is and when to use it

## Technical requirements

For the complete list of requirements that are needed to run the practical examples in this chapter, please see the *Technical requirements* section in *Chapter 1*.

In this chapter, we will be using the web client of Tableau Server or Cloud.

We will be using the following file in the exercises in this chapter:

- `Product Sales.csv`

The files used in the exercises in this chapter can be found at `https://github.com/PacktPublishing/Data-Modeling-with-Tableau/`.

# How to set up and run schedules

We have discussed how to create extracts from both Tableau Prep Builder and Tableau Desktop and each of their corresponding web clients. We will now look at how to schedule extract refreshes for extracts created in Tableau. We will start by creating a published data source from the web client:

1. Sign in to Tableau Server or Cloud. From the home page, click on the **New** button and select **Published Data Source**, as seen in *Figure 14.1*:

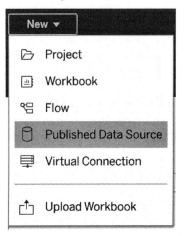

Figure 14.1 – A new published data source

2. Click on the **Files** tab and then on the **Upload from computer** button, as seen in *Figure 14.2*:

Figure 14.2 – Upload file to create a data model

3. When prompted, find the Product Sales.csv file from your computer and click on **Open**. You will be taken to the **New Data Source** web client. Click on the **Data Source** tab on the bottom left-hand corner of the screen, as seen in *Figure 14.3*:

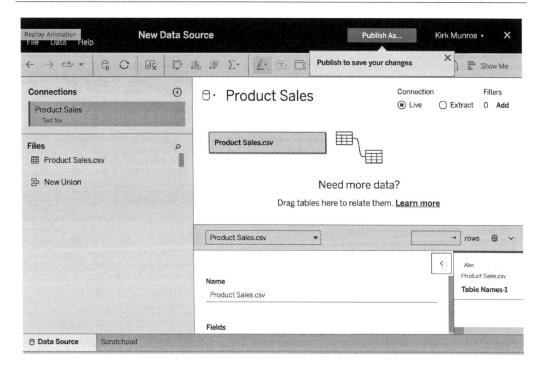

Figure 14.3 – Data source page of the published data source web client

4. Click on the **Extract** button on the top right-hand corner of the data source page. A link to **Create Extract** will appear. Click on the **Create Extract** link, as seen in *Figure 14.4*:

Figure 14.4 – Create Extract button

5. We will then be warned that the extract will take time to create and be given a chance to delay the creation of the extract. We would like to create our extract now, so click on the **Create Extract** button, as seen in *Figure 14.5*:

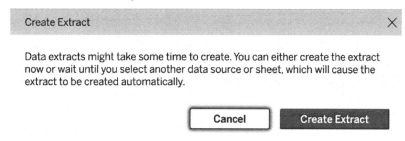

Figure 14.5 – Create Extract warning

6.  After our extract is created, the next step is to publish our data source. Click on the **Publish As...** button, which is on the right in the top ribbon as per *Figure 14.6*:

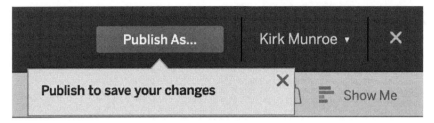

Figure 14.6 – Publish As button

7.  Select the Sales project and leave the name as Product Sales. Click on the **Publish** button, as seen in *Figure 14.7*:

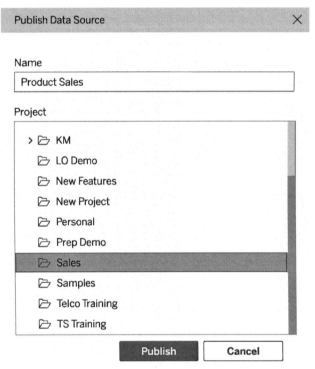

Figure 14.7 – Publishing to a project

8.  We now get a message dialog box telling us that our data source has been published successfully. Click on the **Product Sales** link to go to our data source page, as seen in *Figure 14.8*:

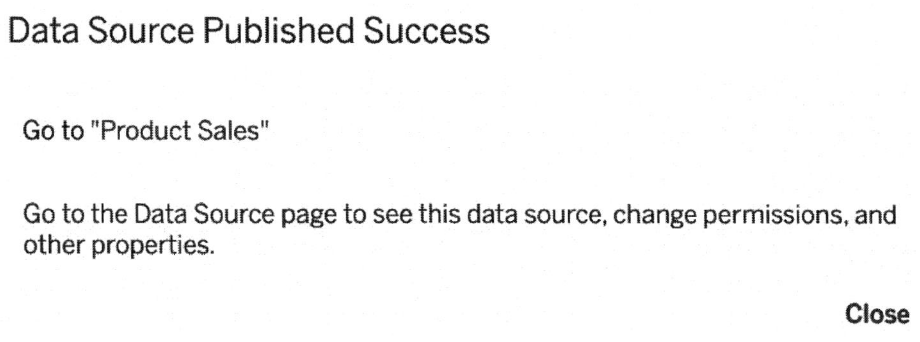

## Data Source Published Success

Go to "Product Sales"

Go to the Data Source page to see this data source, change permissions, and other properties.

**Close**

Figure 14.8 – Publish success dialog

9. We now get a message dialog box letting us know that publishing is complete. The dialog also gives us the option to schedule our refresh. Click on **Schedule Extract Refresh**, as seen in *Figure 14.9*:

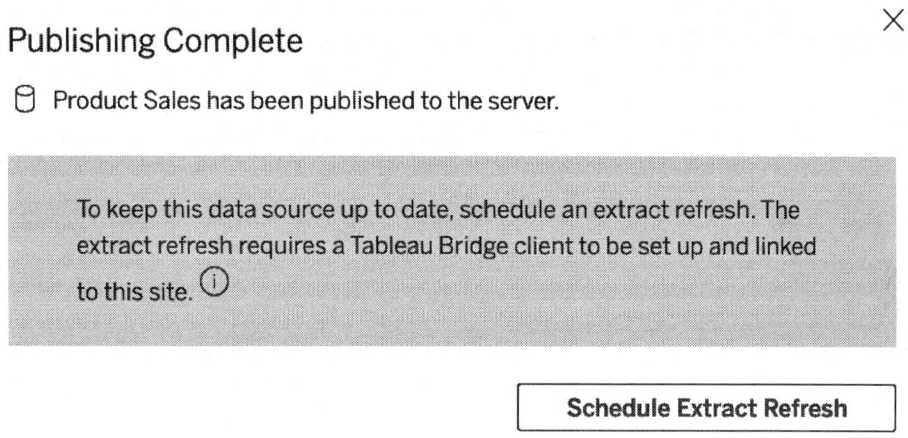

## Publishing Complete                    ✕

🗄 Product Sales has been published to the server.

> To keep this data source up to date, schedule an extract refresh. The extract refresh requires a Tableau Bridge client to be set up and linked to this site. ⓘ

**Schedule Extract Refresh**

Figure 14.9 – Schedule Extract Refresh

10. We are now presented with the **Create Extract Refresh** dialog, as seen in *Figure 14.10*. The scheduler gives us the following options:

- **Full Refresh** or **Incremental Refresh** – In our case, we only have a **Full Refresh** option because we are connected to a file. When we are connected to a data server, we can use a field, typically a data field, and set an incremental refresh to update the data since the last time an extract was run.

- **Refresh Frequency** – If we are using Tableau Online, this allows us to set the schedule at a granular level; we get to set when it repeats, how often, the time of day, and even which days of the week and the time zone. If we are using Tableau Server, we pick from the schedules set up by our server administrator.

Explore the different options and then click **Create** to create our scheduled refresh:

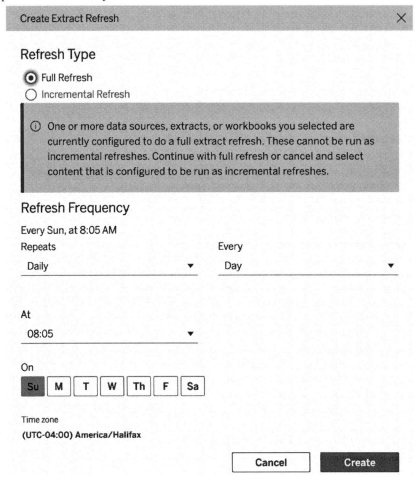

Figure 14.10 – Create Extract Refresh

11. We will now be on the **Ask Data** tab of our data source. Click on the **Extract Refreshes** tab. We will see our refresh in the list. Click on the **...** icon in the **Actions** column, as seen in *Figure 14.11*. We see that we can manually kick off an extract by selecting **Run Now...**, change our schedule with **Change Frequency...**, or **Delete....** For now, click away from the drop-down to dismiss it. Stay on this page as we will pick up from here in the next exercise:

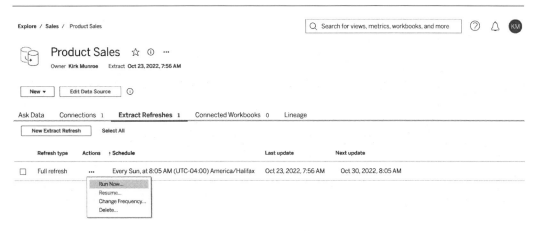

Figure 14.11 – Extract Refreshes tab

In this section, we learned how to create extract refresh schedules on Tableau Server or Cloud. Schedules allow us to automate extract refreshes without having to run them manually.

We will look at how consumers of the workbooks created from our published data sources can create **subscriptions** to let them know when data has been refreshed.

## Using schedules with subscriptions

We often want the consumers of workbooks created from our data source to be alerted when the data has been refreshed. We can enable this through subscriptions. We will now look at how to create a subscription, picking up from where we left off in the previous exercise. In order to create a subscription, we first need a workbook using our published data source:

1.  From our `Product Sales` page on Tableau Server or Cloud, click on **New** | **Workbook using this data source**, as seen in *Figure 14.12*:

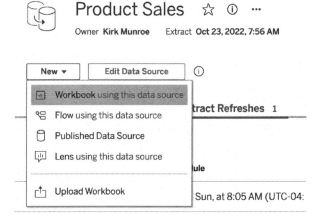

Figure 14.12 – Creating a new workbook

2. Now, we just need to create a simple workbook and publish it to expose the subscription experience. Double-click on `Sales` and then double-click on `Ship Mode`. We now see a bar chart of `Sales` by `Ship Mode`. Click on the **Publish As…** button in the top right-hand corner. When the publish dialog comes up, enter `Subscription Example` in the **Name** field, leave all other default options, and click **Publish**, as seen in *Figure 14.13*:

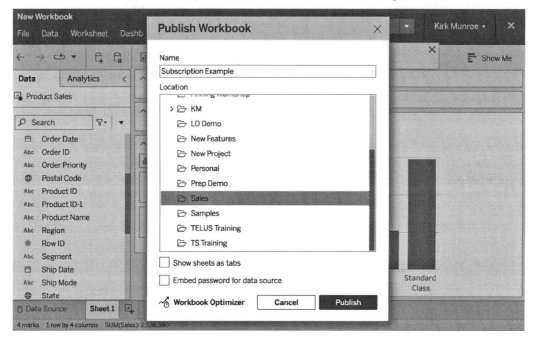

Figure 14.13 – Publishing our workbook

3. We will now see an alert at the top of our screen letting us know the workbook has been published, as seen in *Figure 14.14*. Click on the **Go to workbook** link:

Figure 14.14 – The workbook has been published alert

4. We are now on the page for our workbook. If our workbook had multiple sheets, they would be listed on this screen, as seen in *Figure 14.15*. We only have one sheet, so click on **Sheet 1**:

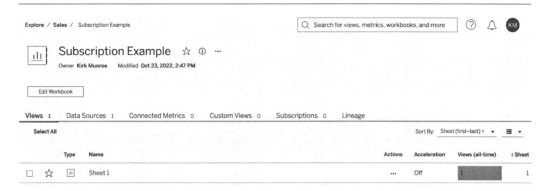

Figure 14.15 – Workbook page

5.   We are now on the screen that is the experience the consumers of the workbook will have. The option that we want to look at now is subscriptions, which can be found under **Watch**. Click on the **Watch** button on the top right-hand side of the screen to see our options, as in *Figure 14.16*. In this exercise, we will be looking at subscriptions. The other options are **Metrics**, which allow users to create and then monitor key numbers that they deem to be important. The **Alerts** function is like subscriptions except they notify only when a certain threshold, which the user sets, is met in the data:

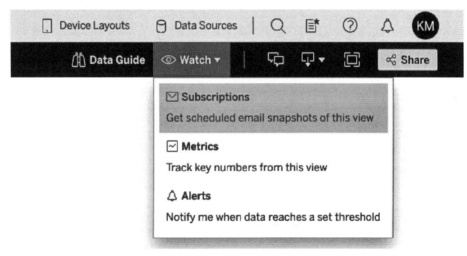

Figure 14.16 – Creating subscriptions

6.   Click on the **Subscriptions** option to bring up the subscriptions dialog, as seen in *Figure 14.17*. We have several options available to us as follows:

   •   **Subscribe Users** and **Subscribe Me** – We can subscribe other users, subscribe ourselves, or both. In our example, canda@company.com has been added to the subscription.

- **Include** – We can include information and the link to the sheet or dashboard from where the subscription is created or to the entire workbook.

- **Format** – Choices are images, PDF, or both.

- **Subject** – The subject of the email. In our example, the text `Data has been refreshed` has been typed into the subject.

- **Message** – Optional text for the body of the email that will be sent.

- **Frequency** – There are two options. The first is to subscribe to a schedule. This option gives the same choices as the schedules we explored in the previous section of this chapter. The second option, and the one selected in our example, is **When Data Refreshes**. This is the option through which we want to let people know that new data is available:

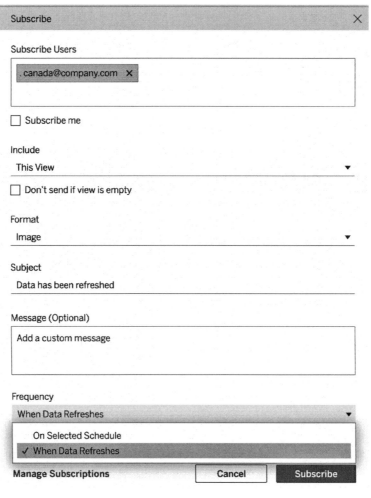

Figure 14.17 – Subscribe dialog

7.  Click on **Subscribe** to create our subscription. We will leave our exercise here as we have seen how to create a subscription on the condition of our extract refreshing.

In this section, we learned how to create subscriptions to notify end users when the published data source in their workbook has been refreshed. This is a key feature that works with extract refreshes to make sure key people are notified when data is refreshed.

We will explore Tableau Bridge to learn how to keep data fresh with on-premises data with Tableau Cloud in the next and final section of this chapter.

## Tableau Bridge – what it is and when to use it

When we are using Tableau Server inside our organization, Tableau Server needs to be able to access the data. A few factors need to be considered. If we are using text files, they need to be in a directory accessible from Tableau Server. If we are using data servers, the drivers for the data servers need to be installed on Tableau Server and Tableau Server needs to be able to access the data server over the network or in the cloud.

When we are using Tableau Cloud, access might need an extra step and Tableau Bridge might be required. If we are using Tableau Cloud with public cloud databases, a direct connection for both live connections and extracts is straightforward if the data server is a listed Tableau Cloud connection. Tableau Cloud already has the drivers we need installed.

When we are using data servers or files from inside our organization (on-premises data) with Tableau Cloud, if we want the connection to be live or if we want to use extract refresh schedules, we need to use Tableau Bridge.

Tableau Bridge is a free client that we can download from `https://www.tableau.com/support/releases/bridge`. Tableau Bridge is only available as a Microsoft Windows application or service. To run it from a Mac, we must run it in a Windows virtual machine.

After installing the Tableau Bridge client, all scheduling works the same as the exercise earlier (see the *How to set up and run schedules* section) in the chapter. The client can be launched from the Windows system tray. The screenshot in *Figure 14.18* shows what the Tableau Bridge UI looks like when connected to a published data source called `Sales for Bridge`. We can decide whether to run Tableau Bridge as an application or a service. If it is run as an application, the user needs to be logged in to the machine for Tableau Bridge to run. If the computer is logged in to Tableau Cloud, refresh schedules will run and live connections will be available:

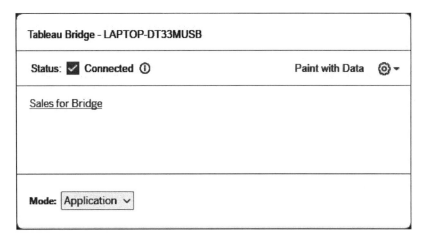

Figure 14.18 – Tableau Bridge client user interface

The Tableau Bridge client can also be configured on the Tableau Cloud site by a Site Administrator, including setting up multiple clients to achieve scale with many published data sources.

Creating an exercise to run a Tableau Bridge connection is beyond the scope of this book as it requires connecting a file from your local network to the cloud which could lead to security concerns. We will leave the learnings on Tableau Bridge at this point.

## Summary

In this chapter, we explored how to set up and run schedules to refresh the data in extracts on Tableau Server and Tableau Online. Schedules are an important part of data modeling in the Tableau platform as they keep our data fresh in an automated fashion, helping us scale.

We also looked at using schedules with subscriptions from within workbooks on Tableau Server and Cloud. Subscriptions are a way for consumers of dashboards to be notified when new data is available.

In the final section of the chapter, we looked at Tableau Bridge. Tableau Bridge is a required component for keeping on-premises data fresh on Tableau Cloud.

The next chapter is the final chapter of our book. It will wrap up all the components we have learned throughout the book by determining which components we need by audience and use case.

# 15

# Data Modeling Strategies by Audience and Use Case

In the first 14 chapters, we discussed the data modeling components of the Tableau platform. We looked at Tableau Desktop, Tableau Prep Builder, virtual connections, published data sources, embedded data sources, lenses, schedules, Tableau Prep Conductor, securing content with projects, securing data with row-level security, and more.

This is our final chapter. We will look at putting it all together by exploring which components of the platform we should use based on the audience and use case. Before looking at use cases, we will discuss the general use cases for Tableau Desktop versus Tableau Prep Builder.

In this chapter, we're going to cover the following topics:

- When to use Tableau Prep Builder versus Tableau Desktop
- Use case 1 – finance user with quarterly financial reporting
- Use case 2 – sales performance management dashboards
- Use case 3 – information systems analytics of internal employee intranet site visits
- Use case 4 – marketing analytics of social media campaigns

## When to use Tableau Prep Builder versus Tableau Desktop for creating our data models

Tableau Prep Builder and Tableau Desktop are the two foundational components for data modeling on the Tableau platform. Each has a place and they overlap in functionality in many areas.

Tableau Prep Builder is the go-to product when you need to transform your data. It uniquely allows for cleaning data, particularly in cleaning up string fields. It has machine learning algorithms to fix dirty data. An example is a field coming from a source where people can type in values such as customer names. It also has features that allow for pivoting rows to columns, adding new rows, and outputting models to destinations beyond Tableau.

Tableau Desktop is the go-to product when you need live connections to your data and when you are combining data that is at different levels of aggregation. Tableau Desktop is also the only place, along with the corresponding web interface, where we can build hierarchies and folders to organize our data.

There are also cases where either product can be used based on the use case. These are joins, aggregations, unions, pivoting columns to rows, filtering data, and integration with data science models. Both products have these capabilities.

A summary of the ideal scenarios for each product and where either can be used can be seen in *Table 15.1*:

| Ideal for Tableau Prep Builder | Use Case Dependent | Ideal for Tableau Desktop |
|---|---|---|
| • Cleaning data<br><br>• Pivot data – rows to columns<br><br>• Data scaffolding (add rows)<br><br>• Output to something other than Tableau<br><br>• String calculations | • Joins<br><br>• Aggregations<br><br>• Unions<br><br>• Pivot – columns to rows<br><br>• Filtering data<br><br>• Integration with data science models | • Live connections<br><br>• Flexible level of detail joins<br><br>• Building hierarchies<br><br>• Creating folders<br><br>• Conditional calculations (for example, moving averages, running totals, year-over-year/month-over-month, percent of total) |

Table 15.1 – The case for Tableau Prep Builder and Tableau Desktop

In the following sections, we will be looking at use cases through the eyes of different audiences. The use case and audience will determine which parts of the Tableau platform we will use to create and share the data model.

> **Note**
> The asterisks in the tables in the next section represent the components that are only available with the Data Management licenses.

# Use case 1 – finance user with quarterly financial reporting

In this and the next three use cases, we will look at the scenario and then the Tableau modeling steps.

**Scenario**:

We have an analyst in finance who must produce monthly financial reporting that is available to the finance department and the executive team. The reports contain profit and loss, balance sheets, and cash flow information. It is combined with the data from the main competitors, who are publicly listed on stock exchanges.

The data comes from both internal and external sources. All internal data is sourced from internal systems and exported to Microsoft Excel. External sources come from PDF documents that competitors need to make available as part of their regulatory requirements and are available on the investor relations pages of their websites.

The company uses Tableau Cloud and has a secure project set up for these reports that limits access to the finance department and the executive team.

**Tableau modeling steps**:

The finance analyst uses Tableau Desktop to pivot rows to columns, join, and potentially union, internal data by connecting to Excel files. They then create a relationship with the competitors' data by using the Tableau PDF connector. On the first build of the report, they use Tableau Desktop to create their tables and visuals and then publish the workbook with the data source embedded. In future quarters, they add new files to the same directory and use unions to bring in historical data. Once the new files are dropped, they only need to hit refresh to publish quarterly.

We can see what is and is not needed from the various data modeling components of the Tableau platform for the finance use case, along with the reason, in *Table 15.2*:

| Component | Use? | Reason |
| --- | --- | --- |
| Virtual connection * | No | Virtual connections are used for sharing data models at scale and helping simplify columns and tables. This complexity is not needed in our use case. |
| Prep Builder | No | Our example is one where Tableau Desktop is sufficient for creating the data model and since we need Tableau Desktop for financial report creation, it is easier to keep everything in a single client. |
| Desktop | Yes | Desktop can handle all the requirements for modeling. |
| Published or embedded? | Embedded | The data model associated with the financial report will only be used in this report. It will not be shared for other uses. |

| Tableau Bridge | No | The data is very sensitive and only produced quarterly. For this reason, the financial analyst will not only refresh new data quarterly but ensure it loads properly (for example, field names didn't change in competitor PDFs). Since they are checking it first, and since it only happens quarterly, a manual republish makes sense. If similar data was being refreshed on a more frequent basis, such as daily or weekly, Tableau Bridge would likely make sense as it connects on-premises files to Tableau Cloud, and Bridge would be needed to automate data refresh. |
|---|---|---|
| Scheduler or Prep Conductor? * | No | The financial analyst will be publishing manually, so the cost of automation is more than manually refreshing once a quarter. |
| Lens | No | The report being created is static and complete. There is no additional data in this use case to enable a free text search. |
| Enable Explain Data | No | The two reasons Explain Data is not needed and should be disabled in the workbook is that the analyst will naturally look for outliers as part of the quarterly publishing. Finally, it is unlikely that there are columns in this type of data to explain any outliers. That is, this is a financial report, not an analysis of financial drivers. |
| Descriptions for Catalog * | Potentially | These audiences likely don't need descriptions to explain the fields in financial reports, but it could be useful in the case of new executive team members. |

Table 15.2 – Finance use case

This use case demonstrates that there are times when data sources are relatively small and are updated infrequently. In this scenario, we do not have to overcomplicate our data modeling strategy by using components of the Tableau platform that aren't needed.

## Use case 2 – sales performance management dashboards

**Scenario**:

We have a request from sales to create a data model for their analyst team to create interactive dashboards for the worldwide sales organization. The dashboards contain sales of all products and services for every customer, in every channel, and every region. The range of users goes from sophisticated sales analysts to sales representatives who aren't always tech-savvy.

The data comes from many sources, but the data engineering team has consolidated all sources into a Snowflake database. The data is messy as the company uses different customer relationship management software in different regions of the world. The rules for data entry validation vary wildly, resulting in messy data in some regions and cleaner data in others. The data engineering team does not have the mandate, resources, and time to clean the data. They will leave this cleaning task to a data steward who works with the business. Finally, regional sales individuals and management should only see the data for which they are responsible, but global sales management should be able to see all regions.

The company uses Tableau Cloud and has groups set up in Azure Directory Services that are synced to Tableau Cloud.

**Tableau modeling steps**:

The data steward for the sales organization first uses Tableau Prep Builder to clean the data, join the necessary tables, and union the tables from different regions. They export to a Snowflake table and set up a schedule in Tableau Prep Conductor to keep the table fresh daily.

The data steward then creates a virtual connection and creates policies to ensure that the right sales groups only have access to the data they should see. They set the virtual connection to live to leverage Snowflake for query performance. They then create a published data source from the virtual connection, add field descriptions for the Catalog, and certify the data source. A lens is then created for more casual users, by eliminating unnecessary and confusing fields for search and adding synonyms that are used in different regions.

The sales analysis and dashboard developer then connects to the published data source to create interactive dashboards. Before publishing, the analysts ensure the proper columns are made available to Explain Data so that consumers in the sales organization are free to explore outliers in their dashboards.

We can see what is and is not needed from the various data modeling components of the Tableau platform for the sales use case, along with the reasons, in *Table 15.3*:

| Component | Use? | Reason |
|---|---|---|
| Virtual connection * | Yes | A virtual connection is used to achieve the row-level security requirements. |
| Prep Builder | Yes | Prep Builder is used to clean up messy fields, join tables, and union table sources from the different customer relationship management software used in different regions. |
| Desktop | No | We created our published data source in Prep Builder. |
| Published or embedded? | Published | This data source needs to be published as it is used in multiple workbooks, Ask Data, and needs to be certified. |
| Tableau Bridge | No | As the data is coming from a cloud database, it can be accessed from Tableau Cloud without needing the Tableau Bridge client. |
| Scheduler or Prep Conductor? * | Prep Conductor | Prep Conductor is used to extract and transform the source data from Snowflake and then load it back into a new Snowflake table after it has been cleaned. |

| Lens | Yes | A lens is required as this is a great use case for Ask Data. |
|---|---|---|
| Enable Explain Data | Yes | Enabling users to find their outliers is a key requirement. |
| Descriptions for Catalog * | Yes | Data definitions are important for the wide use of these data sources across the entire global sales organization. |

Table 15.3 – Sales use case

This sales data scenario was very different than the first example with the finance use case. This scenario had a wide and diverse audience, data security requirements, and big data that changes frequently. In scenarios like this, it makes sense to take advantage of the majority of the Tableau data modeling components.

# Use case 3 – information systems analytics of internal employee intranet site visits

**Scenario**:

We have an information systems analyst who must produce dashboards for the organization to see how employees are visiting and interacting with the organization's internal web properties. The dashboards should be available to the entire organization as executive management has a goal for most employees to help drive employees to web-first interactions.

The data comes from a database that captures all site interactions. This table is then joined to an internal employee and internal systems tables for context.

The company uses Tableau Server and has a secure project set up with all the groups who can see and interact with these dashboards.

**Tableau modeling steps**:

A data steward creates a published data source for information system analysts and dashboard developers that is extracted from the underlying tables at the end of each section of data to improve query performance. The data steward also adds a lens and field descriptions and then certifies the data source after ensuring the data is accurate. The information systems analysts and dashboard developers create interactive dashboards and select appropriate fields for Explain Data.

We can see what is and is not needed from the various data modeling components of the Tableau platform, along with the reason, in *Table 15.4*:

| Component | Use? | Reason |
|---|---|---|
| Virtual connection * | No | The data is not complex enough nor does it need a data policy for row-level security. |
| Prep Builder | No | The data is clean and does not need the transformation features of Tableau Prep Builder. |
| Desktop | Yes | Desktop is used to create a published data source that is extracted. |
| Published or embedded? | Published | The data source is published so it can be used with Ask Data and can be certified. If the use case does not require Ask Data, since it is only being used in a single workbook, embedding it in the workbook would be OK. |
| Tableau Bridge | No | The customer uses Tableau Server, which does not need Tableau Bridge to keep the data fresh. |
| Scheduler or Prep Conductor? * | Scheduler | The published data source is configured to run a schedule to refresh the extract daily. |
| Lens | Yes | To enable broad use, Ask Data is enabled. |
| Enable Explain Data | Yes | To let consumers explore outliers, Explain Data is enabled. |
| Descriptions for Catalog * | Yes | As the workbook will be distributed broadly, data definitions are key to ensure decisions based on the data are based on a solid understanding of the data. |

Table 15.4 – Marketing use case

In this third use case, we have a scenario that falls somewhere between the finance and sales use cases. Like the sales example, we have broad distribution. Unlike the sales example, we don't have the same security concerns about which users can see which data. For this reason, we end up using many of the data modeling components of the Tableau platform without overcomplicating it with unneeded components, such as virtual connections.

# Use case 4 – marketing analytics of social media campaigns

**Scenario:**

We have a request from marketing to create a data model for their analyst team to create interactive dashboards for the worldwide marketing organization. The dashboards contain information on social media click-through campaigns.

The data comes from the social media companies where our campaigns are running, but the data engineering team has consolidated all sources into Google BigQuery. The data is clean and stored at the level of granularity of the day – that is, the data is rolled up to the day and broken down by social media site and campaign name. Sometimes, there are days with no data because the campaigns don't always generate a click-through each day. Finally, everyone in marketing can see all campaign information, regardless of where they are located.

The company uses Tableau Cloud and has groups set up in Azure Directory Services that are synced to Tableau Cloud.

**Tableau modeling steps**:

A data steward creates a published data source for the marketing analysts using Tableau Prep Builder as they need to use it to add new rows for the days where there are no campaign click-throughs, adding zero values on these days. The data steward then uses Tableau Prep Conductor to schedule daily updates.

The marketing analyst and dashboard development team then create the campaign dashboard and publish them to a marketing project on Tableau Cloud for all of the marketing team to use.

We can see what is and is not needed from the various data modeling components of the Tableau platform, along with the reason, in *Table 15.5*:

| Component | Use? | Reason |
| --- | --- | --- |
| Virtual connection * | No | The data is not complex enough nor does it need a data policy for row-level security. |
| Prep Builder | Yes | The data is missing rows for days when there were no click-throughs for campaigns. Prep Builder is used to add new rows. |
| Desktop | No | The dashboard developers will use Desktop but it is not needed for the data modeling step. |
| Published or embedded? | Published | The data source is published from Prep Builder, so it can be used by the marketing dashboard development team. |
| Tableau Bridge | No | The source data comes from Google BigQuery, which can be accessed by Tableau Cloud. |
| Scheduler or Prep Conductor? * | Prep Conductor | The published data source is scheduled through Prep Conductor. |
| Lens | No | Campaign information is consumed through the campaign dashboards. |
| Enable Explain Data | Yes | To let the marketing team explore campaign result outliers, Explain Data is enabled. |
| Descriptions for Catalog * | Yes | As the workbook will be distributed broadly, data definitions are key to ensure decisions based on the data are based on a solid understanding of the data. |

Table 15.5 – Marketing analytics use case

In this fourth case, we can see a case that requires Tableau Prep Builder as the source data is missing rows for days when campaigns did not generate click-throughs. Like the information systems example, we have a broad distribution, but we do not have concerns for row-level security. Security and access can be handled at the project level on Tableau Cloud.

## Summary

In this chapter, we discussed the ideal situations for Tableau Prep Builder and Tableau Desktop based on the strengths and features of each. We also looked at cases where both can be the right fit for the task.

We then looked at four audiences and their use cases to bring together how and when to use the various data modeling components of the Tableau platform. First, we explored a financial analyst who creates quarterly financial reports for a limited audience. This use case does not need many data modeling capabilities as it requires infrequent updates, has a limited audience, and has relatively simple data sources.

Next, we looked at a use case of sales performance data for the entire sales organization. This use case uses most of the data modeling capabilities of the Tableau platform due to a broad and varied audience, complex security requirements, and messy data sources.

Next, we looked at a use case which focused on marketing analytics and is slotted between the finance and sales use cases and audiences in terms of complexity. For this reason, it used many of the data modeling features and components we learned about in this book, but not as many as in the sales use case.

In our fourth and final use case, we explored a case of marketing campaigns where the campaigns don't yield results every day. We used Prep Builder to add rows for these missing days and used Prep Conductor to schedule our flows.

Now that we have experienced all the data modeling components of the Tableau platform through hands-on exercises and explored which to use in different use cases, we are ready to take our new skills and apply them to real-world scenarios.

# Index

Packt.com

Subscribe to our online digital library for full access to over 7,000 books and videos, as well as industry leading tools to help you plan your personal development and advance your career. For more information, please visit our website.

## Why subscribe?

- Spend less time learning and more time coding with practical eBooks and Videos from over 4,000 industry professionals

- Improve your learning with Skill Plans built especially for you

- Get a free eBook or video every month

- Fully searchable for easy access to vital information

- Copy and paste, print, and bookmark content

Did you know that Packt offers eBook versions of every book published, with PDF and ePub files available? You can upgrade to the eBook version at packt.com and as a print book customer, you are entitled to a discount on the eBook copy. Get in touch with us at customercare@packtpub.com for more details.

At www.packt.com, you can also read a collection of free technical articles, sign up for a range of free newsletters, and receive exclusive discounts and offers on Packt books and eBooks.

# Other Books You May Enjoy

If you enjoyed this book, you may be interested in these other books by Packt:

**Microsoft Power BI Data Analyst Certification Guide**

Orrin Edenfield, Edward Corcoran

ISBN: 978-1-80323-856-2

- Connect to and prepare data from a variety of sources
- Clean, transform, and shape your data for analysis
- Create data models that enable insight creation
- Analyze data using Microsoft Power BI's capabilities
- Create visualizations to make analysis easier
- Discover how to deploy and manage Microsoft Power BI assets

**Learning Tableau 2022 - Fifth Edition**

Joshua N. Milligan

ISBN: 978-1-80107-232-8

- Develop stunning visualizations to explain complex data with clarity
- Build interactive dashboards to drive actionable user insights
- Explore Data Model capabilities and interlink data from various sources
- Create and use calculations to solve problems and enrich your analytics
- Enable smart decision-making with data clustering, distribution, and forecasting
- Extend Tableau's native functionality with extensions, scripts, and AI through CRM Analytics (formerly Einstein Analytics)
- Leverage Tableau Prep Builder's amazing capabilities for data cleaning and structuring
- Share your data stories to build a culture of trust and action

## Packt is searching for authors like you

If you're interested in becoming an author for Packt, please visit `authors.packtpub.com` and apply today. We have worked with thousands of developers and tech professionals, just like you, to help them share their insight with the global tech community. You can make a general application, apply for a specific hot topic that we are recruiting an author for, or submit your own idea.

## Share Your Thoughts

Now you've finished , we'd love to hear your thoughts! Scan the QR code below to go straight to the Amazon review page for this book and share your feedback or leave a review on the site that you purchased it from.

`https://packt.link/r/1-803-24802-5`

Your review is important to us and the tech community and will help us make sure we're delivering excellent quality content.

# Download a free PDF copy of this book

Thanks for purchasing this book!

Do you like to read on the go but are unable to carry your print books everywhere? Is your eBook purchase not compatible with the device of your choice?

Don't worry, now with every Packt book you get a DRM-free PDF version of that book at no cost.

Read anywhere, any place, on any device. Search, copy, and paste code from your favorite technical books directly into your application.

The perks don't stop there, you can get exclusive access to discounts, newsletters, and great free content in your inbox daily

Follow these simple steps to get the benefits:

1. Scan the QR code or visit the link below

https://packt.link/free-ebook/9781803248028

2. Submit your proof of purchase

3. That's it! We'll send your free PDF and other benefits to your email directly

Made in the USA
Coppell, TX
02 April 2023